Contents

List of figures   ix
Preface   xi
Acknowledgements   xiii

1   An introduction to the internet   1
Introduction   1
An overview of the internet   1
What the internet is and what it isn´t   2
Search engines   7
Commercial databases   8
Virtual libraries and gateways   8
Newsgroups and mailing lists   9
Weblogs   10
News aggregators   10
Online tools   10
The information mix   11
Better searching   11
Better software   12
Where to go next?   12
Summary   12
URLs mentioned in this chapter   13

Part 1   Mining the internet for information   15
         2   An introduction to search engines   17
              Introduction   17
              The rise of the search engine   18
              Free-text search engines   19
              Index- or directory-based search engines   23
              Multi- or meta-search engines   25
              Resource- or site-specific search engines   26
              Some other points about search engines   27
              Summary   29
              URLs mentioned in this chapter   30

         3   Free-text search engines   31
              Introduction   31
              Google   31
              AlltheWeb   43
              Other free-text search engines explored   46
              Other free-text search engines available   50
              Summary   51
              URLs mentioned in this chapter   52

         4   Index-based search engines   53
              Introduction   53
              Yahoo!   54
              Google Directory   61
              The *Open Directory Project*   63
              Other index-based search engines   65
              Summary   66
              URLs mentioned in this chapter   66

         5   Multi- or meta-search engines   67
              Introduction   67
              What is a multi-search engine?   67
              Characteristics of multi-search engines   68
              ZapMeta   72
              KartOO   75
              Other multi- or meta-search engines   76
              Summary   77
              URLs mentioned in this chapter   77

cph
23/08/04
28·26

The advanced internet searcher's handbook

Third edition

Phil Bradley

facet publishing

© Phil Bradley 1999, 2002, 2004

Published by
Facet Publishing
7 Ridgmount Street
London WC1E 7AE
www.facetpublishing.co.uk

Facet Publishing is wholly owned by CILIP: the Chartered Institute of Library and Information Professionals.

First published 1999
Second edition 2002
This third edition 2004

British Library Cataloguing in Publication Data
A catalogue record for this book is available from the British Library.

ISBN 1-85604-523-4

Typeset from author's disk in 11/15pt Bergamo and URW Topic by Facet Publishing.
Printed and made in Great Britain by MPG Books Ltd, Bodmin, Cornwall.

6 Resource- or site-specific search engines 78
Introduction 78
Site-specific search engines (web pages) 78
Site-specific search engines (databases) 80
Summary 82
URLs mentioned in this chapter 82

7 Searching the 'hidden web' 83
Introduction 83
Search engines 85
Hidden web directories 87
Intelligent agents that help search the hidden web 88
Other resources 89
Summary 90
URLs mentioned in this chapter 90

8 Finding images, sounds and multimedia information 91
Introduction 91
Finding images on the internet 92
Using standard search engines to find images 92
Multi-search engines 96
Image-specific search engines 97
Image collections 98
Image newsgroups 100
Finding sound files 100
Multimedia files 103
Summary 104
URLs mentioned in this chapter 105

9 Finding people 106
Introduction 106
Standard search engines 107
People finders 111
Specific tracking services 112
Summary 113
URLs mentioned in this chapter 113

Part 2   Becoming an expert searcher   115
  10 Weblogs   117
      Introduction   117
      Some examples of weblogs   118
      Librarians and weblogs   120
      Locating weblogs   123
      Creating your own weblog   129
      Summary   131
      URLs mentioned in this chapter   132

  11 Other available database resources   134
      Introduction   134
      Freely available information provided by publishers   135
      Online communities   136
      Commercial information   136
      Online journals   138
      Newspapers   139
      Bookshops   140
      Summary   141
      URLs mentioned in this chapter   141

  12 Virtual libraries and gateways   143
      Introduction   143
      Authority on the internet   143
      Virtual libraries   149
      Virtual libraries currently available   150
      Summary   154
      URLs mentioned in this chapter   154

  13 Usenet newsgroups and mailing lists   156
      Introduction   156
      Usenet newsgroups   156
      The value of newsgroups to the advanced searcher   159
      Reading newsgroups   160
      Mailing lists   165
      Summary   170
      URLs mentioned in this chapter   170

Part 3   The future   173

14 The information mix and into the future   175
Introduction   175
Where do I go first?   176
Some sample searches   177
Incorporating the internet into your overall information strategy   184
Information professionals unite! You have nothing to lose but your books . . . 187
. . . and an internet to gain!   188
Future developments   190
Summary   193
URLs mentioned in this chapter   193

15 Fifty tips and hints for better and quicker searching   195
Introduction   195
Getting online and moving around the web   195
Finding web pages   196
Moving around a web page   198
Saving and printing pages   198
Faster loading of pages   200
Using bookmarks   200
Getting the most out of your browser   202
URLs mentioned in this chapter   205

16 Utilities to help the advanced searcher   206
Introduction   206
Browsers   207
Offline browsers   209
Bookmark utilities   209
Cache viewers   211
Multimedia applications   211
Anti-virus protection   213
Spyware   215
Firewalls   216
Toolbars   216
Deskbars   218
Anonymous browsing   219
Shorter URLs   220
Web page watchers   222
Miscellaneous utilities   224

Summary   226
URLs mentioned in this chapter   226

17 Sources for further help, information and assistance   229
Introduction   229
Search engine news and information   229
What's new services   231
Professional sites   236
Magazines and journals   236
Bookshops   237
Mailing lists   238
Spam   239
Miscellaneous   240
Summary   242
URLs mentioned in this chapter   242

Appendix 1   HTML for a search engine home page   244
Appendix 2   Country codes   249

Index   253

List of figures

Every effort has been made to contact the holders of the copyright material that is reproduced in this text, and thanks are due to them for permission to reproduce screenshots. All brand names and trademarks are the property of their owners. If there are any queries regarding these, please contact the publishers for correct attribution in any revision.

		page
Figure 3.1	The *Google* home page	34
3.2	The *Google* advanced search screen	35
3.3	The *Google* toolbar	39
3.4	The *AlltheWeb* simple search interface	44
3.5	The *AltaVista* simple search interface	47
3.6	The *Teoma* simple search interface	49
3.7	Results of a *Wisenut* search	50
4.1	The major subject headings at *Yahoo!*	55
4.2	Subheadings under 'Reference' at *Yahoo!*	56
4.3	Results of a search using the free-text function at *Yahoo!*	58
4.4	The *Yahoo!* search box within a category	59
4.5	Part of the *Yahoo!* home page	60
4.6	The *Google Directory* home page	62
4.7	*Google Directory* search within a category	63
4.8	The *Open Directory Project* home page	64
5.1	The *ZapMeta* home page	72

5.2 The *Fazzle* results screen   75
5.3 The *KartOO* results screen   76
6.1 The search interface for the author's site at
     www.philb.com   79
6.2 Search results provided by *Atomz* for search
     on author's site for the word 'Google'   79
6.3 Search results from the *FreeBMD* search engine   80
7.1 Search interface for *Direct Search*   85
8.1 The *Google* image search simple interface   93
8.2 The *AltaVista* image search interface   94
8.3 The *Yahoo!* image search interface   95
8.4 The *Picsearch* advanced search interface   97
8.5 The *AltaVista* video search interface   104
9.1 The *Yahoo!* people search function   109
10.1 *TheShiftedLibrarian* weblog   118
10.2 Gary Price's *ResourceShelf* weblog   119
10.3 The *Daypop* results screen   124
10.4 The *Feedster* search engine home page   125
10.5 The author's weblog as an HTML-based page   127
10.6 The author's weblog in RSS format   127
10.7 The author's weblog viewed in a news aggregator   128
10.8 The *Blogger* home page   131
12.1 The *WWW Virtual Library* logo   151
12.2 The *WWW Virtual Library* home page   151
12.3 The *BUBL* home page   153
12.4 The *BUBL LINK* home page   153
13.1 The *Google Groups* search interface   161
13.2 The *Google Groups* advanced search interface   161
13.3 A *Google Groups* newsgroup posting displayed   162
13.4 The *Forte Agent* main interface screen   164
13.5 The form for joining or leaving *lis-link*   167
16.1 The author's page at *Backflip*   211
16.2 *TinyURL* making one of the author's URLs smaller   222
17.1 The *FreePint* home page   232
Appendix
Figure 1 The author's search engine home page   245

Preface

Welcome to the third edition of *The Advanced Internet Searcher's Handbook*! Since I first became aware of the internet over a decade ago I have been fascinated to watch the ways in which it has developed and grown. Since my first faltering footsteps on it I have been aware that it is an interesting but frustrating environment to work in. Despite all the hype about how easy it is to use, and how you can find almost anything you want, I have found that unless you are a skilled searcher this is far from the case. Since the first two editions of the book have been published more search engines have been created (and some have vanished) with the result that, if anything, it's even more difficult to search the internet effectively, since there are so many options available to the searcher. I was therefore delighted to be asked to update this book and provide more help and advice on making your explorations easier and more successful.

The aim of this book is to help you search the internet more effectively by giving you a better understanding of how search engines and related software and utilities work, allowing you to use them to improve your own search techniques. I have given lists of sites that you can visit that will help to further your understanding, and details of utilities that you can use to make life a little bit easier.

This handbook will be of use to anyone who uses the internet to find information. It doesn't matter if you are taking your first step into this new and exciting world, or if you are an expert who uses it every day: you will find information, hints, tips, resources and software that will be of help. Although I have paid particular attention to the use that information professionals can make of the internet you should not feel excluded if you are from another profession – this book is designed to be of use to everyone who needs to find information quickly!

I have spent a lot of time exploring new and easier ways of obtaining information more quickly and effectively by using search engines correctly and by utilizing the many tools available. I trust that I've managed to hit all the highlights of internet searching, even if it's not been possible to cover everything in as much detail as I would have liked.

On this journey of exploration I've discovered some interesting or amusing facts about the internet that I've shared with you; you will find them in the side panels. It has been an enjoyable trip along the 'information superhighway' and, although I have not yet reached a final destination (indeed, I doubt that I ever will), I have witnessed many enjoyable sites (and sights!) and met many interesting people.

You can read the *Handbook* from cover to cover, or you may prefer to 'dip in' and read chapters or sections that appeal to you, or that may help you answer a particular problem or question. At the end of each chapter I have given a list of URLs that I've referred to within the body of the text: these should be a useful resource in their own right, and I have used them quite often myself in my day-to-day work. I have ensured that the URLs listed in the *Handbook* were current before going to press, but the nature of the internet is such that some may well have changed by the time you try to visit them yourself. I hope, however, that your own searching abilities will have improved enough to enable you to locate new addresses for yourself.

The internet is changing all our lives, for better or worse, but mostly I feel for the better. If you embrace the internet, and learn to use it to its best advantage, I firmly believe that you will be all the richer for it. I hope that this book will prove to be of some help to you on your own personal journeys.

Acknowledgements

I should like to thank all the organizations and web authors who gave me permission to use screenshots of their pages and utilities. All screenshots are copyright of their original owners.

I should also like to thank all those people within the information industry who have pointed me along the right track, my clients who were understanding of any delays caused to their projects while I was writing the book, and to the people I have trained in the past for pointing out new places to visit and new software to try.

I should also like to pay particular thanks to the staff at Facet Publishing for their help, advice and encouragement on the production of this third edition.

Finally, as always, most thanks go to my wife Jill Bradley for her continual help and encouragement as I wander around the internet. *The Advanced Internet Searcher's Handbook* is dedicated, with all my love, to her.

Chapter 1 »
An introduction to the internet

Introduction

The internet is not a new phenomenon, despite what you may read in the popular or professional press. It already has a long and involved history; its creation and development profoundly affect the way in which it is used today and indeed how it will be used in the future. As each day passes, it is becoming clear that the internet already affects or will affect almost every possible area of our lives. Pre-eminent among these changes are the ways in which information professionals view and use information. This chapter outlines some of the important developments of the internet in order to provide background information. I do not intend to provide a history of the internet, but if you are interested in this subject you could visit **http://dir.yahoo. com/Computers_and_Internet/Internet/History/** which provides a list of sites that comprehensively cover this.

An overview of the internet

I can still remember the first time that I had an opportunity to 'surf the net'. That is the first and last time you'll read that phrase in this book since it implies skimming over the surface, desperately trying to keep your balance and ensure that you don't get wet or, worse, drown. The skilled user of the internet knows what information is required and how to find it, retrieve it and go on to make good use of it. Perhaps a better description would be that of an underwater explorer (to adapt the surfing analogy) who is able to plot a course in the ocean to a specific point, plan and execute a dive, explore the wreck to obtain any treasure, and come back to the surface quickly and safely. This book will show you how to do just that.

When I first looked at the internet I knew very little other than what I'd been reading in the popular press. My friend Chris had just got an account with an internet service provider and invited my wife and myself around for 'supper and surf'. We planned to eat and then spend a couple of hours seeing what was out there. However, supper was not quite ready, so Chris and I began our first ever tour, while my wife read her book. We spent a long time trying to find something that was interesting (this was in the days before helpful search engines); we downloaded a video of a NASA space launch and generally had an enjoyable, if sometimes frustrating, time. We had become so engrossed that we failed to notice that we'd spent four hours in front of the computer, or that supper had burned to a crisp in the oven, or that my wife had fallen asleep on the sofa!

Frustrating though it had been, I became hooked on the internet that evening and, looking back, I recognize that the problems we encountered were inherent in the system and exacerbated by our very limited knowledge. We didn't really know what we were looking for, and seemed to spend most of our time visiting one site which led us to a second, then to a third, which sent us back to the first one! It took a long time to download the information we wanted to see – the ten minutes it took to retrieve that video clip was rewarded by about ten seconds of moving images. Of course, the internet has come a long way since then, but users still find it a daunting and confusing place in which to work. For the new user it appears to be entirely chaotic, with neither rhyme nor reason behind it, but perseverance does pay dividends in a reasonably short space of time.

What the internet is and what it isn't

It's not a single network

The internet is a collection of networks throughout the world. Academic, military, governmental and commercial networks all combine to create it. All the computers connected to the internet make use of a common protocol, or way of passing data backwards and forwards, called TCP/IP. Data travels across

HINTS & TIPS >>
I have tried to keep jargon terms to the minimum, but if you are puzzled by any of them and want more information you may like to visit a glossary of internet terms at www.matisse.net/files/glossary. html.

ordinary telecommunications lines, and as a result it is very easy for individuals and organizations to connect to it, thus increasing the amount of information available and also making it more difficult to find it! It also means that it is a robust system; when trying to obtain information from another machine somewhere else in the world your computer and software will work out the best routes to get from point A to point B, so even if some routes are unavailable you should still normally be able to retrieve the data that you need.

It's both local and global

The internet isn't interested in geographical locations, and you can find the information that you need regardless of where you happen to be in the world. This is an important change for information professionals. When asked for information in a traditional library setting, an effective searcher will think geographically – is the information in a book on the shelf behind me? If not, is it available elsewhere in the library, or in a sister library down the road, or will it have to be retrieved via an interlibrary loan? All too often this geographical approach is at the expense of time and authority; while it might ideally make sense to talk to the San Francisco tourist board for example, it's generally impractical because of the cost, the distance and the time difference. When using the internet, contacting the appropriate source regardless of geographic location immediately becomes possible; it's simply necessary to find that source and your computer will immediately begin to connect to it and retrieve the data. If you as the information professional feel that the best way of answering a question is to refer the user to a local resource (a newspaper, group of enthusiasts, local history group and so on) this is increasingly possible. The internet enables you to get the most appropriate information quickly, instead of having to rely on less precise information that may be easily at hand within the traditional library environment. Consequently, global information is available on a local desktop.

It isn't a single entity

The internet isn't a single uniform resource. It is a collection of different resources, such as the world wide web (which itself is made up of millions of individual computers), newsgroups, mailing lists, real-time 'chat' facilities and much more. An effective searcher will be able to blend all of these different resources into a single collection, using whichever elements are best to answer a query. A business librarian may prefer to use the web to search financial databases and obtain company reports, while a public librarian may make considerable use of the ready-reference tools that are available, or post a difficult query to a newsgroup, hoping that someone else may be able to come up with the answer.

It's possible to use a wide variety of hardware and software

There is no single standard software package used to access the internet or any of its component parts. In Chapter 16 we'll look at some of the software that is available, some of which is appropriate for some readers and not for others. Effective searchers will create their own library of software tools, specifically designed to provide assistance when seeking information. Similarly, there is no single type of computer which must be used with the internet. It does of course help if you have a computer with a very fast processor speed, large hard disk, lots of memory, a sound card and printer attached, but it is not always necessary. Machines with a lower specification can also give good service without necessarily compromising data retrieval.

It's difficult to say who is in charge

The early networks which eventually combined to create the internet were very often designed to be open systems that people or organizations could quickly and easily become part of. Although some control was exerted (to limit participation to academic institutions, for example), no hard and fast rules were laid down. It is true that there are some organizations which are responsible for various aspects of the internet, such as domain name registration, or for defining the way in which web pages are coded or written, but as far as the information professional is concerned there is no single authority which decides what information should be made available or in what form. As a result, individuals and organizations are, by and large, free to do exactly what they wish. Consequently, information may be sparse in some subject areas, while there may be very comprehensive coverage in others. Information may be current to within a few moments on one site, or it may be years out of date on another.

DID YOU KNOW? >>
Although no one organization 'controls' the internet, the W3 Consortium is an international industry consortium which aims to develop common protocols to aid the growth and expansion of the internet. It can be found at www.w3.org/.

Information may be authoritative or wildly inaccurate; much information will be of no use, or may be offensive or illegal in some countries. The skilled researcher needs to be able to assess value, currency and authority quickly and accurately, but without necessarily knowing the organization publishing the material, the author, or the extent to which the information has been checked by peer review.

It's fast and effective

The internet can be a very fast and effective way to communicate with other people or to retrieve information. A company report can be obtained in seconds, a bibliography can be compiled in minutes, and research that would otherwise take days may be completed in a few hours. Indeed, it's now perfectly possible to listen to your favourite radio station across the internet, and that station may broadcast from the city you live in, or it may be on the other side of the world. As a result of the speed and globalization of the internet it becomes possible to move from a 'just in case' paradigm, in which it is necessary to have a store of information readily on hand in case it is required, to a 'just in time' model, where information is not held locally but is retrieved as and when required to meet the needs of a specific enquiry. Effective information professionals can match their information needs to the availability of data on the internet and as a result may decide that there is no need to subscribe to a range of printed newspapers, for example, since many of them are readily available on the web, together with archival information.

It's easy to talk to individuals or groups

Usenet newsgroups, mailing lists, and more recently weblogs (or blogs) allow people with similar interests to keep in touch, to share knowledge, to express opinions or even just to gossip! Communities of interest are created which facilitate the free flow of information, freed from the confines of time or geographical location. This allows you to make contact with others around the world, to disseminate information to large numbers of people in ways previously not possible, and to draw on the experience of peers and experts in fields that you may never have known about before.

It's not all hard work

Information on the internet covers almost literally every single subject that you could think of, plus a few more besides. Professional information (however you want to define that) and personal or hobby information sit happily side by side, and it is as easy to discover the results of last night's lottery as it is to locate companies that sell chemical compounds. Even a small information centre is in a position to provide access to resources which previously would have fallen outside its remit or budget. This does, however, bring with it the associated problem of ensuring that terminals are used to retrieve appropriate information, and not to download glamour pictures or worse!

It's not just for 'geeks'

Until about ten years ago access to information on the internet was by using a variety of tools that were less than user friendly. *Veronica*, *Archie* and *Gopher* services located and retrieved information, but these tools were difficult for end-users to master. Now, however, graphical interfaces, search engines, intelligent agents and more sophisticated operating systems ensure that even novice users can quickly locate and retrieve information. This ease of use comes at a price – end-users will increasingly require training in the critical assessment of the results they are achieving and the authority of the information they have obtained.

It's not well organized

Since no one 'owns' the internet, everyone can do almost exactly as they please. No centralized authority means that people will publish the same information in different formats, incorrect or out of date information appears as well as accurate current information, and organizations and individuals will arrange their data and access to it in ways that please them. Flexibility on the part of the searcher is therefore paramount, coupled with the ability to quickly identify how information is arranged and to locate relevant data within a site.

It's growing at an enormous rate

There is little point in attempting to provide figures for the number of people who are connected to the internet, simply because it is almost impossible to do so with any accuracy. Even if it could be done, the figure would be out of date by the time you read this. A generally agreed rule of thumb was that the internet was doubling in size every year, in terms of users and web pages, but this is beginning to slow down slightly now. This means that information professionals have to work very hard to keep up to date with that is

DID YOU KNOW? »
If you want to find out how many people currently have access to the internet you should visit a site such as *CyberAtlas* at http://cyberatlas.internet.com/.

happening in this area. In order to be effective it is necessary to spend several hours a week locating new sites and trying new software. However, all is not lost, since there are resources that can help in this process, and I have provided a list of some of them in Chapter 16.

Search engines

One of the characteristics of the internet is the speed at which it has grown in the last few years. No one is quite sure of the size of the internet as a whole, or the world wide web specifically, and I've seen lots of conflicting statistics, most of which are quite out of date. However, a figure that I've seen quoted and am quite happy to believe is about 11 billion web pages (up from five billion in the second edition of this book). Even if this figure is an overestimate at the time of writing, by the time this book is published and in your hands I would expect it to be accurate, or even an underestimate.

In the early days of the internet it was reasonably easy to find information or datafiles using a variety of software packages that were command driven – that is, you needed to type in the command you wanted executed, rather than using a graphical interface. However, with the proliferation of data brought about by the growth of the web, these systems with such names as *Archie*, *Gopher* and *Veronica* became increasingly unable to cope. In order to overcome the lack of retrieval facilities a number of organizations and individuals began to create their own software for searching and retrieving information. Unfortunately, very few of them had any kind of library or information background so, although they were (and are) doing a very sophisticated job of finding and indexing all that information, the early implementations were quite crude. They were not designed for trained searchers, but for people who had never done a literature search in their lives, and as a result they did not make any use of Boolean operators, proximity searching, wildcards, truncation or any of the other things that we take for granted. Users simply entered any keywords that they felt were appropriate and the search engines would retrieve hits based on their perceived relevance. Indeed that's still pretty much what happens today, though some sophistication has crept into the systems.

Over the course of time some of these search engines have hardly moved forward at all, and still the only way of finding appropriate web pages is to throw as many search terms at them as possible and hope that you are lucky. However, some of the others have been through many new versions and upgrades and are achieving the kind of sophistication that we take for granted when searching an online or CD-ROM-based database.

As information professionals the world over know, there is more than one way to classify or catalogue a book, and that's certainly the case when it comes to the data found on the internet. Chapter 2 explains in some detail how the different types of search engine work, and the advantages and disadvantages of using them. The next three chapters then look at particular search engines, how they can be used effectively, and when they should be used.

Commercial databases

The history of commercial databases deserves a study in its own right, since the production of them, their use and subsequent developments closely match technological advances. However, this is not the place for such a discussion, so I restrict my comments here to the way that the internet has affected online commercial databases. As we will see later, database publishers now make their databases available via the internet, usually as the preferred access option. This is also the case for CD-ROM publishers.

This is a logical extension from the early provision of CD-ROM databases in the information centre, since it is another way of moving information out of the libraries and onto people's desktops. Moreover, it is further influencing the job of the information professional, who is moving away from being the 'gatekeeper', or the person who goes away and obtains information for users, towards being the 'facilitator', who no longer performs the search, but establishes systems and trains users to obtain the required data for themselves.

The provision of commercial databases on the internet is closely associated with electronic commerce. Since publishers can make their data available in this way more flexible and varied pricing systems can be introduced. Users may, for example, buy a block of units that can be spent on retrieving any records from a publisher's collection of databases, or they may prefer to continue to subscribe to a particular product. Publishers are having to work harder to keep market share by providing value-added services, and we will explore some of the challenges facing the publishers, information professionals and end-users in more detail in Chapter 11.

Virtual libraries and gateways

As we shall see, one of the problems of using search engines is that they return all the data they can retrieve indiscriminately; the search engines are unable to make any qualitative judgements on the value or authority of the information they find. One of the advantages of the internet is that it is very easy to publish information, and unfortunately this is one of its greatest disadvantages as well. No one owns the internet, so no one is able to say 'this is good' or 'this is bad'; and in any case, what is 'good' for one person may be 'bad' for another. The whole question of authority is one which is mentioned to me at every training session I give, and so in Chapter 12 I explain some ways in which the level of authority of a particular website or page can be quickly assessed.

Information professionals have been taking an important role in this area and over the last few years a large number of virtual libraries have been established. These attempt to gather together links to websites with authoritative, current, trustworthy and useful information. As a result they are a very useful set of resources, which are all too often ignored or badly publicized. The people who maintain virtual libraries have done a considerable amount of work for others in their subject areas, and these resources can provide a useful starting point for searches. Indeed, it may not be necessary to look anywhere else for the information that is required.

Virtual libraries are yet another example of the librarian acting as facilitator, and they can save searchers a lot of time by directing them to hard, trustworthy information. In Chapter 12 I explore the concepts behind them, and list some of those which are particularly useful, as well as explaining how they can best be utilized.

Newsgroups and mailing lists

If the internet is about anything, it is about people being able to talk to people. Much work is currently being undertaken in the fields of video conferencing and internet telephony, for example, and though they have a long way to go before being fully functional they are a good indication of the importance we all put on being able to talk to each other when, where and how we want.

Newsgroups and mailing lists are not as visually exciting or as 'sexy' as these recent innovations, but they have a long history and are still perhaps the best way we have at present to talk to each other across the internet. Unfortunately, they are also an under-used resource, perhaps because they have been around since the early days of the internet; it may be a case of familiarity breeds contempt. In Chapter 13 I go into much more detail about what exactly newsgroups and mailing lists are, and explain how they can be of real assistance to the information professional. I also give you some pointers on the different ways they can be used (both in technical and professional terms), and what software is required.

Weblogs

These are a recent innovation which, as with so many things on the internet, have been around for a long while, but have only just come into focus as an important development in the growth of the internet. Put simply, a weblog (or 'blog') is an online diary that other people can read. Consequently, a lot of weblogs are simply collections of 'got up late today, didn't do much, went to bed late' which are of no interest to anyone – probably not even the people who write them. However, other weblogs are rather more useful – some are written by experts in particular areas who write about developments in their subject area, so they can be a very useful way of keeping up to date with what is happening. Other weblogs are used by people to discuss what is happening in a particular subject area, and they are a good way of keeping a finger on the pulse of public opinion. I discuss these in more detail in Chapter 10.

> **DID YOU KNOW?** >>
> There are approximately 50 million internet users worldwide and it took only four years to reach that number. By contrast, it took radio 38 years and television 13 years to attract the same number (www.perfectisite.com/surprise.html).

News aggregators

Following on from weblogs, various individuals and companies are producing utilities commonly referred to as 'news aggregators'. These are an extension of intelligent agents (see Chapter 7), and indeed are an interesting development of them. They make it easier for people to create their own information feeds, covering subjects and resources that are of particular interest to them. Consequently it's possible to quickly scan multiple news resources every day, or indeed every hour to see what new information is available. They are, therefore, a new resource that information professionals can use in their arsenal of utilities.

Online tools

One of the joys and frustrations of the internet is that, because it is such an open system, organizations and individuals are always adding new resources, facilities and utilities that can be used. I've already mentioned news aggregators, but we can also include such things as toolbars, pop-up killers, bookmark managers, spam filters and so on. Chapter 16 is an opportunity to look at some of these in detail to see how some of them can be used to make life a lot easier.

The information mix

As I have already said, the internet is not one thing; it is a collection of different types of software, resources, data and utilities, used by many millions of people, all of whom have their own particular reasons to be using it. Never was this more true than when looking at how the information professional utilizes this collection of resources.

As a profession, we are faced with an almost bewildering array of resources: traditional book-based sources, online databases, CD-ROM and DVD technology, search engines, virtual libraries, newsgroups, mailing lists, intelligent agents (see Chapter 7) – the list could go on and on. However, our key role has not changed; information has to be gathered, sifted, checked, rechecked and made available in one form or another for our users. The question of how this is done though, is becoming more and more complex as each new facility is made available.

Once you have explored some of the sites that I mention, and have installed and become familiar with the software needed, the next step is to make some sense of it all. As users also engage in the same process, and technology continues its rapid development, this problem becomes more acute. It is necessary to blend and mix these resources together into a coherent package which is appropriate for your own user community. Where should the information be found? Should information be made available in a variety of formats? Is it possible to dispense with some traditional information resources and replace them with something else? How can users be encouraged to find information for themselves? What advances do we need to be at least aware of, if not actively planning, to embrace them? I attempt to answer these questions in Chapter 14, and also point out where the internet is perhaps leading us.

Better searching

A full understanding of the internet and its resources is obviously invaluable, and a searcher cannot work effectively without this knowledge. I hope that this book will help you obtain this understanding, but a broad overview is only part of the picture. Sometimes it is necessary to explore some of the minutiae of systems and software. It is surprising just how much time can be saved daily by reducing each search by two minutes, or by using a shortcut here and there. In Chapter 15 I've collected together a number of hints and tips that should make searching and using the internet a little bit easier and a little bit faster. I estimate that you may be able to save yourself several hours each week by incorporating them into your normal daily work routines.

Better software

The internet, and in particular the world wide web, is constantly growing and increasing in complexity as people explore new possibilities. In its early stages, the web was text based, but it did not take long before still images, animated graphics, sound and multimedia were brought into play. Browser software has also become more sophisticated, with ever greater functionality.

Consequently, web designers are always pushing the boundaries of what is possible, and commercial organizations, always seeking revenue, are providing ever more intelligent and powerful software to take advantage of the web. In order to remain effective and to gain the most out of the system it is necessary to keep as up to date as possible. The only way of doing that is to install new software and upgrade older versions.

In Chapter 16 I look at resources on the internet that can help you in this area, and examine in more detail some packages that can make a very real difference to searching and using the internet.

Where to go next?

The speed at which the internet is growing means that it is not possible to stop still; if you do that you will find that you are out of date within a matter of days. The internet is a little like a treadmill; once you have got on it and started to walk it becomes difficult to get off. Worse than that, the treadmill just goes faster and faster, and you have to run harder just to keep from falling behind. There are a number of internet resources that are worth using to help keep you current, as well as organizations providing training courses. Chapter 17 goes into detail on these resources, with the intention of ensuring that you don't fall behind – or, if you do, that you are able to catch up again!

Summary

In this introductory chapter I have identified some of the key elements that affect the way in which the information professional is able to use the internet, and have alerted you to the major areas that this book covers. I expect that you will find some chapters more interesting than others, so feel free to explore those; each chapter stands on its own, and, while they do make reference to each other, you can read them in any order you choose.

URLs mentioned in this chapter

http://dir.yahoo.com/Computers_and_Internet/Internet/History/
www.matisse.net/files/glossary.html
www.w3.org/
http://cyberatlas.internet.com/
www.perfectisite.com/surprise.html

Part 1 »

Mining the internet for information

Chapter 2 »
An introduction to search engines

Introduction

The internet is often referred to as the 'information super-highway'. The term gives the impression that it is fast and effective, getting you quickly from A to B in the twinkling of an eye. Furthermore, it implies that the ride is going to be a smooth one, with no bumps or potholes, and certainly no chance of breaking down or taking an incorrect term.

Unfortunately nothing could be further from the truth. In point of fact, I think that a closer and rather more accurate analogy is that of the library I would expect to find in the type of gothic house you see in horror films; huge and rambling, with long corridors leading off into the middle of nowhere, small rooms packed with frequently used material in little order and yet other places shrouded in darkness from which you hear rather nasty noises. The whole grand edifice is presided over by a half-insane librarian who is constantly coming up with new classifications and cataloguing schemes. These are implemented on a few hundred titles before our insane librarian begins again with a different scheme on some new materials that have just been dumped in no order on the floor of the library. Meanwhile, the minions of our librarian are busily working away in different rooms constantly arranging and rearranging their own collections, without reference to each other, and each convinced that they have the best collection and best scheme for its arrangement.

Unfair? Yes, perhaps it is, but only a little. We've already seen just how fast the world wide web is growing, and it is easy to let your eyes glaze over at the sheer amount of data that we're talking about. The web is large and it is growing at a tremendous rate, and gathering speed under its own anarchic mass, but strangely enough it is, in the main, going in one direction. As a result it is possible to impose some control over it, and to put some structure in place. Chief among these are the different search engines, which prove to be of great assistance in allowing us to quickly find the exact piece of information that we require, sometimes in less time than it took to articulate and type in the query.

I do not pretend that the search engines are perfect – very far from it! As we will discover, they all have their own shortcomings, and we are a long way from having a perfect interface or comprehensive index to the internet. Indeed, I doubt that we ever shall. However, while we continue to strive for that holy grail we have to work with the tools that are available to us, and in this chapter I give you an overview of the way in which the search engines actually do their jobs; the more you understand about search engines, the easier they are to use and the more effectively you can retrieve information.

The rise of the search engine

I'll start by asking you a question: 'How many search engines do you think that there are out there?' The chances are that your immediate reaction will provide a figure in the region of a few hundred. If you've read the previous chapter you'll already know not to underestimate the size of the internet and the speed at which it grows, so you may be a little more confident in giving a larger figure, perhaps in the region of a few thousand. You would still be a long way short of the mark, since I've seen figures that suggest there are in the region of 150,000 search engines.

If you find this figure just too remarkable to believe, I'd ask you to hold back on your scepticism for a moment or two. While my question wasn't

> **DID YOU KNOW?** >>
> In the last edition of this book the figure that I gave was 20,000 search engines, and in the first edition, published in 1999, the figure was 2500!

exactly a trick, I expect that you were thinking of one specific type of search engine, such as *Google* or *Yahoo!* That is to say, a search engine that attempts to index as large number of pages as possible. If you'd said that you thought there were a few hundred of that sort, or even just a handful of really 'large' or 'important' search engines, you wouldn't be too inaccurate. However, when I posed the question, I was thinking much more broadly than just that generic type of search engine – I was also thinking of smaller engines that might search one particular site, or one particular resource, such as a dictionary. Once you redefine search engines into this broader category the figure of 150,000 becomes rather less implausible. If you're still doubtful, take a look at the *Yahoo!* listing for search engines at **http://dir.yahoo.com/Computers_and_Internet/Internet/World_Wide _Web/Searching_the_Web/Search_Engines_and_Directories/** which gives a fairly impressive listing, but which is still just a drop in the ocean.

Let's discuss this business of definition in a little more detail. If you are considering search engines as tools to find information (rather than as a promotional tool for your website, for example) there are basically four different types of search engine available to you:

- free-text search engines
- index- or directory-based search engines
- multi- or meta-search engines
- resource- or site-specific search engines.

Free-text search engines

Free-text search engines are very easy to describe. You can simply search for a single word, a number of words, or a phrase perhaps. You are not limited in any way as to your choice – you may search for the name of a company, a line of poetry, a number, a person's name, a word in a different language, just about anything. You are therefore *free* to type in any *text* you want.

This approach has both advantages and disadvantages, as you would expect. Free-text search engines are very useful if you know exactly what you are looking for, or if you are looking for a concept that can be defined in a small number of words. They are less useful if you want a broad overview of a subject, or are searching in an area that you don't know very well and consequently have no idea about the best terms to use. There are a great many free-text search engines available for you to use, and we'll look at some of them in later chapters, but for now, if you want to break off reading and try one out, I'd suggest going to *Google* at **www.google.com/** although I expect you've already tried that one out. If you have but would like a break from reading anyway, try another favourite of mine, *AlltheWeb* at **www.alltheweb.com/**.

Most of the free-text search engines are still, unfortunately, quite primitive in their approach, and if you have used online or CD-ROM-based resources you might be a little surprised. They are improving over the course of time however – with leading engines it's possible to use Boolean operators, and in some cases even wild cards! However, since search engines are aimed at the lowest common denominator, which is people who have never done any kind of searching before, their designers may well feel that there is little point in adding in a great deal of advanced functionality when 97% of users won't use or understand that functionality.

How free-text search engines collect their data

In order to use these search engines effectively, it is necessary to have some background knowledge of how they work. Most of them make use of 'spider' or 'robot' or 'crawler' utilities which spend their time crawling around the web, going from link to link looking for new pages, or pages that have been updated since they were last visited by the spider. When they find these new or updated pages they copy this information back home to be included in an updated version of the index at some point in the future. The spider will also follow any links that it finds and repeat the process until it can't find any more, at which point it will retrace its steps and follow a new route.

Search engines can also be alerted to the existence of new pages if a web author goes to a particular search engine site and informs the engine of new pages or a new site. These pages will then be put on a list for visiting at some point in the future. If an author is particularly keen to add their site or pages to the search engine index they can pay the engine(s) a fee to be put on a priority list for indexing.

This has a number of implications as far as the searcher is concerned. Given the size of the world wide web, the collection of new data and maintenance of existing information is a full-time job, and even the fastest computers have trouble keeping up with the flood of new pages and sites onto the web. As a result, pages and sites may have been published on the web for months before they are found by search engines. Consequently, when searchers use search engines they are not doing a 'real time' search – they are searching through a snapshot of the web as it existed at some period of time in the past. Worse, it's not even a complete listing of all the pages that are publicly available. At the time of writing, *Google* indexes and makes available data from 4,285,199,774 pages; one of its main rivals, *AlltheWeb*, does the same with 3,151,743,117 pages. Now, this is a lot of data and it is highly likely that a searcher will find what they need somewhere within that amount. However, that is not always the case; it may be because that information does not exist, or the searcher has created a poor search strategy, or it may simply mean that the search engine being used does not know of, and has not indexed, the one particular web page that perfectly answers the question being asked. No one knows how many web pages are publicly available (as opposed to those on intranets or which are password protected), but I have seen figures ranging between eight and 13 billion pages. Even if we are conservative and take the lower figure, it means that even the biggest of the search engines are finding and indexing fewer than half of all the pages on the web. In comparative terms, therefore, four billion web pages isn't actually a great deal.

Returning to the issue of currency, it's depressing to say that the searcher is not much better off here. As we have already seen, search engines do not update their indexes every second of the day; indeed an update of the index is a major event and takes a lot of work, so much so that when *Google* is doing this it's generally referred to as the 'Google Dance'. Depending on the subject that the searcher is looking for this may be a major problem or a minor inconvenience, but it should always be kept in mind. It may be necessary in some cases to change the overall search strategy completely; if the information required relates to the latest earthquake, or the death of a celebrity, you may find that it's quicker and easier to go directly to one of the news broadcasting sites – or even that old faithful, the daily newspaper!

The content of web pages is the responsibility of the organization that owns the site, or of the individual author. It's therefore up to them to decide when to update the information on their site. Sites that are frequently updated tend to be visited more often by search engine spiders, and sites that are seldom updated are consequently visited less often. As a result the information retrieved by the search engine will not be an entirely accurate picture. Inevitably, some of the pages returned by the engine will not exist any longer, because they will have been removed by the author, for example; but as the engine hasn't been back to check it doesn't know. The same situation will occur if the text on a page has been changed by the author; if the search engine hasn't been back to update the data the searcher may well be confused, since the information returned by the engine isn't what the searcher will view on the page when they visit.

DID YOU KNOW? >>

It is difficult to work out which are the most popular search engines, but one company in particular, Nielsen/NetRatings, estimates that, based on its figures for the US home market, the current most popular search engines are *Google, Yahoo!, MSN, AOL* and *Ask Jeeves*. More details can be obtained from www.nielsen-netratings.com/.

Relevance ranking

You may therefore wonder how it is possible to retrieve any information of value from your searches, given that the indexes are out of date and not everything is indexed anyway! However, it's worth remembering that the search still has over three billion pages to play with and, even if a search engine hasn't indexed the most current version of a page, it's still likely that searchers will find the information they require. We'll look later in more detail at individual search engines to see how to use their syntax in an effective search, but before we get to that point there is one final area that needs to be discussed when looking at free-text search engines, and that is relevance ranking.

Given the number of results a search is likely to return (often into the millions), it would be unrealistic for an engine to return those results in no order at all. Therefore, engines try to work out which pages are going to be more helpful than others, and they will put those at the top of the list. The criteria that they use are constantly changing, and they tend to keep the exact algorithms secret, but it's possible to point out a few of the things that they do take into account. Some examples are:

- search terms appearing in the title of the page
- search terms repeated several times on the page
- search terms in important positions on the page, such as headings or close to the beginning
- search terms close to each other
- links to pages from other sites.

HINTS & TIPS >>
If you search for two words, such as President Bush, most search engines will default to a search for President AND Bush, giving a higher ranking to pages that contain both of those terms together. However, it is possible that a search engine may search for President OR Bush, giving a very different set of results.

This is only a small number of examples – *Google* uses over 100 different algorithms to rank pages – but it will give you some ideas as to why you get the results that you do. It's also important to be aware that each search engine will use different weighting and algorithms, so even if all the free-text search engines used the same database (which of course they don't), you would get a different set of results with each of them. Consequently, it's always important to be flexible when searching – if one engine doesn't give you the information that you need it's always worth trying another engine (or indeed several!) before giving up the hunt.

Index- or directory-based search engines

These search engines take a rather different approach to providing you with information on the sites that you might want to visit. Their emphasis is on classifying knowledge under a series of major subject headings, and then subdividing these into a tree structure of more specific headings, and sites are then listed as appropriate in this directory structure. If this approach sounds familiar, that is because it is, as anyone who has ever used a library classification scheme will know.

The advantages of this approach are obvious. The subject headings and subheadings can be used to guide the users through the vast mass of information until they are able to locate exactly the right section that covers the area they are interested in. An in-depth knowledge of the subject is not required since the users can stop drilling down through the trees at any point they wish, check one or two sites to see that they are in the right kind of area, and then continue to focus and re-focus until they get to a reasonably small number of sites which can then be viewed as necessary. Probably the most famous of these index search engines is *Yahoo!*, and you may wish to break off from reading to go and have a look at it (although I'd be surprised if you've not used it at least once or twice). You can find it at **www.yahoo.com/**. The UK and Ireland version is at **http://uk.yahoo.com/**.

Another advantage of this approach is that it is very easy to obtain an overview of sites in a particular category. For example, if you wanted to know which UK newspapers had websites it would be difficult to use a free-text search engine to quickly give you that information. However, by drilling down through the subheadings at *Yahoo!*, it's only a few mouse clicks before you can see a fairly comprehensive list – although of course it's important to remember that it will not be a complete list.

> **DID YOU KNOW? >>**
> The name *Yahoo!* is an acronym for 'Yet Another Hierarchical Officious Oracle'.

With advantages there are always disadvantages, of course. One of these lies in the way in which the headings and subheadings have been constructed, and these may well show up individual biases. For example, if you are looking at *Yahoo!*, one of the main subject headings together with its subheadings is:

Government
    Elections
    Military
    Law
    Taxes.

American readers are probably wondering what is wrong with it. This is perfectly understandable, because from an American viewpoint there *is* nothing wrong with it. However, a British reader might look slightly askance at the subheadings, since we would expect to find them in rather different places in a hierarchical structure. To be fair to *Yahoo!* though, this has been recognized, and country-specific versions of the search engine have been created with a different structure. Therefore, if you take a look at the same heading in *Yahoo!* UK and Ireland, it looks something like this:

> Government
>> UK
>> Ireland
>> Politics
>> Law.

However, while this does (to British eyes) make more sense, the basic point still stands – you are at the mercy of the people who put the structure into place. If the searcher assumes that a particular subject is going to be found under a particular heading, they may spend a lot of time drilling down into one section of the index, only to discover that what they are actually looking for is contained somewhere else entirely. Therefore, it's quite easy to waste time, unless careful thought is given to the best approach. Many of the organizations that have produced search engines of this type have recognized that this may be a problem for their users and have created a free-text-style search box which can be used to quickly identify exactly where within a hierarchy the users will find information about their subject of interest.

Another major disadvantage of the index-based search engine is that it doesn't provide access to web *pages*, but rather to web*sites*. Searchers therefore need to think rather more broadly when trying to find information: they must first use the index search engine to identify a useful site, then visit the site and hope to find the exact information that they are looking for. Consequently, unlike a free-text search engine that will direct a searcher to a precise page, index-based engines can act only as the first stage in a two-stage process.

A third important disadvantage of index- or directory-based engines is that they are quite small, as a result of the way in which they obtain the data, and we'll look at that in more detail in a moment. However, suffice to say at this point, even large index-based search engines will give access to only a few million websites, which is not quite in the same league as the billions of pages that can be directly accessed via free-text engines.

How index-based search engines obtain their data

Well, in actual fact they don't. 'Obtain' implies a level of proactivity that they simply don't possess. An index-based search engine will essentially just sit and wait for a web author to come to it, decide on the subject of their website, find the correct category and then submit their site for inclusion into that heading. Depending on the search engine it may simply be added with hardly any checking, or at the other end of the spectrum the submission may be rigorously checked before inclusion. Consequently, searchers are to some extent at the mercy of web authors to make sure that they have submitted their sites to the correct category. This can be pushed even further, because searchers are also at the mercy of web authors who may not even submit their sites at all.

A second problem is to do with currency. We've already seen that this is a problem with free-text search engines, and it's a problem with this type as well. From submitting a website for inclusion into the database to it actually showing up for people to visit can take anything upwards of three months, although you can pay for an express submission service. (This doesn't mean that the site will be included in the database, just that it will be looked at and assessed more quickly.) It's worth remembering, then, that it's quite likely that any new websites that you hear about in the news, for example, may well not be found in an index search engine for some time.

Once a site has been submitted, the index search engine may well just include the site the next time it updates its index (whenever that may be), or alternatively it may look at the site in more detail. Aspects of a site that may be checked are the HTML coding, content of the site, originality of the data and coverage in comparison to sites already included in the database. It's therefore possible to make the case that sites found in an index search engine are of a higher calibre (in terms of coding and content) than pages that may be returned with a free-text search engine, though it's not a point that I would want to push too far.

Multi- or meta-search engines

The next type of search engine isn't really a search engine at all, since a multi-search engine doesn't search anything itself. Instead, it takes your query and passes it onto a selected group of search engines. Once the results start coming in from these individual search engines, a multi-search engine will display these on the screen. The more advanced engines will collate the results, remove duplicates and put them into some sort of sensible order. The most advanced ones of all will allow users to display the results in different ways.

Search engines in this category are useful if you want to obtain a comprehensive listing of websites that cover a particular subject. Individual search engines may well not be fully comprehensive (in fact I would not expect them to be), and one may index sites that another has missed, and vice versa. Searching each of them individually is going to take time – you must locate the URL, visit the engine, input the search, wait for the results and then visit the pages that you find useful before repeating the whole process somewhere else. Using a multi-search engine means that it's only necessary to visit one site and all the results are brought back to your screen, therefore limiting the amount of work you have to do.

Unfortunately, this strength is also a major weakness of search engines in this category. The searcher is submitting their search to a number of different search engines, and consequently each engine needs to be able to understand the syntax used. Therefore, searchers need to know that each engine used by the multi-search engine will understand what is being asked of it. As a result, it's necessary to run searches at the lowest common denominator, which may well just be a series of terms, without using syntax to focus the search more closely. Some of the more sophisticated multi-search engines are now able to translate your query into the correct syntax for each search engine, but this cannot be guaranteed, so you should check rather than automatically rely on this happening.

There is a second type of multi-search engine which is perhaps even less like a search engine than the type that I have described above. These engines simply provide you with links through to lots of other search engines, without even giving you the opportunity to input search terms to be forwarded to them. If I were being pedantic I would refer to such sites as 'launchpad sites', rather than search engines in their own right. They can, however, be useful by providing you with links to search engines and other resources which you might otherwise have never found at all – or, if my experience is anything to go by, which you would have found the day after you really needed them!

If you are keen to try out a multi-search engine, you could visit one at *ZapMeta* which can be found at **www.zapmeta.com/**, or if you want to have a look at them in more detail, pay a visit to Chapter 5.

Resource- or site-specific search engines

The final category of search engines is without a doubt the largest, but paradoxically perhaps the least used, probably as a result of their diversity. A resource-specific engine may well have been created simply to search one particular resource such as the Bible, a dictionary or an encyclopaedia. The data that is retrieved is therefore static information, in that it doesn't change at all, or only on an irregular basis. A second type of engine is one that will search a database, such as a yellow pages or a genealogical database, and the data that is retrieved will change more frequently. The final type of engine in this category will just search a single site.

There is very little that can be said about these engines, since they are all different to look at and to use. One point which it is important to make, however, is that generally the resources that they make available will not be found by other, more general search engines, and the reasons for this will become clear in Chapter 7, which explores 'the hidden web'.

Some other points about search engines

Who owns the search engines?

Search engines are created by anyone who has the time, money, skill and inclination to devote to creating one. The internet has few rules and regulations, so anyone can (to a greater or lesser extent) do exactly what they want, and some organizations and individuals have decided that, for a variety of reasons, they wish to establish and maintain search engines for people to use. Many engines will provide you with some sort of detail as to their origins and background, but in most cases they are created because someone wanted to; it really is as simple as that. Of course, money does raise its head at this point, since they are a way of making money; though, given the number of search engines that are launched and then quietly disappear, they're even better at losing it!

How much do search engines cost to use?

Search engines take a considerable amount of time to establish and maintain. This requires full-time staff, expensive computer equipment, advertising and communications – everything in fact that any large corporation requires. It may, therefore, come as something of a surprise to discover that there are very few search engines that charge end-users to search them. People are free to connect to their search engine(s) of choice, interrogate the database and move on to view the sites or pages that they think will be helpful. In the training sessions that I run, people often express amazement that all of this information is given away freely, so if you are surprised by this, don't worry

– you're not alone! Given that search engines do need to make money, if they don't make it through the users, there have to be other ways in which this is achieved.

The answer to this conundrum is very simple and can be summed up in a single phrase: 'advertising revenue'. The internet is, despite its early developments and academic origins, driven by commerce, and this is best demonstrated by looking at the number of advertisements on websites. Almost all search engines include some sort of advertising from sites enticing viewers to visit them, and of course once you visit the site you will be faced with more skilful attempts to part you from your money. Advertisers work on the theory of maximum exposure for maximum profits, and nowhere is this more evident than on a search engine page. If an advertiser has a product for sale that costs £/$100 and places an advertisement for it on a site that is visited 10,000,000 times a day (which isn't uncommon), if only 1% of visitors to that site click on the advertising link and visit the advertiser's site, and if only 1% of them buy the product, that would mean a revenue stream of £/$100,000 a day. Consequently, the advertisers will be prepared to pay significant sums of money to the owners of a site that commands that many visitors.

Search engines also make money by advertisment placement, and this can be very sophisticated. If you go to a search engine and run a search for keywords such as *gardens, gardening, flowers* it is likely that a sponsored link will displayed before the results, for a site that sells gardening equipment, or for an internet florist, for example. This can be useful if you are actually searching for a product to buy, but in general terms most searchers' eyes glaze over these links. To generate the maximum advertising revenue possible it is in the best interests of the owners of search engines to encourage as many visitors as possible, which means having increasingly powerful search software, easy and advanced interfaces, larger databases and so on. Indeed, many engines are now offering e-mail addresses for life, web space, personalized news services and anything else they can think of to encourage visitors to return time and time again. Therefore, although in one sense searching is entirely free, in another sense you do actually pay by having to download and view an advertisement (or probably several) every time you view a page of results.

Search engines also make money by licensing other organizations to use their database of results. Not every large organization with a large presence has the inclination to produce its own search engine, but it may appear to do exactly that by paying a search engine for access to the data and simply producing its own front end. If you go to one search engine and run a query and get a specific number of responses, and go to another engine and get exactly the same number, it's doubtful that it is a coincidence; it's much more likely that you're looking at the same results. Therefore, choose one engine or the other, but don't waste time searching both since it will be a duplication of effort.

Natural-language search engines

In the two previous editions of this book I included a section on natural-language search engines – that is to say, a search engine that accepts a question written in straightforward English and that gives an answer in straightforward English. There used to be several search engines that fell into this category but, with the exception of *Ask Jeeves*, these have all but disappeared.

If you visit most search engines and type in the question *What is the longest river in the world?* search engines will try and find web pages that match the search string. *Ask Jeeves*, however, will first of all give you the answer to your question before going on to suggest various sites for you. Obviously, it can only do this for very straightforward factual queries – the question *What is the best football team in the world?* does not provide such a clear-cut answer, so the use is limited. However, it is a good search engine and, even if the category has virtually disappeared, the search engine itself is still going strong.

Country and regional search engines

If a searcher has a specific requirement for country-based information there are a number of ways of getting it. Many of the larger search engines have versions for different countries which, when used, will default to just returning results from sites based in that country, or they may have an advanced search option to allow searchers to limit to a country or a particular region. Finally, there are more than 1500 search engines (mostly index or directory based) that just list sites from a particular country or region. A good listing of these can be found on my own site at **www.philb.com/countryse.htm**.

> **HINTS & TIPS >>**
>
> If you want to get to a country-based version of a search engine, just try replacing the .com element of the URL with the commercial extension and country code for the country you're interested in. For example, the UK version of *Google* can be found at www.google.co.uk/.

Summary

In this chapter I have outlined the major types of search engine, how they gather their data, and in general terms what their strengths and weaknesses are. In order to search the internet effectively, it is necessary to match the search you wish to do against the type of engine, and your level of knowledge of the subject. Each search engine will provide different results, based on the data contained within its database and the way in which it ranks results.

None of the search engines are perfect, and all have their own particular advantages and disadvantages. The successful searcher will have a good understanding of the rationale behind their design and working methods. In the next five chapters I will be looking at the different types of engine in more detail, and will focus on a number of particularly important and popular ones.

URLs mentioned in this chapter

www.quoteland.com/

http://dir.yahoo.com/Computers_and_Internet/Internet/World_Wide_
   Web/Searching_the_Web/Search_Engines_and_Directories/

www.google.com/

www.alltheweb.com/

www.nielsen-netratings.com/

www.yahoo.com/

http://uk.yahoo.com/

www.zapmeta.com/

www.pacific.net.ph/pacific_trivia/

www.philb.com/countryse.htm

www.google.co.uk/

Chapter 3 »
Free-text search engines

Introduction

In this chapter I look in more detail at free-text search engines; how they can assist the searcher, search methodologies and so on. I'll look at several engines in some detail, but will also point readers towards some other engines that are perhaps not quite so well known. To briefly summarize from the previous chapter, free-text search engines:

- will accept any term(s) or phrase(s) a user wishes to search for
- can search for terms in any combination
- can include or exclude terms
- allow very focused searching
- are not comprehensive
- are not current.

Google

The first two editions of this book contained scant, if any, reference to *Google*. That isn't because I wasn't doing my job properly and had somehow 'missed' its existence, and it isn't because *Google* was in some way a bad search engine. It is simply that it was quite new and was very much in the second division of search engines, being totally eclipsed by the 'greats' such as *AltaVista*, *Yahoo!*, *Lycos* and *HotBot*. Now the situation is entirely reversed, and any book on any aspect of the internet has to pay great attention to *Google*, and indeed several books have already been written just about this one search engine. Before we get into the nuts and bolts of using it, let's get a little of the trivia out of the way, which will also help illustrate how important it is to, not only to searching the web, but to the whole internet.

Google came out of beta testing on 21 September 1999. More than 55 billion searches were run on *Google* in 2002 (**www.google.com/press/ zeitgeist2002.html**) and over 200 million searches are run on it per day. It is one of the ten most popular websites in the world; has at least 88 different language interfaces; has at least four billion indexed web pages; provides access to at least 425 million images; and has archived at least 800 million Usenet messages. I say 'at least' not because of any uncertainty, simply because Google adapts, changes and evolves so quickly there's a very good chance that these numbers will be incorrect by the time you read this. These facts are from **www.google.com/corporate/facts.html**. There is even a search engine about *Google*, called *Google World* (**http:// google.indicateur.com/**).

Google – the basics

Google, both in historical and functional terms, falls squarely into the free-text search engine category. That is to say that you're free to type in any term or terms that you think are appropriate to find pages that will answer your query. At the simplest level, a single word search, however obscure, will result in a lot of results. Since *Google* indexes over three billion pages the major problem with the search engine is too many results, not too few!

Consequently, a good search will be for several terms, to help *Google* define and narrow down exactly what you are looking for. The search engine uses an AND approach, which is to say that if you put two or more terms into your search, such as *richmond holiday* it will look for pages that contain both 'richmond' and 'holiday'. Consequently, the more terms you add, the more precise the search becomes, resulting in fewer results. *Google* will accept up to ten search terms – any more than that and it will ignore the eleventh onwards. Since it does an automatic AND search, an easy way to reduce the number of results (other than narrowing by adding terms) is to exclude terms from your search, using the minus (–) symbol. Therefore, a search for *richmond holiday – september* will search for web pages that contain both 'richmond' and 'holiday', but if any of them also contain the term 'september' those pages will be excluded from the results returned. This works in the same way as the Boolean operator NOT and should be treated with care. If you're interested in pages that are about diabetes in adults and not in children, a search for *diabetes adults – children* may look a good idea, but as well as excluding pages that talk about diabetes in children it will also exclude a web page that states

'This page is about diabetes in adults and not in children.' Do, therefore, use it with some caution, though it can be particularly useful to exclude American-authored pages if you're looking for British–English material, or vice versa.

The number of returned results can be narrowed further, and with more precision, by the use of the phrase syntax, and this can best be explained by searching for a person's name. A simple search for *mark green* will return a lot of pages that mention 'mark' in one place on the page and 'green' in another. (You'll notice that I'm not using capital letters here – *Google* doesn't distinguish between the two.) When I ran this search at *Google* it returned 4,390,000 records, and most of those pages will be of no interest to me. However, by putting the two words into a phrase by the use of the double quote symbol thus – "*mark green*", *Google* now knows that it should simply return pages that contain that exact string of characters in that order, and I end up with 64,000 results – still an awful lot, but it's certainly better than several million.

The phrase option is therefore a very useful way to focus a search, not only by reducing the number of pages returned, but by specifying the order of the terms. "*cattle breeding*" is not the same as "*breeding cattle*" for example, and using

the terms in the correct order will result in a smaller and, importantly, more focused search than simply searching for *cattle breeding* which will return pages that talk about either subject. Of course, the phrase option isn't perfect – our search for "*mark green*" will also return pages that contain text that might look a little like this: *Jones, Mark. Green, David*. But then, nothing is perfect – certainly not in the world of internet searching!

A phrase can of course be excluded from a search by using the minus symbol immediately before the opening double quote mark. So, to exclude references to the United States of America, one would only have to include the following search statement: –"*United States of America*", although an experienced searcher would also exclude other variants, such as USA.

Let us now put all this together into a search to see how these different functions can be used in conjunction with each other to give us a small, but useful set of results. Suppose that we're interested in taking a holiday in the quaint English town of Richmond. Google gives us the following sets of results (if you do this search yourself you will get different numbers, though the trends should be exactly the same – downwards!):

10,100,000	*richmond*
527,000	*richmond holiday*
268,000	*richmond holiday –virginia*
845	*richmond holiday –virginia "yorkshire england"*
618	*richmond holiday –virginia "yorkshire england" –"self catering"*

We could of course continue to add or exclude more terms, but I think the point is clearly made. Just remembering to use those three search tips – more terms rather than fewer, excluding terms, and phrase searching – will dramatically reduce the time spent on searches. You will get fewer results but, most importantly, more focused results.

There are many more things that can be done with *Google* and, while many of them can be done at the simple search screen, there is greater flexibility by moving to the advanced search interface. Just before we do that, just in case you're curious, if you press the 'I'm Feeling Lucky' button on the *Google* interface screen in Figure 3.1, it takes you directly to the first site returned by the search engine. This can save you a few moments of your time but, if you're not particularly lucky, you then have to backtrack and start again.

Figure 3.1   The *Google* home page, showing the simple interface
© 2004 Google

HINTS & TIPS >>

Most search engines are now using the plus and minus symbols to include AND or NOT, but you should check with individual search engines to see if this holds true, since it is a convention, not a rule. It's not necessary to use the plus symbol with *Google*, since it defaults to an AND search naturally, but you can use the minus symbol to exclude words from the search.

Google – advanced searching

The first section of the advanced search screen is shown in Figure 3.2

The first box is really not that different from the simple search function. Indeed, if you type in some search terms, or a phrase, or exclude some terms (or of course a combination of all three) in the simple search box and then click on the advanced search function you'll see those terms already in the appropriate boxes for you. However, to briefly go through them:

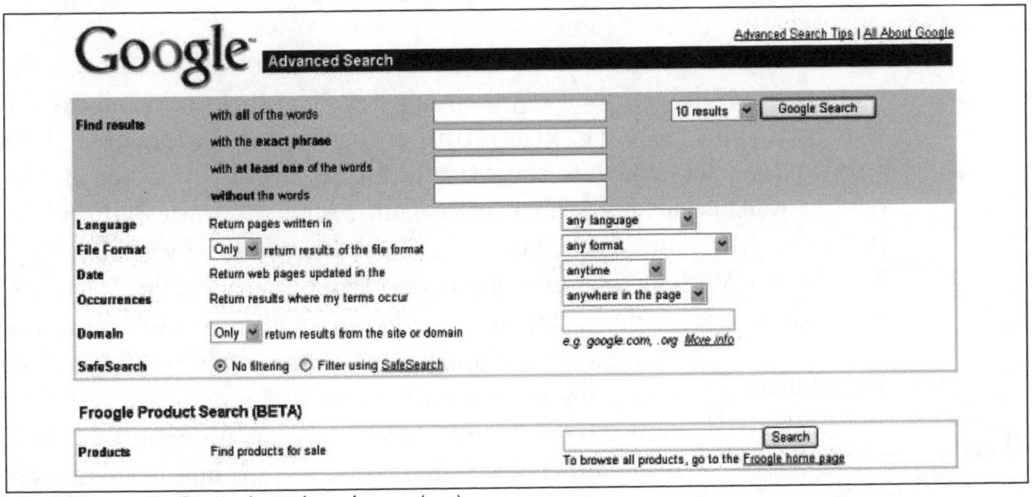

Figure 3.2 The *Google* advanced search screen (part)
© 2004 Google

- 'Find results with **all** of the words' is the *Google* default. A search for *dog puppy cat kitten* will find pages that have all four words in them, anywhere on the page, in any order.
- 'Find results with the **exact phrase**' means that a search for *dog puppy cat kitten* will just return pages that have that exact string of characters in that exact order, anywhere on the page.
- 'Find results with **at least one** of the words' will result in a search for *dog puppy cat kitten* returning web pages that contain one or more of the terms on the page.
- 'Find results **without** the words' would find pages that did not include *dog puppy cat kitten* anywhere in them. This would obviously only be useful if you'd also included one or more search terms in the other boxes.

- The final option available to searchers in the first series of boxes is to change the number of results returned in one go; the options are 10, 20, 30, 50, 100. I don't think that there is a particular advantage or disadvantage here, other than personal taste.

The next option down, Language, allows searchers to limit to a specific language. This may be useful if a searcher speaks another language and wants to limit results to that language (for example, it would be a simple way to limit searches to the perspective of a German, or at least German speaker). Alternatively, a search for *Berlin* would result in a lot of German-language pages which could be excluded if the search was limited to just returning English-language pages.

The File Format option can prove to be a very useful way of reducing the number of results and focusing them quickly. The first option allows the searcher to limit a search to a file format or to exclude a file format, and the second allows the searcher to chose the file format they are interested in. The options available are any format (the default), Adobe Acrobat PDF, Adobe Postscript, Microsoft Word, Microsoft Excel, Microsoft PowerPoint, Rich Text Format. Without too much of a stretch of the imagination, limiting results to any of these file types will tend to produce particular sorts of results. For

example, government departments often publish official documents in an Acrobat format, as do companies with their annual reports, and educational establishments with their course brochures. Running a search and limiting to this format will tend to lead to a higher proportion of results that contain that type of data. Similarly, if a searcher is looking for financial or statistical data, limiting a search to Excel spreadsheets might provide a very useful set of results.

Date is the next option available to the searcher. *Google* allows searchers to limit results to pages that were updated in the last three months, six months, the last year, or the default option, anytime. This is not an area that *Google* is particularly strong in and, as we shall see later, other search engines are rather better at this.

Searchers can choose where occurrences of a term are to be found on a web page. The options available here are anywhere on the page (the default option); the title (which with the way in which relevance ranking in *Google* works will almost always come close to the top of the list of results); in the text of the page (which is so broad as to be almost meaningless); in the URL of the page (a search here for library in the URL would produce a hit for a page like www.philb.com/library/hours.htm); and in links to the page. This last means that if someone writes linking text to another site that viewers can click on, such as 'read about the *library opening hours*' this would be a hit. In most cases I don't tend to use any of these with the searches that I run, since I think they're either too broad to be of much use, or they're already taken into account when *Google* relevance ranks the pages that it has found.

The last option in this section, Domain, is very useful. The first variable is 'only return results from the site or domain' or 'don't return results from the site or domain' and the second variable is where the searcher writes their choice into the blank box. There are three very useful ways of using this option. Let us suppose that we want to know what the Microsoft position is on security flaws in its Windows XP product. Just doing a search for something like "*security flaws*" "*Windows XP*" is going to result in lots of pages (over 6000 when I ran this search in fact), and most of these will not be from Microsoft sites. Refining the search to "*security flaws*" "*Microsoft Windows XP*" does reduce this number somewhat (to over 500). However, by limiting the search to Microsoft.com in the Domain box, our search drops to only 15 results. 6000 results to just 15 – it makes you think, doesn't it!

The second way that this search option can be used is to limit the search to just .com or .net sites, for example. Given that the whole domain naming convention has broken down now, there does seem little point in trying to use this to limit a search – it's as likely that a non-profit-making organization will have a URL that ends in .com as in .org. However, if this is combined with the third option, of limiting to a particular country code, such as .uk or .de, the value becomes clearer. Consequently, a searcher can limit to .gov.uk or .ac.uk to simply get British government or academic websites.

A number of other options are available to the advanced searcher from this page, and I'll go through them briefly. The first of them can be seen in Figure 3.2, Froogle, which also has its own site at **http://froogle.google.com/**.

In brief, it's a new service from *Google* that makes it easy to find information about products for sale online. If you're looking to buy particular products it might be an option worth exploring, but as I imagine it's unlikely many readers of this book will have a clientele that asks for the best and cheapest widget I think we can pass on by.

There are two page-specific options provided by *Google*. The first of these, called Similar, allows users to locate pages similar to one that they are familiar with. The theory is that other pages will be equally as useful as the one that you know of. This is sometimes the case, but not always. However, if you are having difficulties finding other resources, this may help point you in the right direction. The second search option is entitled Links, and allows searchers to find pages that link to a specified page. Again this works by assuming that similar pages are connected, in this case by links. There is a lot of logic behind it, because an author will not link to a page that has no relevance. However, it quickly becomes clear that the pages are not returned in any particular order, so it isn't as useful as it might at first appear. *Google* also doesn't actually give a complete listing of pages that link to another page; just pages that it considers to be particularly important (known as PageRank).

Google shortcuts

The advanced search functionality is therefore reasonably powerful, and it does allow searchers to quickly focus on pages that are likely to be useful to them. However, it is not necessary to go to the time and trouble of going to the advanced search screen; the majority of these advanced searches can be done from the simple search page, once you are aware of the syntax that is required. Since we have already discussed the merits of the different options I won't go through them again, but list the syntax used:

- filetype:pdf
  filetype:ps
  filetype:doc
  filetype:xls
  filetype:ppt
  filetype:rtf
- allintitle:keyword
  allintext:keyword
  allinurl:keyword
  allinanchor:keyword
- site:google.com
  site:.com
  site:.uk
  site:.ac.uk
- related:www.google.com/help.html
- link:www.google.com/help.html.

Options for language and time period are included in the set of results as options on the screen, rather than command line options with the other search syntax listed above. Google also offers an option for searching for synonyms. This is done by using the tilde (~)symbol immediately before the appropriate keyword. Therefore, to search for, say, guides for a novice in some area the syntax would be ~*guide* ~*novice*. This returns web pages that use terms such as tutorial, guide, guides, novice, beginner, tips and so on. Not only does this work for synonyms, but for related terms. A search for ~*confederate* returns pages that not only talk about confederate and confederacy but also civil war.

The *Google* toolbar

The *Google* toolbar is a very useful application, and one that makes the lives of many searchers much easier. It is a small utility which can be freely downloaded from **http://toolbar.google.com/** (the current version is 2.0) and installed directly without any fuss – in fact it was the quickest and easiest installation of any software that I have ever done. When installed it sits neatly in the browser window. In order to run it your computer needs to be using Microsoft Windows 95, 98, ME, NT, 2000, XP or 2003 Server with MSIE version 5 or later. I'm using ADSL and the download and automatic install over my current version took less than 30 seconds. One thing that you should be aware of is that to use some of the advanced functions of the toolbar it's a requirement that you allow the toolbar to 'talk' to *Google* to let the search engine know what pages you're viewing. It does this anonymously, but I know that some people get a little freaky about this. You can disallow this function, but it does mean that you won't be able to use all of the functionality of the toolbar, which seems a shame, but it's your choice of course. The *Google* toolbar is shown in Figure 3.3.

Figure 3.3   The *Google* toolbar
© 2004 Google

Google search

This is a small search box on the left hand side in which you type your search terms. If you click on the down arrow next to the box you can view the last 20 searches that you ran, and can if necessary click on one of them to rerun it, which

I find extremely helpful. There's also an option (which I think is new to this version, at least I've not seen it before), which allows you to clear the search history. Useful if you've been searching for something confidential. The search defaults to the *Google* easy or simple search function, but it's possible to move directly to any of the other *Google* search functions such as Advanced, Groups, Images and so on, simply by clicking on the 'Google' button on the extreme left of the toolbar. It's a nice simple straightforward function that's always appealed to me

To the right of the search box is the 'Search Web' button, which you can click when you've typed in your search. Alternatively, you can use the pull-down menu to utilize the 'I'm Feeling Lucky' option, just search for your term(s) within the site that you happen to be on (which has to be useful, though of course limited to those pages that Google is aware of), or you can search Dictionary.com for a particular word.

New *Google* toolbar features

These functions allow you to get to places in *Google* more quickly and easily than by remembering URLs, or following links or even pulling down your list of favorites. There are some interesting new additions which deserve a mention. You can now get to the *Google* Zeitgeist page, which is full of interesting titbits relating to popular searches, searches decreasing in popularity, top image queries, international queries and so on. I'm not sure just how useful it is, but it's fun to browse through now and then. There's also a link to Blogger.com which is no surprise, given *Google*'s recent acquisition, and is further supplemented by the addition of a 'Blog it' icon on the toolbar which allows users of Blogger to quickly and easily add something to their blogs directly from the web page they happen to be looking at. This feature has been available for some time via Blogger.com but it's nice to see it included. There's also an option to save your search preferences, and it was only when I clicked on this that I realized that my preferences weren't quite what I thought (I had filtering turned to moderate, which I hadn't realized. No wonder I wasn't seeing stuff that other people had been complaining about!). Finally, there is an 'Options' button, which allows you to change just about anything and everything to do with the toolbar.

Moving along the toolbar, the next icon up by default is the 'News' icon, which takes you directly to the news page. It would be nice if this had been integrated with the search option; it seems logical to me that I should be able to type a term into the search box and click on the 'News' icon, but if I do this my search term is ignored, and I just go directly to the *Google* News home page. To be fair, I can achieve exactly what I want by choosing a term and then using the pull down menu to choose *Google* News to run my search that way.

PageRank is the next icon on the toolbar. This is a small icon, based on a sliding scale, of how important *Google* thinks a particular page happens to be. It's useful for searchers who want a quick indication of authority (though it's easy enough to misunderstand, and it's also used by website developers for relevance ranking purposes.

The next icon which I activated for myself, a default in the current version but not in the new beta version, is the option to query *Google* about the

site you happen to be on. Simply clicking on the icon gives you the opportunity to see *Google*'s cached snapshot of the page, similar pages, backwards links and the opportunity to translate the page into English. (I've never tried to get *Google* to translate a page already in English into English. It's got to be an experiment worth trying sometime!) I've always liked this particular function since it's useful for authority checking, and to see what the general internet community thinks about a particular page or site.

A new feature is an automatic pop-up killer. I already have a pop-up killer, which works very well, but I always forget to turn it on – I don't have it set as a default, mainly because I run so many applications and don't have that much free memory to spare. This is delightful though, since it does the job neatly and without any fuss. When it blocks a pop-up it lets you know by sounding a little chime, the cursor briefly changes and the count on the blocker is increased by one. If you wish to allow pop-ups for a particular site (if, for example, it uses pop-ups for help screens), it's easy to turn it off for that site, and then turn it back on when you leave. What I haven't been able to find yet though is any way of seeing a list of exactly what I've blocked, or a way of unblocking a specific pop-up that I may have blocked in the past. Consequently, while I think this is a very useful function I'd prefer to see a little more flexibility. But there is no doubt that it's going to prove a very popular feature with users.

Another new option is 'Autofill' which you can use to autofill forms. If you get fed up with typing in your name and address details you can get autofill to do this for you. It can even remember your credit card details and input those as well. (Though having a little utility that can remember all that is just asking for trouble!) While you can set a password for this particular application it's one that I think in the main I'll leave well alone.

Automatic highlighting of search terms is another icon that I find invaluable. In fact, there are two ways in which this works on the toolbar. The first icon (in the form of a highlighter pen) simply highlights all the terms that you've searched for on the page. The second approach is that your search terms are temporarily added to the toolbar and you can click on them individually and you'll be taken to the section of the web page where the term appears. Both approaches are simple and easily implemented; I find them invaluable.

Google toolbar extra options

Well, that's the default for the toolbar but, as I mentioned earlier, there is an 'Options' facility. A great deal is hidden in there; more options, autofill details and so on. First up is the option of choosing which version of *Google* you search with. Most people will choose the .com version I should imagine, but there are all the various country versions including .co.uk. Other basic options are the ability to open a new window to display the results every time you search (no thanks, *Google*, I've usually got more than enough windows open as it is), options to turn on/off page ranking, page information, and all the other features that I've mentioned, such as the Blogger icon, news and pop-up killer.

The 'More' option is truly impressive, giving you the ability to add icons such as 'I'm Feeling Lucky', search images, search groups icons and so on. Of course, you can get these via the pull-down menus, but it's very nice to have them available as icons. A number of other options are pretty much hidden; one example being *Google* Compute, which is a little like the *Seti@home* project in that it allows your computer to be used to help compute data on a large scale. It's a nice idea, and in theory I have nothing against it, but I'd rather keep control over my computer, if it's all the same. Fortunately it is, since it's an option that's turned off by default. Another hidden option is a voting button – you can either vote for or against a particular page. At the moment my understanding is that Google isn't proactively using this information, but I can see it may well do in the longer term, and use it to assist in working out page rankings. There are a few other options, but I've pretty much covered the main ones.

Other *Google* functionality

Google is one of the most powerful search engines available to searchers – and indeed many would argue that it is the most powerful. It has gained this reputation not only because of the size of the database and the accuracy of the results, but because it does a lot more than simply search web pages. Rather than address all of the other functions in this chapter, I think it is more useful to cover them as appropriate in other chapters. However, if you prefer to read everything about *Google* in one go, you can find information on the image search function in Chapter 8, the directory function in Chapter 4, and *Google Groups* in Chapter 13.

Google offers various other search options, such as narrowing your search to universities or schools, a translation service, and a tool for software developers to automatically query *Google*. All of these can be located at **www.google. com/options/**.

AlltheWeb

AlltheWeb simple search

AlltheWeb at **www.alltheweb.com** is another search engine that was not mentioned at all in the previous edition of *The Advanced Internet Searcher's Handbook*, and for the same reason as Google; it was very new and had made virtually no impact on internet searchers. However, it has very quickly risen through the ranks and is now one of the most important free-text search engines, in some ways rivalling and surpassing *Google*. *AlltheWeb* was developed by Fast Search and Transfer, a Norwegian company, before being bought by Overture.

The simple search interface, shown in Figure 3.4, is very similar to that of *Google* – it is very straightforward, uncomplicated and clean.

Many of the comments previously made about searching using *Google* are applicable to *AlltheWeb*, and it's fair to say that if you can use one, you can use the other. *AlltheWeb* also works on an AND principle – if you type in two or more terms *AlltheWeb* will find pages that contain all the terms searched for. The search engine also understands the use of the double quotes marks to indicate a phrase search, and the minus symbol to exclude words from the search. *AlltheWeb* does not, however, have the same ten-word limitation that *Google* has. *AlltheWeb* does have an extra option which defaults the search to English, which *Google* does not, and this is balanced up against the fact that it doesn't have an equivalent of the *Google* 'I'm Feeling Lucky' button.

Figure 3.4   The *AlltheWeb* simple search interface
              © 2004 Overture Services, Inc.

AlltheWeb displays the list of results in a similar style to *Google*, with what it considers to be the most relevant at the top of the list. After the page title the keywords are shown in context, and there is then (in some cases) a description of the site. The searcher can then choose to see more pages from the site in question, and finally can also see the size of the web page concerned.

AlltheWeb tries to improve search results by rewriting them in some situations. This rewriting will include the addition of quotes around common phrases that are detected from its phrase dictionary. This option can be customized if required. Generally the rewrite does improve the focus of the search results, but the way in which *AlltheWeb* alerts users to the fact that it has done this (a small sentence hidden at the top of the page) is not always clear, and it may cause confusion sometimes.

AlltheWeb advanced search

Although the layout is slightly different, searchers will find very similar functionality between *Google* and *AlltheWeb*. The first option is a simple choice of searching for all the words, any of the words or the exact phrase. Alternatively, searchers can run a Boolean search using AND, OR, ANDNOT and RANK. The last option is not strictly speaking a Boolean operator at all, and it is used by *AlltheWeb* to give further weighting to search results which contain one particular term and also preferably one other term.

Other functions are available to focus the search more closely. *AlltheWeb* provides searchers with the option to limit to any one of over 70 language options and character sets. Word filters are included to allow users to choose to do a search that 'must include', 'should include' or 'must not include' in the fields title, text, URL, link or host name. The difference between 'must include' and 'should include' is, according to *AlltheWeb*, that pages with this word or phrase are prioritized if using 'should include' (essentially the same as the Boolean operator OR) and 'must include' means that pages without this word or phrase are discarded, which means that it works the same way as putting a + symbol or AND in front of the term.

AlltheWeb also offers an option to limit by domain, in exactly the same way that Google does (that is to say, the option of limiting to a particular domain such as **www.allthweb.com**, or to .com sites or .ac.uk sites, for example). Unlike *Google*, it offers the further opportunity of excluding a specific domain from the search, though it is fair to say that this can also be achieved with *Google* by putting a minus symbol in front of the search syntax. The *AlltheWeb* version is slightly neater though. *AlltheWeb* also allows users to to limit a search to a specific geographic area. As we've already seen, it's possible using the domain filter in *Google* to limit to a particular country, but *AlltheWeb* gives the option of limiting to Africa, Asia, Canada, Central America, Europe, the Middle East, North America, Oceania, South America, Southeast Asia or the United Kingdom. *AlltheWeb* offers an option for limiting results to certain IP addresses or ranges. To be perfectly honest, I can see no particular reason for using this search option, and I've never used it – nor has anyone that I know. Consequently, I'm going to ignore it but, if you're curious, the help page at **www.alltheweb.com/help/faqs/advanced.html** goes into more detail, though don't blame me if you're still puzzled at the end of the explanation.

Of more interest and use is the option of limiting results to those pages that have different types of media embedded in them. This allows users to include/exclude media such as images, audio, video, flash, Java applets, JavaScript or VBScript. Again, this provides a little more flexibility than is currently on offer with *Google*. The results of a search on whooping cough, for example, may well provide the option of hearing a sound file of someone who has the complaint if the audio box has been ticked. (Readers will find more discussion of various different media in Chapter 8.) However, like a good game of tennis, *Google* comes back with more sophistication when it comes to searching for file types, since *AlltheWeb* is limited to Adobe, Flash and Word files.

The balance tips again though when looking at the next advanced search option offered by *AlltheWeb*, which is the date limit function. The *Google* option is limited to the rather basic three months, six months or one year. *AlltheWeb* offers the choice of choosing any specific dates from 1 January 1980 onwards.

AlltheWeb ends the advanced search page with a small number of other options: the (file) size of a page, the number of results displayed per page, and a toggle for offensive content. And *AlltheWeb* allows users to save their settings, which is an option that *Google* does not currently have.

Finally – just like *Google* – *AlltheWeb* offers other functionality, such as the ability to search for images, multimedia and so on. For the sake of consistency, discussion of these functions can be found in the appropriate chapters in this volume.

Other free-text search engines explored

Despite the existence of the all powerful *Google*, and almost all powerful *AlltheWeb*, there are still plenty of other search engines available for searching. I don't think that there is any point in going through each of them in great detail, mainly because they are similar and all try to do the same job in the same way. However, it is worth outlining a few key examples to give some indication of the length and breadth of this category, and one or two people may be tempted to explore some search engines that they have not previously looked at. Consequently I'll limit myself to brief pen pictures, to draw out notable features that make them stand out.

AltaVista

AltaVista at **www.altavista.com** is still one of the best known, and one of the oldest search engines available on the internet; it was launched on 15 December 1995. The *AltaVista* Search Public Service was the brainchild of researchers at Digital Equipment Corporation's Palo Alto Laboratory. The search engine has been bought and sold since then, and is now owned by Overture Services, Inc. For many years it was considered to be the innovative search engine, but fell into something of a decline with the increasing popularity of *Google*. It is now trying to recapture former glories, but in most instances is not producing anything particularly innovative now; while it has many useful search features, these are often produced in response to the work other engines have already done.

DID YOU KNOW? >>

The name *AltaVista* was the code name of the project and was not adopted as the name of the service until two days before it was launched.

The simple search interface can be seen in Figure 3.5 and, in common with *Google* and *AlltheWeb*, it has a simple uncluttered look, which is easy to follow. As you would expect, the search syntax and method of searching are the same as for the previously men-

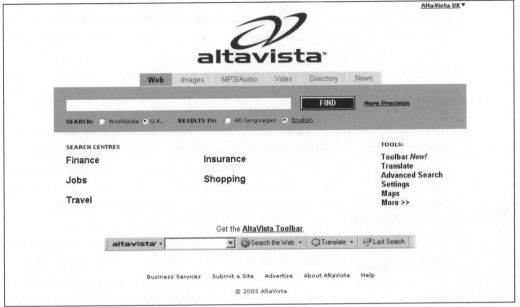

Figure 3.5 The *AltaVista* simple search interface
© 2004 Overture Services, Inc.

tioned engines – *AltaVista* uses the AND approach with keywords, double quotes for a phrase and the minus symbol to exclude words from the search. However, *AltaVista* does have one particular advantage over the other major engines, in that it is possible to run a search that is upper- or lower-case specific – indeed it is the only search engine that currently offers this feature. In order to use it, it is necessary only to put the word into double quotes. Moreover, if you include an accent in a query word, *AltaVista* only matches words with that particular accent. If you do not include an accent, *AltaVista* will match words both with and without accents. This means you can search for French, German or Spanish words, even if you have an English-only keyboard.

The advanced search function is almost identical in many respects to the two that we have already seen, with options for 'all these words', 'this exact phrase', 'any of these words', 'none of these words'. There is also a search box that is used for typing in your own search, using Boolean operators. This is another area that *AltaVista* has always been strong in, and where it is still perhaps more attractive than its larger competitors. The usual operators, AND OR AND NOT are available, as is NEAR (to within ten words, although the exact number cannot be specified). *AltaVista* also allows the use of truncation (the symbol used being the asterisk) to replace any number of letters at the end of a word, or in addition as a wildcard in the middle of a word. Use parentheses to group complex Boolean phrases. For example, (*peanut AND butter*) *AND* (*jelly OR jam*) finds documents with the words 'peanut butter and jelly' or 'peanut butter and jam' or both. (It is worth noting that these options are also available in the simple search function as well; it is just that if they are used in the advanced search function they should be used in the Boolean operator box.) One final point here, and that is that *AltaVista* will not sort the results that are returned using this function. Once the search strategy has been compiled it is also necessary to add terms into the 'Sorted by' box, at which point *AltaVista* will then relevance rank accordingly. Other options include searching restricted by language, and limited to the United Kingdom.

DID YOU KNOW? >> Seventy-six per cent of Americans searching the internet use a search engine to find what they are looking for (http://sanfrancisco.bizjournals.com/ sanfrancisco/stories/2004/02/23/daily1. html?jst=b_ln_hl).

Further options worth noting include the ability to search by time period – *AltaVista* is as good here as *AlltheWeb*, and is better than *Google*, since the options are a week, two weeks, a month, four months, eight months or a year, or a specific time period. *AltaVista* also has a toolbar option, but this has only recently been introduced, so is not as advanced as the *Google* offering.

The list of retrieved records also shows a particular difference to that of either *AlltheWeb* or *Google*, and that is from a function *AltaVista* refers to as *AltaVista* Prisma. This lists the main topics within your search results. These are the most common terms from the pages that best match your query. Each term is a link you can use to refine your search. Consequently, when running a search for "*Robert E Lee*" Prisma will offer such terms as "*General Lee*", "*General Robert E Lee*", "*American Civil War*" and so on. This can be particularly useful if a searcher is stuck for search terms, or does not have any kind of in-depth knowledge about the subject they are looking for.

Therefore, *AltaVista* does have a particular appeal to experienced searchers who still like to use Boolean operators. Although the database of websites may not be as large as the two main engines, it more than makes up for this in terms of search sophistication.

Teoma

DID YOU KNOW? >> *Teoma* means 'expert' in Gaelic.

Teoma, found at **www.teoma.com**, was designed by computer scientists from Rutgers University in the USA in April 2000, and launched a year later. It was acquired by Ask Jeeves, Inc. in September 2001. By 2002, according to

Nielsen//NetRatings, it had become the third most widely used search technology in the USA.

The simple search function is shown in Figure 3.6.

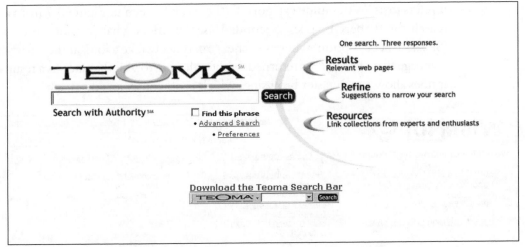

Figure 3.6   The *Teoma* simple search interface

The interface looks rather more cluttered than that of the other search engines we have looked at so far – particularly since the 'options' on the right hand side of the screen (results, refine, resources) are not options at all, but general details on how the engine works. As usual, the search engine works using AND as a default, with double quotes for a phrase (though *Teoma* has a checkbox to indicate this as well) and the minus symbol to indicate NOT, or that a term should be excluded.

Once a search has been run and the results are displayed the difference between *Teoma* and an engine such as *Google* is clear, since *Teoma* offers two additional listings – a Refine feature which is very similar to the Prisma offering from *AltaVista*, and a Resources listing of link collections from experts and enthusiasts. Both of these are helpful for searchers who are not clear on exactly what they are looking for and who may need a little help and guidance to identify appropriate material.

WiseNut

WiseNut at **www.wisenut.com** is a search engine owned by Looksmart (**http://aboutus.looksmart.com/about.jhtml?**) that is unusual in that it doesn't have an advanced search function, so it's fairly basic in the manner in which it can be used. However, it does have one or two interesting features. In common with *AltaVista* and *Teoma* it provides a mechanism whereby searchers are prompted with ways to focus a search more clearly using what it refers to as 'WiseGuide categories' (these can be seen in Figure 3.7 from a search for Robert E. Lee). Second, *WiseNut* offers what it refers to as a 'Sneak-a-peek' option, where searchers can quickly take a look at the particular page that *WiseNut* has returned, without having to visit that site. As a result it does allow much faster browsing, which is obviously an advantage.

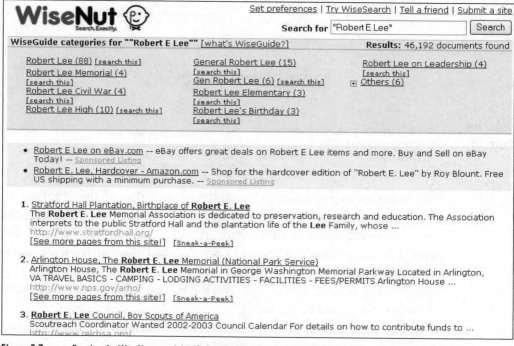

Figure 3.7   Results of a *WiseNut* search for 'Robert E Lee' showing the WiseGuide categories

Other free-text search engines available

There is almost no limit to the number of free-text search engines that are available, and it would be quite possible to write an entire book on them alone. If you do not feel inspired to use any of those that I've already mentioned you may wish to explore some that I've listed below. Please note that this is not a complete list:

- *AOL Search*   **http://search.aol.com/aolcom/index.jsp**
- *Euroseek*   **www.euroseek.com/**
- *Gigablast*   **www.gigablast.com/**
- *HotBot*   **www.hotbot.com/**
- *Lycos*   **www.lycos.com/**
- *MSN Search*   **http://search.msn.com/default.aspx.**

Before trying out a new search engine for the first time it's always advisable to spend a little while being nosey. See if it has a link to some sort of 'About us' page where you can check out the history of the engine; see who owns it (and if it's been owned by someone else in the past); when it was started; and so on. Take a look at any help screens to get a quick overview of what is and what isn't possible. Before you try and use it 'in anger' try out one or two test searches to see how well it copes with them; if you use the same searches every time you test a new search engine you should have a very clear idea as to how many results you should get from one of the big two or three; if you get a consistently substantially smaller number with your test searches it's likely that the new engine has only a very small database, and may not be worth using.

It's also worth checking to see if anyone else has been talking or writing about the engine. There are several good sites to check here, such as *Searchengineshowdown* at **www.searchengineshowdown.com/** which is run by Greg Notess, who has a background in information work. The site is always up to date and Greg provides some excellent resources and information on the current situation with regards engines. *Searchenginewatch* at **www.searchenginewatch.com/**

> **HINTS & TIPS >>**
>
> For a more complete listing of websites that provide you with information on search engines, see Chapter 17.

is another excellent resource which provides hints and tips on using search engines, news snippets, and various other resources. I also write a column for the online quarterly magazine *Ariadne* at **www.ariadne.ac.uk/** on various aspects of search engines as well.

Summary

In this chapter I have detailed how to use free-text search engines, with particular emphasis on two or three major ones. Some are more advanced and sophisticated than others, but they all work on the same principle. If you have a clear idea of what you are looking for, and can define that using some keywords or phrases, a free-text search engine will always be a good place to start.

Remember, however, that they're not perfect; if you are unable to get the information you need from one, simply try another to see if you have better luck elsewhere. By all means have one particular engine that you use as your favourite, but don't just rely on that one to the exclusion of the rest – as an information professional you wouldn't just use one reference book to answer all the things you get asked, so why do it with a search engine?

URLs mentioned in this chapter

www.google.com/press/zeitgeist2002.html
www.google.com/corporate/facts.html
http://google.indicateur.com/
www.peak.org/~jeremy/dictionary/dictionary/
http://froogle.google.com/
http://toolbar.google.com/
www.alltheweb.com/
www.alltheweb.com/help/faqs/advanced.html
www.altavista.com/
www.teoma.com/
www.wisenut.com/
http://aboutus.looksmart.com/about.jhtml?
http://search.aol.com/aolcom/index.jsp
www.euroseek.com/
www.gigablast.com/
www.hotbot.com/
www.lycos.com/
http://search.msn.com/default.aspx
www.searchengineshowdown.com/
www.searchenginewatch.com/
www.ariadne.ac.uk/

Chapter 4 »
Index-based search engines

Introduction

Free-text search engines are, as we have seen, one very good way of searching the internet. At least – they are very good if you know exactly what you are looking for and can identify it using a small number of keywords or phrases. However, they are less useful if you require a broad overview of a subject, or if you are unfamiliar with a subject and its technical jargon. For example, if you need to obtain a list of all UK newspapers that have websites, while this isn't a difficult query in itself, the choice of terms to search for most certainly is. Appropriate terms would include newspaper, newspapers, tabloid, tabloids, broadsheets, press, journalism, UK, United Kingdom, England, Wales, Scotland, Northern Ireland, list, listing, collection, collections and so on. Trying to construct a sensible search from a combination of these is going to take a considerable amount of time. This is where index-based search engines are much more appropriate. Index-based search engines:

- arrange data in a structured fashion
- make use of headings and subheadings going from the general to the specific
- usually rely on web authors to submit sites directly to the engine
- depend on their category structure for their success
- are simple to use
- appeal to novice searchers

- are useful if a broad approach to a subject is required
- are valuable if the searcher is unsure of the most appropriate keywords to use.

As in Chapter 3, I look at some examples of this type of search engine in detail, with illustrations of how to get the most out of them.

Yahoo!

The first index-based search engine that I look at in detail is *Yahoo!*, established in 1994 by two students at Stanford University, David Filo and Jerry Yang.

It can be found at **www.yahoo.com/**. The UK and Ireland version is at **http://uk.yahoo.com/**. *Yahoo!* started when the two decided that they needed a sensible way of keeping track of their own interests on the web, rather than continuing to use large and cumbersome lists of websites. They developed software to allow them to quickly locate, identify and edit materials, and over the course of time *Yahoo!* has evolved into a highly effective and valuable search engine.

This list-based approach is still quite obvious when you look at the search engine's front page showing the top-level subject headings. These are:

- Business and Economy
- Computers and Internet
- News and Media
- Entertainment
- Recreation and sports
- Health
- Government
- Regional
- Society and culture
- Education
- Arts and humanities
- Science
- Social science
- Reference.

Below these 14 major headings there are 45 second-level headings, and so on. You can immediately see a major difference between the approach taken by

Yahoo! (and of course all other index-based search engines) and free-text search engines in that you can immediately see the type of information which is available. (See Figure 4.1.) With a free-text search engine it is necessary to run a search before being in a position to see the data the engine covers.

Web Site Directory - Sites organized by subject   Suggest your site

Business & Economy
B2B, Finance, Shopping, Jobs...

Regional
Countries, Regions, US States...

Computers & Internet
Internet, WWW, Software, Games...

Society & Culture
People, Environment, Religion...

News & Media
Newspapers, TV, Radio...

Education
College and University, K-12...

Entertainment
Movies, Humor, Music...

Arts & Humanities
Photography, History, Literature...

Recreation & Sports
Sports, Travel, Autos, Outdoors...

Science
Animals, Astronomy, Engineering...

Health
Diseases, Drugs, Fitness...

Social Science
Languages, Archaeology, Psychology...

Government
Elections, Military, Law, Taxes...

Reference
Phone Numbers, Dictionaries, Quotations...

Buzz Index - **Yahoo! Picks** - **New Additions** - **Full Coverage**

Figure 4.1   The major subject headings at *Yahoo!*

Human indexing, not computer generation

A second major difference between *Yahoo!* and a free-text search engine is that all the headings and subheadings are created by people. There is a much greater human input into index-based search engines than you will normally find with free-text engines. This is both an advantage and disadvantage. The advantage is that it is easier to work out the way in which another human being thinks, than it is to second-guess a computer; so, if you think of a subject, you can probably guess with a reasonable level of accuracy which of the major subject headings will cover that subject. Paradoxically, the disadvantage is exactly the same; the success of an index-based approach depends on the user thinking in the same way that the creator of the index does. If the creator of the index has a different bias (cultural or geographic, for example), it's possible to spend a long time searching for the required information in entirely the wrong place. I go into this in more detail later in the chapter.

However, for now, let's look into *Yahoo!* in rather more detail. Clicking on any of the subject or subheadings will return another page, providing you with a further breakdown of the subject and so on, until you finally reach a page which gives you a list of sites for which you can read a brief description (provided by the person who submitted the site), and you can then click on one that interests you and visit it, leaving *Yahoo!* behind. Figure 4.2 illustrates what happens when you click on the top-level heading 'Reference'.

INSIDE YAHOO!

Reference: visit <u>Yahoo! **Reference**</u> for encyclopedia, dictionary, thesaurus, and more

CATEGORIES

- <u>Acronyms and Abbreviations</u> (23)
- <u>Almanacs</u> (10)
- <u>Arts and Humanities@</u>
- <u>Ask an Expert</u> (1208) NEW!
- <u>Bibliographies</u> (4)
- <u>Booksellers@</u>
- <u>Calendars</u> (76)
- <u>Codes</u> (25)
- <u>Country Profiles@</u>
- <u>Dictionaries</u> (154)
- <u>Directories</u> (10)
- <u>Encyclopedia</u> (29)
- <u>English Language Usage@</u>
- <u>Environment and Nature@</u>
- <u>Etiquette@</u>
- <u>FAQs</u> (8)
- <u>Finance and Investment@</u>
- <u>Flags</u> (15)
- <u>General</u> (14)
- <u>Geographic Name Servers@</u>

- <u>Health@</u>
- <u>Journals@</u>
- <u>Libraries</u> (6948) NEW!
- <u>Maps@</u>
- <u>Measurements and Units@</u>
- <u>Music@</u>
- <u>Parliamentary Procedure</u> (12)
- <u>Patents@</u>
- <u>Phone Numbers and Addresses</u> (145)
- <u>Postal Information</u> (28)
- <u>Quotations</u> (188)
- <u>Research Papers@</u>
- <u>Science@</u>
- <u>Searching the Web@</u>
- <u>Standards</u> (61)
- <u>Statistics</u> (28)
- <u>Student Resources@</u>
- <u>Thesauri</u> (27)
- <u>Time@</u>

Figure 4.2   Subheadings under 'Reference' at *Yahoo!*

The number in brackets after each subheading indicates the total number of websites listed, and the @ symbol indicates that the heading is also used elsewhere within the index, so it is possible to move between different subjects easily in order to find the information that you require. This is particularly the case with commercial categories, which are linked to their appropriate non-commercial counterparts.

This last point is an important one with respect to *Yahoo!* When site owners register their site(s) with the search engine, they can choose up to two categories within which to list the site, and if it's a commercial one it must be placed in a commercial category. This needs to be taken into account when using the engine. For example, if you have an interest in baseball cards it may be necessary to check both the non–commercial category Collectibles>Baseball Cards and the commercial category Shopping>Collectible Baseball Cards, although *Yahoo!* will of course link the two categories together.

The same concept works for regions of the world, and is an area that can cause some confusion. If you have an interest in the British general election of 1997, the most sensible place to begin your search may at first glance appear to be in the Government>Elections hierarchy. However, unless you are a sharp-eyed user of the system and notice the link to 'By Region' you may start searching in the wrong category. It may then be necessary to backtrack, find the regional subheading and work down through the hierarchy to Regional>Countries>United Kingdom>Government>Politics>Elections>1997 in order to find websites that cover the subject.

If a website is in any way regional in coverage or scope *Yahoo!* will always place it in the appropriate regional category, rather than directly into a main subject category; the only time this rule is superseded is when a subject or an organization is global in nature. In most cases you will need to remember to check under the appropriate regional heading, although in most instances *Yahoo!* will cross–reference directly to the subject area as well. An alternative approach would be to use the appropriate local *Yahoo!* The search engine has over 20 regional versions which are tailored to a more local approach to and understanding of the classification of knowledge. (As we saw in Chapter 2, the sections in the .com and .uk versions for Government are very different.)

The basic approach to using *Yahoo!* is therefore quite simple; decide on the major heading your subject comes under and follow the links through the hierarchy until you reach it. As a result of this simplicity it is a very good search engine to direct novice searchers towards, and as long as they are made aware of some of the idiosyncrasies of the system they should be able to retrieve good results quickly.

Free-text searching in *Yahoo!*

Even very early on in the history of internet search engines developers real-

ized that in order to appeal to the widest possible audience it would be necessary to offer varied search techniques. Even in the early versions of *Yahoo!*
dating back to 1996 a free-text search box was prominently displayed towards
the top of the home page, in exactly the same way that it is today.

Consequently, it is possible to run a free-text search at *Yahoo!* although the
results are not provided by *Yahoo!*, but by a third party vendor. (In the past this
has been *Google*, although *Yahoo!* has used different ven-
dors.) Figure 4.3 shows the result of a search for the phrase
"Robert E Lee" using the *Yahoo!* search box. Although the set
of returned pages looks very similar to that found when the
search is undertaken using a free-text search engine, there are
one or two important points to make. First, at the very top
of the screen you will see a series of tabs: Web, Images,
Directory, Yellow Pages, News, Products. These allow the
searcher to quickly move from one type or set of results to
another. Clicking on the Images option takes the searcher to a large number
of images that match the search; the Directory option displays the top 20
results from the *Yahoo!* directory; Yellow Pages takes the searcher to organizations that would sell a particular product (though in this case it is not applicable);
News would display any news stories about the Confederate general; and
finally Products displays a variety of related products.

> **DID YOU KNOW?** >>
>
> If you want to see what a website or page
> looked like months or even years ago
> you can. Simply visit the *Internet Archive*
> site at www.archive.org/ and type in the
> URL of the site that interests you. If you're
> lucky it will have been archived, and you
> can go right back to 1996 in some cases.

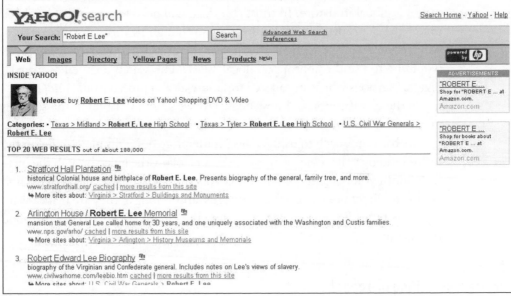

Figure 4.3   Results of a search using the free-text function at *Yahoo!*

As well as those varied options it is also possible to click on the link 'More sites about' which takes the searcher to the appropriate section of *Yahoo!* This can obviously be useful if, for example, you want more information on other American Civil War generals, but do not know the names of any – clicking on the link US Civil War Generals>Robert E Lee immediately jumps you deep into the *Yahoo!* hierarchy at Arts>Humanities>History>U.S. History>By Time Period>19th Century>Military History>Civil War (1861–1865)>People>Generals>Lee, Robert Edward (1807–1870).

Although *Yahoo!* offers an 'Advanced Web Search' this is limited to the usual 'All these words' 'The exact phrase' 'Any of these words' 'None of these words' and focusing on finding them anywhere on the page, in the title or in the URL. Results can further be limited to the past three months, six months, one year or anytime. Domains can be restricted to .com, .edu, .gov, .org or any other specified URL or domain. *Yahoo!* also allows for the use of a 'Mature content filter, searching by country (any one of 24), and by choice of language (35 options). Options also exist for finding web pages similar to, or linked to, another web page address as specified by the searcher.

Yahoo! also allows you to do a search within a specific subject area. There will be times when you may be quite clear on the particular approach that you wish to take on a specific subject, but even when the search has been narrowed down using the hierarchical structure there may still be many hundreds or indeed thousands of websites listed. It is possible to limit a *Yahoo!* search to a specific category; when you navigate through the hierarchy *Yahoo!* always displays a box similar to the one shown in Figure 4.4 in the section Animals, Insects, and Pets.

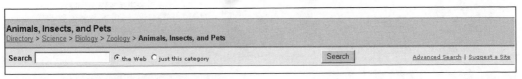

Figure 4.4   The *Yahoo!* search box within a category

The option given to the right allows the user to search either the web in general, or to restrict the search to just that specific category. A search just on the term *enterprise* is going to result in a great many hits; but, if I firstly narrow the category to Entertainment>Television Shows>Science Fiction and Fantasy>Star Trek>Enterprise, this will substantially reduce the number of results that I get.

Other *Yahoo!* functions

As you can see, *Yahoo!* is not a difficult search engine to use; in fact it's very straightforward. However, the value in using it does not rest only on its simplicity, but also on the fact that it has a number of other very useful features as well. *Yahoo!*, in common with other major search engines, is always attempting to broaden its user base, and as a result has a regular programme of updating and adding new features. Some of these have little relevance to us as searchers, but others can prove to be most useful. If we briefly take a look at the home page of the search engine as shown in Figure 4.5 we can see that *Yahoo!* is more than just a search engine.

Figure 4.5   Part of the *Yahoo!* home page
© 2004 Yahoo! Inc. All rights reserved

The functions are as follows:

- 'Personalize' (*My Yahoo!*) allows users to personalize their own content, including news headlines, weather reports, stock prices, sports results, television and cinema listings, yellow pages and maps, for example. This

HINTS & TIPS >>

If you want a geographic search, use a local version of *Yahoo!*, but if you want a comprehensive view, make use of the main version.

is restricted to the USA, and therefore is of little use if you reside elsewhere – indeed on the UK and Ireland version this option is not available. However, if you are based in the USA this is a very useful and effective way of collating a lot of relevant and personal information together in one place. Moreover, since it is accessed by user name and password, it is not limited to one particular machine; it can be used from any terminal anywhere in the world.

- 'Finance' is a page of information on financial information (there's a surprise!), which gives details on stock and shares, bonds, investing, top financial stories and so on. It also has the ability to allow users to track stocks and share prices. There is a version for the UK and Ireland site, and the emphasis tends towards British and European financial information.
- 'Shop' is a useful search function for finding the best deals on many different products. However, it is focused on the American market, so may have little value for anyone else.
- 'Mail' is, unsurprisingly, an e-mail service that *Yahoo!* offers, similar to *Hotmail* or *Talk21*.
- 'Messenger' is an instant messaging service, allowing you to chat/type real time to your friends.
- 'Hotjobs' is self-explanatory, but once again is American biased.

Yahoo! has many other features as well as those listed above – it has many local *Yahoo!*s for different countries and regions and some subject-specific information, such as football or cricket. It is worth spending some time looking at it in detail, since it's much more than a standard search engine – indeed, it could easily be described more as a portal or gateway service. I talk more about these in Chapter 12.

Google Directory

The *Google Directory* at **www.google.com/dirhp** is composed of over 1.5 million URLs arranged in a hierarchical method, with 15 main headings and 45 second-level headings, as can be seen in Figure 4.6. There are also several World (more correctly entitled Regional or Country) versions as well. The directory has been created by *Google* in conjunction with the *Open Directory Project* at **http://dmoz.org/**. The sites listed in the directory are arranged according to *Google*'s PageRank technology, which places what *Google* considers to be the most 'important' of the pages at the top of the listings, unlike other

Google™
Directory

| Web | Images | Groups | **Directory** | News |

[   ] Google Search   • Preferences
                                         • Directory Help

The web organized by topic into categories.

Arts
Movies, Music, Television,...

Home
Consumers, Homeowners, Family,...

Regional
Asia, Europe, North America,...

Business
Industries, Finance, Jobs,...

Kids and Teens
Computers, Entertainment, School,...

Science
Biology, Psychology, Physics,...

Computers
Hardware, Internet, Software,...

News
Media, Newspapers, Current Events,...

Shopping
Autos, Clothing, Gifts,...

Games
Board, Roleplaying, Video,...

Recreation
Food, Outdoors, Travel,...

Society
Issues, People, Religion,...

Health
Alternative, Fitness, Medicine,...

Reference
Education, Libraries, Maps,...

Sports
Basketball, Football, Soccer,...

Figure 4.6   The *Google Directory* home page
© 2004 Google

index- or directory-based search engines which arrange them alphabetically. This is indicated by the use of a small coloured bar to the left of the site; the more the bar is coloured green, the more important the site is considered. All of the sites that are listed in the directory have been reviewed by *Open Directory* editors (it has over 20,000 volunteer editors who take responsibility for reviewing site submissions to the different categories), so users can expect an indication of quality or at least an unbiased observation of the sites that are included.

The directory can be searched in one of three ways; by clicking on the appropriate heading or subheading, then moving down the categories until the searcher finds a list of sites which can then be directly visited; by adding keywords into the search box above the headings; by clicking on one of the subject headings, then choosing to search just in the category, as can be seen from Figure 4.7.

This last approach does of course allow a searcher to specify a particular subject area and focus solely on that, which can be very useful if looking for a subject that may cross many boundaries.

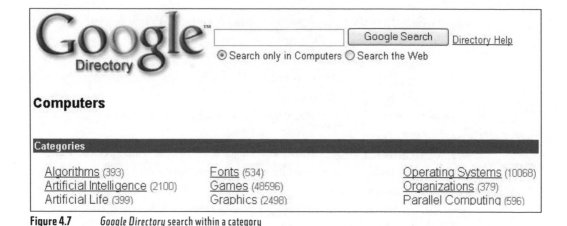

Figure 4.7 *Google Directory* search within a category
© 2004 Google

The *Open Directory Project*

Having already mentioned the *Open Directory Project* (at **http://dmoz.org/**), several times, and knowing that I'll be referring to it again when referring to other index- or directory-based search engines it seems to make sense to spend some time looking at it. It says of itself: 'The *Open Directory Project* is the largest, most comprehensive human-edited directory of the Web. It is constructed and maintained by a vast, global community of volunteer editors.' It powers the core directory services for some the most popular index- and directory-based search engines on the web, such as *AOL Search*, *Netscape Search*, *Google*, *Lycos*, *DirectHit* and *HotBot*. A full listing of engines using the data can be found at **http://dmoz.org/Computers/Internet/Searching/Directories/Open_Directory_Project/Sites_Using_ODP_Data/**.

It is run by staff from Netscape Communication Corporation which administers it as a non-commercial entity. Categories are run and administered in conjunction with volunteers who are experts in their own particular areas. It currently indexes over 3.8 million sites, with 58,827 editors and over 460,000 categories. The home page can be seen in Figure 4.8, and it is very similar to *Yahoo!*, for example. It can be searched either by drilling down into the categories and subheadings, or by using the free-text search box. There is an advanced search function, although this is very limited, allowing a searcher to look for results in a category, or in a site or both. Results can also be limited to sites suitable for children, teenagers or mature teenagers. Results are returned in hierarchical order, with subheadings displayed first, with sites that are within a particular category below these. The strength of the system is that the reviews are not written by the authors of the websites themselves, but by the *Dmoz* editors. Searchers therefore have a reasonably unbiased view of a site. My own site has three entries, and it's described variously as:

1. **Bradley, Phil** – A librarian whose Web site helps other librarians search and make sense of the Internet.
   -- *http://www.philb.com/ Reference: Libraries: Library and Information Science: Librarians (1)*
2. **Phil Bradley's Blog** – Links and news for librarians and people interested in search engines, searching the net, design issues and general whitterings and rants.
   -- *http://www.philb.com/blog/blogger.html Reference: Libraries: Library and Information Science: Weblogs (1)*
3. **Phil Bradley**: Internet for Beginners – Articles on the basics of the Internet. Includes advanced search techniques, writing web pages, web tools that will be useful for authors, and many other articles written with the information professional in mind.
   -- *http://www.philb.com/Computers: Education: Internet: Help and Tutorials: Internet Beginners Guides (1)*

Figure 4.8   The *Open Directory Project* home page
© 1998–2004 Netscape

Other index-based search engines

The structure of *Yahoo!* is very appealing, both for organizations establishing web search engines and also for those people who are new to searching. Consequently, it is an approach which is very widely used. As we have already seen with *Google*, traditional free-text search engines often incorporate a directory, but there are one or two other index/directory-based engines worth mentioning just in case you're not happy with *Yahoo!* or the *Google Directory*, or would simply like to compare them with other engines.

AltaVista

In common with *Google*, *AltaVista* also has a directory-based facility at **http://uk.altavista.com/dir/default/** and, like *Google*, it is based on the *Open Directory Project*. I don't feel that this is as comprehensive as the *Google* version, so would tend to continue to use *AltaVista* for more complex Boolean free-text searches.

AOL Search web directory

AOL offers a web directory search facility at **http://search.aol.com/aolcom/browse.jsp** and, as you may be coming to expect, the directory structure is based on the *Open Directory Project* categories.

Lycos

The *Lycos* search engine at **www.lycos.com/** also offers the same functionality as the other index search engines, using as it does the *Dmoz* system, although it refers to the *Lycos* Topics. *Lycos* has also added some of their own, which tend to relate to popular subject areas such as Movie Trailers and Models.

MSN Search

MSN Search at **http://search.msn.com/** is another very popular search engine and, like *Yahoo!*, offers both a free-text search function and an index/directory-based approach. *MSN Search* has ten major headings and over 50 secondary headings.

Netscape Search

Netscape Search is located at **http://channels.netscape.com/ns/search/default.jsp** and is another index-based search engine based on the *Open Directory Project*.

Summary

Index-based search engines provide users with a straightforward approach to finding information by guiding them through a series of headings and subheadings until they are able to locate a listing of websites. Users can then go directly to the websites that interest them in order to obtain an answer to the question that troubles them. Consequently, such search engines are rather more of a 'stepping stone' in the retrieval of information, by pointing searchers in the right general direction, rather than taking them directly to a specific page in the way that a free-text search engine would do.

They are very useful if it is necessary to obtain an overview of a subject, or if the searcher has very limited knowledge on a particular subject. While all the engines in this category provide headings and subheadings, some are more in-depth than others, or, if they take the *Dmoz* classifications, may have added their own twist to them. The choice(s) searchers take when using engines in this particular category should therefore reflect this.

URLs mentioned in this chapter

www.yahoo.com/
http://uk.yahoo.com/
www.archive.org/
www.google.com/dirhp
http://dmoz.org/
http://dmoz.org/Computers/Internet/Searching/Directories/Open_
    Directory_Project/Sites_Using_ODP_Data/
http://uk.altavista.com/dir/default/
http://search.aol.com/aolcom/browse.jsp
www.lycos.com/
http://search.msn.com/
http://channels.netscape.com/ns/search/default.jsp

Chapter 5 »

Multi- or meta-search engines

Introduction

We have now looked at a variety of different search engines, and it is worth emphasizing that they make up a very small percentage of the total number that are available. Each of them has its own strengths and weaknesses, and you will have discovered that you may need to use several of them to be confident that you have found everything that you need. This can be a time-consuming and frustrating experience, since you will have to go from one search engine to another, rerunning the same search, checking off the results against each other, getting increasingly annoyed.

However, there is a solution to this problem, which is to make use of multi- or meta-search engines. This chapter concentrates on explaining what they do and how they do it. In common with the previous chapters I shall take a look at one or two of them in detail.

What is a multi-search engine?

As the name implies, it's an engine that searches across multiple search engines on your behalf, displaying records on the screen in any one of a number of different formats. As you're probably coming to expect by now, there are a variety of multi-search engines available, all with their own strengths and weaknesses. Strictly speaking though, they're not really search engines at all, since they don't go out and collect data in the way that free-text engines do, nor do their creators put together headings and subheadings – they act like post boxes, sending out your query, gathering back the results and giving them to you. They administer, rather than search.

The simplest form is a collection of links to different search engines, and this may or may not even include a dialogue box to enable you to input search terms. Once the search has been input you'll be taken directly to the chosen search engine's home page to view the results.

The second type of multi-search engine allows you to input your search term(s) into a single search/dialogue box and perhaps even choose the search engines that you want to be interrogated. The multi-search engine then passes the query onto the chosen engines and then displays the results, usually arranged in order of search engine. This saves a little time, but does result in a very long page of results, and it's still going to be necessary to wade through them, trying to find the information that is actually needed.

The final type of multi-search engine is rather more sophisticated – it does all that the previous type does, but then de-duplicates the records to remove pages that are mentioned twice or more, and attempts to sort all the records into a more useful order. This usually means that the result that comes at the top of the list of returned pages will be the one that has been found in the top ten results of most of the search engines. A page that has been found by four engines will be regarded as more relevant than one found by three, for example. A secondary ranking system is also used, which is to order pages by their position within the top ten. It's easiest to explain when you actually run some searches, but consider for a moment that a multi-search engine returns three pages as a result of the search that's been run – 'a' and 'b' have been located by four different search engines, and 'c' by only three engines. Of the first two 'b' was found in 1st, 1st, 2nd and 3rd positions and 'a' in 1st, 2nd, 3rd and 4th positions. Consequently, the final ranking of the three pages would be 'b', 'a' and 'c'.

Before moving on to look at some examples, let's start by looking at a few defining criteria in a little more detail.

Characteristics of multi-search engines

I have tried putting together a list of the different elements that one might expect to appear on a multi-search engine page. Unfortunately, few if any search engines exhibit all of these criteria, but they'll all exhibit some.

Number and quality of search engines used

The number of search engines that a multi-search engine will call on varies dramatically; small ones will use no more than four or five, while a larger one may use upwards of a dozen. On the other hand, others that just list search engines may run into the hundreds or even more. This is no indicator of quality, however; it depends much more on the particular search engines that are used, rather than sheer number. I would much prefer to use a multi-search engine that just called on a small number of high-quality free-text or index-based engines, rather than several hundred that I do not know.

Nonetheless, it's an acceptable criterion to use when evaluating the effectiveness of a multi-search engine; while more is not necessarily better, less could in some situations be considered worse. While I wouldn't normally evaluate success in terms of the number of hits, this is one of the reasons for using a multi-search engine, so it is justified. There may, however, be times when the advanced searcher has to make a choice between more results and higher-quality results, and using multi-search engines will bring this choice out into the open.

> **DID YOU KNOW? >>**
> Ever wondered what people are actually searching for? Visit www.metaspy.com/info.metac.spy/metaspy/ to see the search terms people use. There is a filtered link and an unfiltered link, and the results are updated every 15 seconds.

Elements of the internet that are searched

It seems almost automatic these days to regard the phrase 'Search the web' as a synonym for 'Search the internet'. Of course, while this is understandable give the hype and attention surrounding the world wide web, it behoves us to remember that there are a number of other aspects of the internet that deserve consideration as well. Examples are usenet newsgroups, news, various forms of media and so on. Multi-search engines are at the mercy of the search engines they choose to use but, given that a good number of these do concentrate on specific aspects such as those just mentioned, there is no reason why they shouldn't be made available for searching as well.

Any words, all words, phrase searching

Most, if not all, search engines now work on the principle of searching for a number of terms using AND as the default; that the minus symbol excludes a term from a search; and that a phrase should be contained within sets of double quote marks. Therefore, any fairly straightforward search should be passed directly onto the individual engines by the multi-search engine, and they should all produce sets of results that, while different, are all doing the same thing.

However, while we can make the assumption that they'll all work in the same way this *is* the internet after all, and expecting consistency is optimistic to say the least! It does, therefore, make sense to double-check that the search engines being used for a search will all understand it correctly. A failure to do so by the searcher may well end up with a set of results that is inaccurate or just downright wrong.

Boolean operators, truncation, proximity searching

Here we are on much thinner ice. Search engines have their own ways of working, and while one search engine may well know that a search for *libraria** will include words such as librarian, librarianship, librarians, another engine may well simply look for the string of terms as given, including the asterisk. It is therefore best to limit search strategies to the simpler search techniques mentioned in the last section.

Focusing a search

There are many occasions when the user will not wish to do a global search, but will want to focus on one specific aspect, such as searching in a particular domain, or within a geographical area such as Europe, or the UK. Some search engines do allow this level of specificity, though it is unusual. If a searcher requires this, it would be necessary to find a multi-search engine that uses (for example) UK-based engines, or those that focus on a different region. A good example of a multi-search engine that uses a lot of UK-based engines to create its listings is *Ixquick* at **www.ixquick.com/**.

Choice of subject area

This approach is very familiar to anyone who has ever used the index approach to search engines, by taking a broad subject area and drilling down through various subject headings until the specific subject is reached. Some multi-search engines either provide examples of headings/subheadings for searchers to click on, or they offer the opportunity of limiting a search to a smaller number of specialized search engines. The *CNET Search.com* engine at **www.search.com/** deserves being singled out for being quite superb here.

Time taken and hits returned

These are two very important elements when looking at multi-search engines. Free-text engines boast the number of pages they index; an index engine may well emphasize the number of headings it has; and a multi-search engine makes great play of how quickly it works. Most engines allow the searcher to choose the length of time the multi-search engine can spend communicating with the engines it's using, and this can vary between one and ten seconds. An example of a multi-search engine that offers this in its list of preferences is *ez2Find* at **www.ez2www.com/**. If a multi-search engine doesn't get a reply within the specified time period it will ignore that search engine and will create a set of results based on the pages that have been returned by the other, less tardy engines. Consequently searchers may find that they get variable results because of this. It therefore helps if the time limited can be extended for as long as possible. And, after all, if it's necessary to get results inside ten seconds it's probably already too late!

Display and ranking

Multi-search engines display results in their relevance-ranked order as described above. However, an increasing number of more sophisticated engines also allow users to display the results in other ranked orders, such as popularity or title. Moreover, when results are pulled from search engines that provide categories or focused searches these may also be displayed for the user as well. *Vivisimo* at **http://vivisimo.com/** is one such engine that uses what it terms its 'clustering engine'.

Collating results

When you use a single search engine it is not uncommon to find the same site turning up several times, though most engines now take this into account and offer a facility to allow searchers to see more pages from the same site. A good multi-search engine will also ensure that it only displays one particular page once, rather than several times. However, there are still engines that simply display a listing of everything that they've found, which I've never found to be a very helpful way of providing data. An example of this type of multi-search engine is *Dogpile* at **www.dogpile.com/**.

ZapMeta

ZapMeta at **www.zapmeta.com** is a multi- or meta-search engine that has
been around since 2002. The home page is very Spartan, as can be seen in
Figure 5.1, and reminds me of the way in which *Google* used to look when it
first came out. There is a search box, options to search the web or go shopping, links to preferences and advanced searches, and that's just about it.

Figure 5.1   The *ZapMeta* home page

Preferences

Let's start by taking a look at the preferences to see what we can do with this
creature. You can set a timeout of anything between one and 20 seconds, which
is very reasonable – many multi-search engines don't give you that option at
all, or you're limited to a smaller set of options. Results can be grouped, or
they can be displayed – this means that results will remove duplicates by grouping pages with the same URL under one match. The number of results per
page can be a number of options from eight to All, which is nicely flexible.

Results can be sorted by relevance, which you'd expect, but also by title and source, and either in ascending or descending order. I like this – it's rather unusual, but I can see ways in which this could allow a searcher to jump much more quickly to particular pages or sites. Keywords can be highlighted or not; quite why someone wouldn't want keywords highlighted is a bit of a mystery to me, but if you're one of those folk, it's an option for you. Pages can be opened in the same or a new window – a useful feature, but nothing startling. You can choose to display description, sources, URL and page preview. This again is a nice feature, giving you more flexibility than you'll find with many other engines. Finally, we have a choice of nine search engines that *Zap-Meta* uses to search from. Oddly enough, not all of these are checked. The nine are *AltaVista* (unchecked), Yahoo (checked), *AlltheWeb* (checked), *WiseNut* (checked), *AOL* (checked), *MSN* (checked), *HotBot* (checked), *Open Directory* (unchecked) and *Gigablast* (unchecked). I do find this a little strange since the strength of a multi- or meta-search engine is surely to search as broadly as possible as a default, with an option of narrowing down to specific engines afterwards? Of course, you can easily set the default to search all the available choices, but I suspect that a lot of people won't think of doing this at once. The other major point is that *Google* is missing from the list, but since *AOL* is included (and is powered by *Google*) it's not quite the omission that one might at first assume. One slight annoyance is that once you've set your preferences it's not immediately clear how you can get back to the search screen (by clicking on the *ZapMeta* logo), which may cause some confusion or frustration.

Advanced search function

The advanced search function is not terribly exciting, and is what you'd expect to find. We have the usual boxes for 'Must contain the words', 'Match the exact phrase' and 'Exclude the words' with the options of 'Anywhere', 'In the title' and 'In the URL' which are fine – a couple of years ago this would have been worth particular mention, but this is fairly pedestrian now. There's a Domain filter, with options to limit by any one of eight regions (it's a shame there isn't an option to choose a couple of regions though), by Domain (.com, .co.uk, .org and so on) or by Host (philb.com or dell.com). Nice, but nothing fancy. The next option allows users to sort by relevance, URL, Popularity, Title and Source. This is an interesting option, and one that I'll come back to later when I'm talking about the results that we get from the search engine. The final options are again uninspiring – results per page, display options, timeout and sources used. So, nothing special – it would have been nice to have seen search criteria based on media, news, images and so on.

Searching

Moving onto the search function now. I did a search on *Everton* and got several sponsored listings before the 'proper' results which weren't really appropriate at all, though to the right was a small box of 'related searches' which did include 'Everton football' and 'Everton fc', so I'll give it marks for getting that right – or rather, picking up those options from *AlltheWeb*. I had the main body of results ranked by order of relevance, and *ZapMeta* used the standard approach of ranking by number of search engines and position in the top ten. A nice function is the 'Quick View' of the page, which an increasing number of search engines are offering, providing you with an opportunity to view the page without having to actually visit it. The last section of the page offered me some Related categories, which seem to have been culled mainly from *Dmoz*.

I reranked the search results by clicking on the 'Popularity' option, and *Zap-Meta* managed this very quickly, reranking the results to give me the official club website as top of the listing. Quite what it based that on I don't know – a failing of the site is that it's not actually that forthcoming about such things. Reranking by title was less useful, since I then had *1UpTravel.com* as first in the list, which is logical, but of little interest to me. The Source option again put the official site back at the top of the listing, while the Domain option once again gave me *1UpTravel*. Several other searches confirmed what I was already thinking – relevance and popularity are probably the most useful options, followed by title. Another useful option is 'Search within these results' which is good to have available.

The layout of the results page was quite clear, although I did have one minor gripe, related to moving to the next page of results. The options given are: 1 2 3 4 5 6 7 8 9 10 next > next 10. Clicking on 'next 10' did not take me to results 20–9, but to 101–10. Clearly, the 'next 10' option refers to pages 11 12 13 and so on. Logical when you think about it, but, until you do, I can guarantee a quick double-take when you look at the results!

ZapMeta is a useful search engine with considerable functionality. However, if for some reason it doesn't appeal, another engine with similar functionality is *Fazzle* at **www.fazzle.com/**. Figure 5.2 illustrates the results search screen.

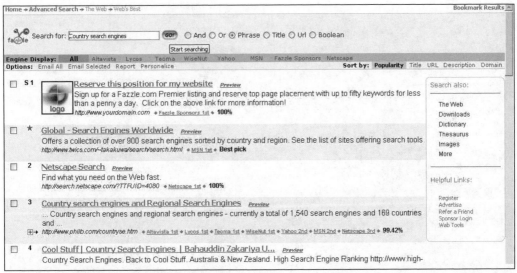

Figure 5.2 The *Fazzle* results screen
© 2001–4 Anvil Development Group, LLC

KartOO

KartOO which can be found at **www.kartoo.com/** is an unusual meta-search engine; in fact it's an unusual search engine however it's considered, since it's the only one currently on the internet which gives its default search screen results in a graphical format, rather than a textual format. In fact, it styles itself as a 'visual meta-search engine'. Consequently, it's worth looking at it. The search interface is not unlike those of other engines – a simple box for search terms. However, once the engine returns the results, and we can see this in Figure 5.3 for a search on the term *dyslexia*, things become rather different.

The larger the 'ball' or circular button, the more important *KartOO* considers the particular site to be. *KartOO* also attempts to make links between different sites, based on what they do, so in Figure 5.3 it's possible to see that there is a link between the International Dyslexia Association and the Dyslexia.com site. On the left hand side of the screen is an indication of what the particular site is (this changes as the mouse moves over different sites), top sites and, in some cases, ways in which the search can be focused. While this approach will not be to everyone's taste, it's an interesting and refreshingly welcome addition to the various search engines that are available.

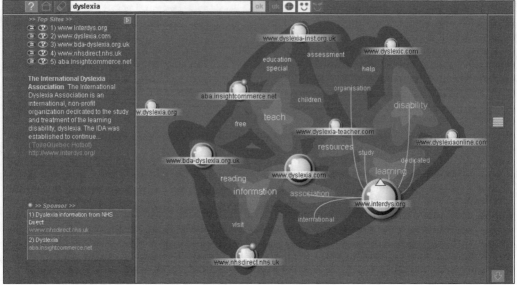

Figure 5.3   The *KartOO* results screen
                   © KartOO

Other multi- or meta-search engines

While, from a technical standpoint, not being as easy to create as index- or directory-based search engines these engines are not, I am assured by my programmer friends, a difficult proposition. Consequently, searchers have a reasonably large choice when it comes to finding a multi-search engine. If, after having looked at the engines that I've discussed in this chapter, you don't like any of them, you might like to explore some others. The following is not an exhaustive list, but it will give you reasonable choice:

- *1Blink* **www.1blink.com/**
- *AllSearchEngines* **www.allsearchengines.com/**
- *Beaucoup* **www.beaucoup.com/1geoeng.html**
- *Eureka!* **www.gocee.com/eureka/**
- *iTools* **www.itools.com/**
- *Highway61* **www.highway61.com/**
- *Keyword* **www.keyword.com/**
- *MaMMa* **www.mamma.com/**
- *Metacrawler* **www.metacrawler.com/index.html**
- *MonsterCrawler* **www.monstercrawler.com/**
- *Ungoogle* **www.ungoogle.com/**

- *Supercrawler* **www.supercrawler.com/**
- *Web Search* **www.web-search.com/**.

Summary

Multi-search engines are a powerful and easy way of running a comprehensive search across a reasonably large number of search engines. They create a relevance ranking that is a collaborative result. And I am more likely to believe such a result than one of a single search engine.

Of course, these engines are not perfect; if they were we'd all be using one of them, rather than still going to individual engines. They are limited by the fact that they're only as sophisticated (in search syntax) as the most basic of the engines that they query, and they are not always reliable because of their insistence on getting results back to the enquirer quickly.

URLs mentioned in this chapter

www.ixquick.com
www.search.com/
www.ez2www.com/
http://vivisimo.com/
www.dogpile.com/
www.zapmeta.com/
www.fazzle.com/
www.kartoo.com/
www.1blink.com/
www.allsearchengines.com/
www.beaucoup.com/1geoeng.html
www.gocee.com/eureka/
www.itools.com/
www.highway61.com/
www.keyword.com/
www.mamma.com/
www.metacrawler.com/index.html
www.monstercrawler.com/
www.ungoogle.com/
www.supercrawler.com/
www.web-search.com/

Chapter 6 »

Resource- or site-specific search engines

Introduction

As we discussed earlier, there are many thousands of search engines available to the keen searcher – many more than one would at first think. The search engines that are the largest set numerically may be overlooked entirely. That's because they are so integral to a particular website that they are hardly even noticed, which may well be a tribute to the designer of the site.

Engines in this category are particularly important, because they may well be the only way for a searcher to find a specific piece or type of information, as we shall see shortly. Moreover, because the amount of data they index is usually quite small (in relative terms) it's reasonable to assume that it's accurate and current.

Site-specific search engines (web pages)

Almost any good-quality site these days has its own site-specific search engine. This may be supplied by the company the site uses to host its pages, or it may be based on a program written by members of the organization, or, as in my case, it may be a utility supplied by a third party.

A site-specific search engine is useful to search the pages produced by that site. Consequently, the searcher has focused on a very specific data set, and so should get very good results at once. Another advantage is that the engine probably updates every day, or at least once a week, so that the searcher is getting the most recent data possible. This depends entirely on the search engine and the way in which it is put together, of course. Rather than spending time creating the search engine on my site, I simply used the facility offered by a company called *Atomz* at **www.atomz.com/**. Once a week it updates the engine that visitors to my site use. An *Atomz* spider visits the site, takes a new copy of each of my pages and then creates a small database of my pages, indexed to the word level. The search engine interface, as can be seen from Figure 6.1, is very basic, but it does the job. The results, seen in Figure 6.2, are perfectly acceptable.

Companies that offer free services such as this make their money from selling their search solutions to larger commercial organizations, and often look on the free versions as a good way of advertising their product; in this case, it has most certainly worked!

Search my site

You can now search my website, courtesy of an excellent little gizmo provided by Atomz.com *Please note: this just searches MY SITE; not the whole of the web!*

[Search]

Figure 6.1 The search interface for author's site at **www.philb.com**
© The author

SEARCH RESULTS 1 - 10 of 27 total results for **Google**

SITE SEARCH BY ⟨Atomz⟩ FIND OUT MORE   Sort By Date | Hide Summaries
                                                                        Next 10

1. Phil Bradley: Google Toolbar - new beta version 2.0 ••••
The new Google Toolbar version beta 2.0 Introduction Toolbars are not exactly new these days – several search engines have them, the most well known one...
   The new **Google** Toolbar version beta 2.0 Introduction Toolbars are not exactly new these days – several search engines have them, the most well known one...
   ...search engines have them, the most well known one of course being **Google**. In fact, the **Google** toolbar is what finally kicked me over from using...
   ...I've used the **Google** Toolbar ever since; I do it pretty much automatically these days and I get confused for a few seconds if I'm using a computer that...
94% Sun, 29 Jun 2003 11:21:25 GMT http://www.philb.com/gtoolbar.htm

2. Phil Bradley's Blog •••
Phil Bradley's Blog about For librarians and people interested in search engines, searching the net, design issues and general whitterings and...
   ...Search Deskbar looks like it's in immediate and direct competition with the **Google** toolbar. It seems to have more functionality, allows you to search...
   ...Phil Bradley: **Google** Toolbar - new beta version 2.0 Further to my posting on the toolbar, I thought I'd try it out. I've now written a fairly short...
   ...People are often surprised when I say that I prefer Allthweb over **Google** (toolbar notwithstanding!). I'm glad to see that I'm not the only person who...
70% Mon, 30 Jun 2003 15:50:51 GMT http://www.philb.com/blog/2003_06_01_blogarc.htm

Figure 6.2 Search results provided by *Atomz* for search on author's site for the word 'Google'

The major disadvantage of search engines in this category is that they work rather differently, and so the keen searcher has to experiment – can you only put in a list of words, or can you include a phrase, or use Boolean operators? It takes trial and error in most cases to work this out and, if time is tight, it can be very irritating.

Site-specific search engines (databases)

I make a very particular distinction between site search engines that search web pages, and those that search databases. The pages on my site that *Atomz* indexes are exactly the same ones that *Google* or any of the other search engines can visit, and they index them in exactly the same way. It make take rather longer for my pages to get added to the index, but they will eventually get there; they are what are termed 'publicly accessible' pages – anyone can find them. However, there are other web pages that you will have looked at which are perhaps not all they seem. Let's use an example from a genealogical website. Figure 6.3 shows a page from the *FreeBMD* (Births, Marriages and Deaths) website at **http://freebmd.rootsweb.com/** which lists the birth of Emily Mary Highfield.

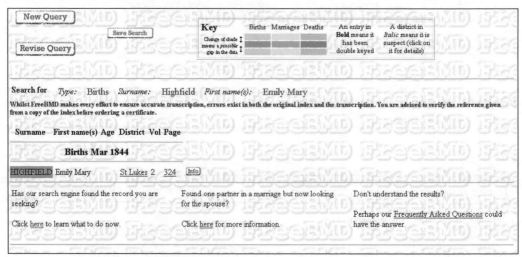

Figure 6.3   Search results from the *FreeBMD* search engine
© 1998–2004 The Trustees of FreeBMD

Although this looks like any other web page that you might come across while searching the internet, it's not a page that actually exists in its own right. That is to say, it is a web page that has been created as a result of the search that was run on the genealogical database. While searches in *Google* or *AlltheWeb* may turn up other pages that mention Emily Mary Highfield (although at the time of writing neither of them do), they will not include this page, because it exists only as a result of a search. As soon as the user points the browser at another web page, or runs another search, that page will be stored in the browser's cache for a day or so before being deleted, and will no longer exist, not even in a temporary form.

The reason for this is quite simple; a search engine spider is able to visit a page and index the data that it finds. However, it is not intelligent enough to realize that there is a search box that it could put words into (and how would it know which ones to use?), and index the page that was created as a result. Indeed, it's an impossibility because, although the amount of data contained within a database sitting behind a website is finite, the number of different combinations of terms and resultant web pages is essentially infinite. Consequently, the information contained in the database is often referred to as the 'hidden web' or the 'invisible web', because search engines cannot see it. The only way that a searcher can get access to this information is to find a search engine on a website that can interrogate a database with the appropriate information in it.

A good searcher will think laterally when it comes to searching for material of this nature. Let's take another example. If you wanted a list of plumbers in Glasgow, a visit to *Google* for a search on *plumber Glasgow* results in over 10,600 web pages that refer to plumbers in Glasgow Scotland, Glasgow Montana and Glasgow Kentucky. Even a search for *plumber Glasgow ~list* doesn't help very much. However, by thinking rather more broadly, to the type of site that would have that sort of information, such as an electronic yellow pages, a quick visit to *Yell.com* (the UK Yellow Pages online business database) at **www.eyp.co.uk/** results in 60 matches – many of which don't have web pages anyway.

Since there are so many search engines that could and do fit quite happily into this category, it's not possible to provide any sort of listing at all. However, there are plenty of search engines out there, particularly of the multi-search variety that do offer very good listings of specialist search engines, in particular *TheBigProject* at **www.thebigproject.co.uk/** and *CNET Search.com* at **www.search.com/**.

Summary

Site- or subject-specific engines are a very good way of getting good-quality, accurate and current information. It's reasonable to assume that the owners of the data ensure that they keep the information quality high. This is because they may be staking their reputation on the information, or they are hoping to sell a commercial product (a train ticket, for example). The actual information contained within such a database may be difficult to get hold of any other way, or it may not be possible to access it using any other search engine.

Of course, a site- or subject-specific engine will only be of value in one very specific area, but that's often exactly the information that a searcher is looking for. Once the appropriate engine can be located (which is often the difficult part of the search), finding the exact data needed should be much easier. A good or advanced searcher will keep an up-to-date listing of these engines close by them at all times.

URLs mentioned in this chapter

www.atomz.com/
www.philb.com
http://freebmd.rootsweb.com/
www.eyp.co.uk/
www.thebigproject.co.uk/
www.search.com/

Chapter 7 »
Searching the 'hidden web'

Introduction

The 'hidden web', often referred to as the 'invisible web', is the information
that is available on the internet that is not indexed or found by the traditional
free-text, index-based or multi-search engines. There are several reasons
why pages will not be found by these engines:

- Searchable databases. Some websites provide access to information that is
  contained within a database on their site, such as genealogical information,
  telephone numbers, train times and so on. The information you retrieve
  from a search is created for you as a result of the specific query that you have
  run, and the page doesn't actually exist as a stand-alone page. In order for
  a search engine to be able to index this information it would be necessary
  for the spider to visit the site, recognize the existence of a database sitting
  in the background, run searches and then index the results. Unfortunately, this really isn't possible, so the data does not get indexed and
  remains 'hidden' from general view.
- Password-protected pages. Passwords are used by web authors to protect
  data that they want only authorized people to view, either because the content is commercial, so you need to pay to get a password, or because the
  information is deemed appropriate only for members of an organization.
  Since the search engine spiders don't know the password they cannot
  visit that part of the site and so cannot index the data there.

- Author-excluded pages. It is possible for a web author to issue instructions to spider programs not to index certain pages on a website. For example, when I create a website for a client I often put a test version of the pages onto my own site for the client to view, and it's not appropriate for a search engine to index this material.
- Format of pages. The way that data have been made available may mean that some search engines are unable to index the data on them. One example is those pages that have been formatted in Adobe Acrobat; some search engines are unable to recognize and visit these pages (though generally search engines are now getting much better at this), so they are excluded.
- Scripts. Sometimes, when you've been searching a site, you may find that the URL of the page that you're looking at contains a ? symbol. This is because the page has been formatted or created for you by the use of a script, and most search engine spiders will not try and index the page beyond that question mark: some scripts may be poorly created and might 'trap' the spider in a loop (either intentionally or more often by accident), forcing it to index the same information over and over. To ensure that this doesn't happen spiders have been programmed to stop indexing when they find such a page.
- Pages excluded by search engines. Some search engine developers have made a decision not to index certain pages or sites. The reasons for this are many and varied. A search engine will not index a page (or will exclude it from its database) if the page is trying to trick the search engine into giving it a higher ranking than it deserves. So if a spider identifies that a page contains hidden text (by making the text colour the same colour as the background for example), it may not index it. Spiders may also decide not to index pages found on a particular server if they are aware that the server hosts (for example) a lot of pornographic material. Even if a site does not contain pornographic material, and may be a perfectly innocent site, because it's hosted on a server that is predominantly pornographic in nature it may be overlooked by the spiders.
- Frames-based sites. This is much less of a problem than it used to be, but may still trip up some search engines. A frames website is a site that has several panes of data available, contained within the browser window, and these work independently of each other. A common example is a situation where you have a menu bar in one frame which, when an option is clicked on, will open another window in the main body of the page. Most search engines are able to cope with this, but not all, and if the frames site has been poorly coded it may confuse the spider.

DID YOU KNOW? >>

Recent studies estimate the size of the hidden web to be about 500 times larger than the size of the known 'surface' web indexed by search engines.

Consequently, there is a lot of information available to searchers on the internet which is not immediately obvious. Happily, however, there are plenty of resources available to the advanced searcher that identify and search for material that would otherwise remain hidden, and in the rest of this chapter we look at some examples.

Search engines

Direct Search

This is a resource compiled by Gary Price, an acknowledged expert in the area of the hidden web. It is a list of links to the search interfaces of resources that contain data not easily or entirely searchable/accessible from general search tools. *Direct Search* is located at **www.freepint.com/gary/direct.htm**. The search engine links into such resources as *Fast Facts*, *Price's List of Lists*, *Speech and Transcript Center* and so on. The interface is shown in Figure 7.1.

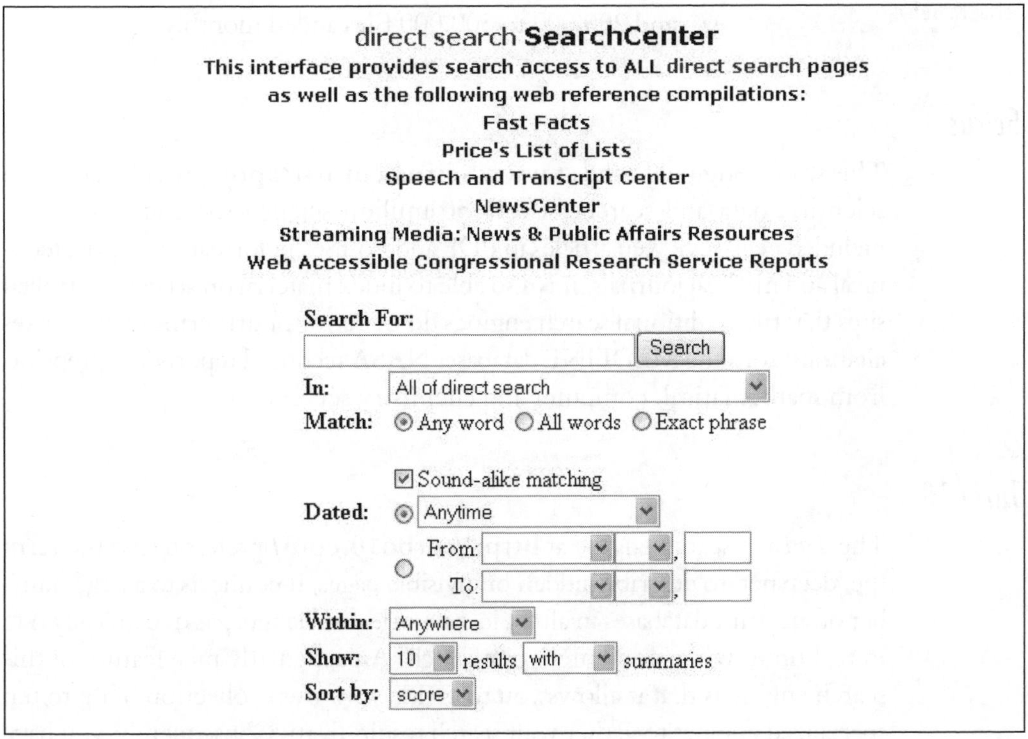
direct search SearchCenter
This interface provides search access to ALL direct search pages
as well as the following web reference compilations:
Fast Facts
Price's List of Lists
Speech and Transcript Center
NewsCenter
Streaming Media: News & Public Affairs Resources
Web Accessible Congressional Research Service Reports
Search For:
Search
In:
All of direct search
Match:
Any word
All words
Exact phrase
Sound-alike matching
Dated:
Anytime
From:
To:
Within:
Anywhere
Show:
10
results
with
summaries
Sort by:
score

Figure 7.1 Search interface for *Direct Search*
© Gary Price

As can be seen from Figure 7.1, the interface has considerable functionality and it provides access to a lot of data that would otherwise be unobtainable with a more traditional search engine.

Infomine

Infomine at **http://infomine.ucr.edu/** provides access to information and data that is appropriate for students and research staff at university level. The resources that it searches cover databases, journals, books, bulletin boards, mailing lists, online library catalogues and so on.

Singing Fish

This search engine, located at **www.singingfish.com/**, helps searchers to find audiovisual files, music files, movie trailers, sports highlights, news casts and other streaming media. The search engine offers the world's largest index of streaming media, with currently over ten million streams, mp3s and downloads, and 200,000 to 300,000 files added monthly.

> **DID YOU KNOW? >>**
> Streaming media is content delivered over a network that can be played on a receiving computer prior to the delivery of the entire file.

Scirus

This search engine, found at **www.scirus.com/srsapp/**, provides access to scientific data and searches over 150 million science-specific web pages, included peer-reviewed articles in PDF and PostScript format, scientific, technical and medical journals. It is also able to index material on access-controlled sites that the traditional search engines do not cover. Furthermore, it indexes citations from the MEDLINE database, NASA technical reports and preprints from mathematical, computer and chemistry servers.

Turbo10

The *Turbo10* search engine at **http://turbo10.com/** prefers to use the term the 'deep net' to describe hidden or invisible pages. It connects to a large number of specialist databases in all topic categories and languages dynamically (i.e. in real time) when you enter your search. A particularly nice feature of this search engine is that it allows you to create your own collection of up to ten specialized engines to gather your search results from. Consequently, you have much greater control of the type of results that are returned to you by limiting to only those engines that you think are going to give you pertinent results.

Hidden web directories

As you would expect, as well as search engines that connect to specific resources and search them for you there are a number of directories that identify appropriate databases and resources that you can go to directly in order to run a search. These compilations can be particularly useful in identifying resources that you would probably not otherwise be aware of.

CompletePlanet

The *CompletePlanet* resource at **www.completeplanet.com/** provides access to 103,000 searchable databases and speciality search engines in a 7000 category directory structure.

Invisible-web.net

This site, at **www.invisible-web.net/** is a companion site to the book *The Invisible Web: Finding Hidden Internet Resources Search Engines Can't See* by Chris Sherman and Gary Price. To quote from the site: 'It includes a directory of some of the best resources the Invisible Web has to offer. The directory includes resources that are informative, of high quality, and contain worthy information from reliable information providers that are not visible to general-purpose search engines.' The directory lists various subject headings such as 'Computers and the Internet', 'Reference', 'Science', 'Legal and Criminal' and 'US and World History'. The subcategory on US History lists about 20 databases that cover aspects of the subject from the 'Abraham Lincoln Primary Source Material Database' to 'Western History Photographs'.

LincOn.com

This search engine, at **www.lincon.com/srclist.htm** lists over 3000 speciality search engines in 34 different categories. It covers a wide variety of different subject areas, particularly those that are not covered by other search engines, such as Fuel and Energy, or Large Industry.

Intelligent agents that help search the hidden web

If you compare this edition of the book with one of the previous editions you'll note that there isn't a separate chapter this time on intelligent agents. There are a number of reasons for this, but the main one is that intelligent agents have not taken off in the way that many people (myself included) had expected them to. While these utilities are still extremely useful and important for the advanced searcher they have in some respects dwindled in number in comparison to the increase in other resources. Having said that, they are still an excellent way of finding information that would otherwise remain hidden. The intelligent agents that I refer to in this section are, in the main, utilities that you can download onto your own computer with which, using the interface provided, search a wide variety of search engines, databases and other resources in one go; almost like a multi-search engine in fact, but with a much larger pool of databases at their disposal. Some of these are free, while others are commercial in nature.

Copernic

The *Copernic Agent*, currently version 6.1 comes in three varieties: Basic, Personal and Professional. The Basic version is free of charge and can be downloaded from the website at **www.copernic.com/en/index.html**. It queries leading search engines for you (up to 1000, depending on the version), combines the results (removing duplicates as it does), relevance ranks them, and then displays the results. It can also search the invisible web, including resources such as market-research databases, business news, company information, news, reviews and patent information. The data returned can be managed, analysed and summarized, eliminating broken links, filtering irrelevant material, grouping and sorting results, summarizing and presenting key concepts. *Copernic Agent* can track new information, e-mailing the results to you, and track pages that you've found to be of particular interest.

Deep Query Manager

This utility, provided by *BrightPlanet* at **http://brightplanet.com/products/dqm.asp** has access to over 60,000 unique databases; one query can search hundreds or indeed thousands of these resources in one go. Searchers can create various search patterns for press clippings, competitive intelligence and job tracking, for example. The results can be shared, combined, annotated and archived as necessary.

FirstStop WebSearch

This is a new utility, first released in 2003, and is to be found at **www. firststopwebsearch.com/**. As with the other utilities, it is a desktop utility (that is to say, you download the software onto your computer, rather than using a website) and it searches multiple search engines and websites for the information that you require. There are three different versions, Standard, Deluxe and Visual; the latter two being commercial products, while the first is a free version, with limited functionality.

Other resources

There are many more resources available than I am able to cover in this section. However, if this is an area that is of interest to you, I would certainly suggest taking a look at some of the following.

Guides to Specialized Search Engines

This site at **www.searchability.com/** provides an excellent annotated list of multi-subject guides to over 30 specialized search engines in such areas as multi-subject guides, children's search engines, and guides to specialized engines.

Librarians' Index to the Internet

The motto of this site, at **http://lii.org/**, is 'Information you can trust'. It is a searchable, annotated subject directory of more than 12,000 internet resources selected and evaluated by librarians for their usefulness to users of public libraries.

Resource engines and the hidden web

Dawne Tortorella of *Bellcow* has created an excellent listing of several hundred resources in the field of the hidden web. The list of URLs at **www.bellcow. com/Resources/Presentations/CLS/HiddenWeb2003URL.htm** is now slightly dated, but still provides an impressive and easy-to-use starting point for further explorations in this area.

WebLens Search Portal

This site at **www.weblens.org/invisible.html** provides access to thousands of research tools, organized by theme or type of resource. It also contains information on various specialized searches, tutorials, articles, products and services.

Summary

It is important for the advanced searcher to know about the hidden web because of just that fact – it's hidden. It's all too easy to rely on the information that you find searching *Google*, and to stop looking at that point. However, there is so much more information available than you'll find with the traditional search engines and, in order to be comprehensive, it is necessary to spend time getting used to some of these hidden web search engines and utilities.

URLs mentioned in this chapter

www.freepint.com/gary/direct.htm
http://infomine.ucr.edu/
www.singingfish.com/
www.scirus.com/srsapp/
http://turbo10.com/
www.completeplanet.com/
www.invisible-web.net/
www.lincon.com/srclist.htm
www.copernic.com/en/index.html
http://brightplanet.com/products/dqm.asp
www.firststopwebsearch.com/
www.searchability.com/
http://lii.org/
www.bellcow.com/Resources/Presentations/CLS/HiddenWeb2003URL.
    htm
www.weblens.org/invisible.html

Chapter 8 »
Finding images, sounds and multimedia information

Introduction

Images form an integral part of the internet, appearing on just about every page you look at. There are probably two reasons why you might be looking for an image: either to include them in a web page, in which case the search will be for icons, bullets, backgrounds and so on, or in order to answer a query that you have been asked.

Sound files are also available in abundance on the internet – as brief snippets of sound, or as full-length songs, or other sound recordings. You may download them to sing along to, or for rather more serious uses; rather than just read a description of what whooping cough sounds like, it might be rather more effective to be able to hear the sound.

Video files are also becoming a common format on the internet, particularly since broadband connectivity becomes more widespread. Although it can still take many hours to download a full-length movie, even with the fastest of connections, much shorter clips, film trailers, or snippets of historical filmed material are all readily accessible.

At this point, I should add a disclaimer: much of the material that you find on the internet (particularly sound files such as music files produced by pop groups) will have been placed there without the agreement of the copyright holder. Copying this data may therefore be in breach of various copyright acts and, unless you are certain that you are legally entitled to copy and use the file for the purpose(s) you require, it makes sense to contact the copyright holder and seek specific permission. Copyright owners are becoming less tolerant of abuses of their material and are increasingly seeking legal recourse to protect their data.

Finding images on the internet

Image formats

There are essentially two different types of image on the internet, and they have the file extension .gif or .jpg. A small number of other types of file are slowly becoming more popular, but I'd be prepared to say that over 95% of all the images you find will be in one or other of these formats.

> **DID YOU KNOW? >>**
> The extension 'gif' is short for Graphical Interchange Format and 'jpg' means Joint Photographic Group.

Photographs are generally found as .jpg images, while icon, cartoon and block colour images are more likely to be made available in a .gif format. For the most part you can ignore this, although it may be important if you want a specific type of image for use on a web page, for example. If you're looking for photographs, they will most likely be found if a search is focused on the .jpg format. (You may also see the extension .jpeg, but it's referring to the same type of file.) However, this isn't a hard and fast rule, so while limiting yourself to a particular file type may give you a smaller number of hits, you may be excluding other images that would work perfectly well for your purpose.

> **HINTS & TIPS >>**
> An excellent listing of different file formats and the programs that open them can be found at http://members.aol.com/donnaskani/filetypes.html.

Using standard search engines to find images

Google image search

Google is rather more than just a text search engine, because it can be used to find images as well. The search engine has indexed over 425 million images culled from web pages. The interface can be found at **http://images.google.com/**. *Google* uses a variety of different factors to identify images and match them to the search terms, such as text that is adjacent to the image, image caption and so on. The simple image search function looks very similar to that of the web page interface, as can be seen in Figure 8.1.

Simple searches can be run in exactly the way you would expect – by typing in descriptive words or terms. The resulting page(s) of returned results shows thumbnail images that match the search term(s) and the user can then

Figure 8.1   The *Google* image search simple interface
© 2004 Google

click on one and go directly to its page. The advanced search function has options to focus the search by all words, any word, the phrase or to exclude words. It is also possible to limit the search to a particular type of image so, if you just want to see photographs of flowers (rather than cartoons or drawings), a reasonable search would be to search for *flower filetype:jpg*. *Google* can also limit the search to images of a particular size, such as small, medium, large or wallpaper sized, and to colours, black and white or greyscale. Finally, the advanced search function also allows users to limit searches to particular domains.

AltaVista image searching

The *AltaVista* image interface at **www.altavista.com/image/default/** can be seen in Figure 8.2. You'll notice that it claims to be the 'largest image search on the web', a claim that *Google* may wish to challenge. However, since *AltaVista* doesn't say how many images it has indexed, it's rather hard to comment!

Figure 8.2   The *AltaVista* image search interface
© 2004 Overture Services, Inc.

As can be seen from Figure 8.2 the interface is simple to use and doesn't have an advanced feature. Images can be located simply by typing in appropriate words or terms in exactly the same way that one would search for web pages. The search can be limited/widened to photographs, graphics and buttons/ banners, by ticking the appropriate boxes. *AltaVista* can limit to only black and white, colour or 'all colour'. The 'Sources' option allows users to limit their searches to News resources, the *Corbis* collection (discussed below), Rollingstone.com or web pages. *AltaVista* does allow users to choose from 21 different files sizes, however (most of which are various wallpaper sizes).

AltaVista displays only 15 images per page of returned results, rather than the 20 provided by *Google*. There are two options when it comes to display-ing the image – clicking directly on the image will take the searcher to the web page that contains that exact image (rather than showing it in a window in the *Google* manner), or users can click on the link 'More info'. This dis-plays a page of information about the image, such as its file name, image size, pixel size and file type. One other very nice feature is that users can choose to see all of the media from a particular page. If this option is chosen *AltaVista* generates a new page, with thumbnails of all the images or audiovisual data for a searcher to view in more detail. This is a very neat feature, and it is a def-inite incentive for the multimedia searcher to focus their attentions on *AltaVista*.

Yahoo!

Yahoo! has an excellent image search function, the main problem being that it's quite difficult to locate! There are three ways of locating it. Firstly do a 'normal' search using the free-text search box at the top of the screen, then click on the 'Images' tab and redo the search, which is irritating because it's obviously necessary to do the same search twice. A second approach is to scroll to the bottom of the home page, to the second occurrence of the free-text box, input the search term(s) and choose 'Images' from the pull-down menu. The third way of searching is to go directly to the 'Images' search function at http://images.search.yahoo.com/ which can be seen in Figure 8.3.

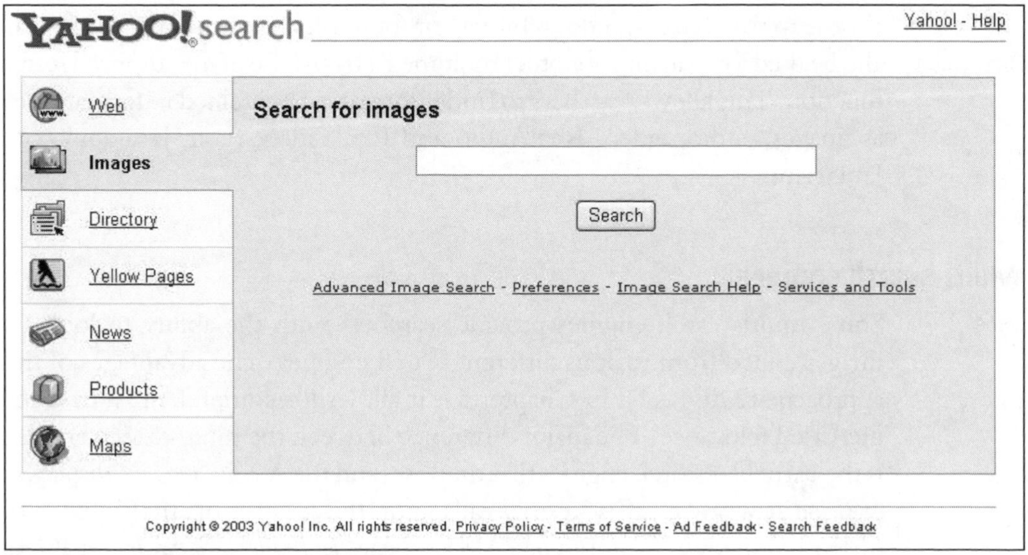

Figure 8.3   The *Yahoo!* image search interface
© 2004 Yahoo! Inc. All rights reserved

The advanced image search function allows searchers to limit search terms to the usual all words, any words, phrase, exclude words options, and to various size options. *Yahoo!* also allows searchers to limit searches to .jpg, .gif or .png files, and to any one of four colour types (full colour, any colour, greyscale or black and white). A final option, and one that doesn't appear with any of the other engines that I look at, is to limit results to websites that are .com, .edu., .gov, .org or a specific domain. Finally, and in common with all other engines, *Yahoo!* gives searchers the option of filtering returned images, to block the more unpleasant ones.

One final *Yahoo!* image search option, also hidden deep in the search engine, is the ability to search for, or limit

> **DID YOU KNOW? >>**
> A '.png' extension stands for Portable Network Graphic. These files are the standard files in Macromedia's Fireworks software, and can be seen in many commonly used browsers. .png files are the most recently accepted image file format on the internet, but are still quite rare.

images to news images. The easiest way to access this function is to point the browser to **http://search.yahoo.com/news/** and click on the 'News Photo' option before running the search.

AlltheWeb

AlltheWeb has almost exactly the same image search interface as *AltaVista*, and the only difference with the advanced search function is that searchers can also choose to search for Windows bitmap or .bmp files. However, *AlltheWeb* can also be used for searching for other multimedia by the use of the advanced search function. This allows searchers to find information contained in formats such as images, audio, video, RealAudio and RealVideo, flash, Java applets or JavaScript.

Multi-search engines

Some multi-search engines provide searchers with the ability to look for images culled from various different search engines. The advantages of this approach are discussed in Chapter 5 – it allows for comprehensiveness and increased relevance. The major difference between the multi-search engines is the particular search engines that they use, and the way images are displayed. *ez2Find* at **www.ez2find.com/** calls upon the services of *AltaVista*, *Corbis* (discussed below), *Lycos Pictures*, *NASA Image Exchange*, *Picsearch* and *Yahoo! News Photos*. *Ixquick* at **www.ixquick.com/** is rather disappointing, since it is limited to *Gograph* and *Picsearch*. *Fazzle* on the other hand, at **www. fazzle.com/**, collates results from *Lycos* images, *Webshots* and *Picsearch*. In common with its web search interface, searchers can then sort returned images by popularity, title, description or domain.

FaganFinder

FaganFinder is a multi-search engine that has a remarkably large number of image search engines at its disposal; it can be found at **www.faganfinder.com/ img/**. As well as providing searchers with the option of searching for keywords with the image function of the main search engines, it also provides links to graphics and clip art, educational images, artwork, stock photographs, regional and historical images, science, nature and body images and links to several dozen other resources. It is an excellent engine for providing the novice searcher with a wide variety of opening options when it comes to searching for images.

Image-specific search engines

Stopstock

This website at **www.1stopstock.com/** gives access to various commercial image providers; their databases can be accessed through the *Stopstock* front end. You can do either a multi-search across all the providers or, if you prefer, search each individually, and limit the search to 'all royalty free' or 'all rights protected'. After the search has run you are presented with a display of images which are kept at low resolution and/or are watermarked. However, having said that, the quality is quite acceptable for general viewing, and it is certainly good enough to decide if it is worthwhile purchasing the use of the image.

Picsearch

Picsearch at **www.picsearch.com/** has been mentioned before; it's used by various multi-search engines, but of course can be searched directly. *Picsearch* only searches for, and indexes, images from web pages. It has an automatic filter in place, so it should be rare to view pornographic images. Consequently, this is a good search engine to direct children towards (though of course it's always sensible to monitor or sit with a child who is searching the net) if they need to search for pictures.

Picsearch allows the use of the plus and minus symbols to focus searches, but oddly enough doesn't use the phrase option. It does have an advanced search function, which can be seen in Figure 8.4.

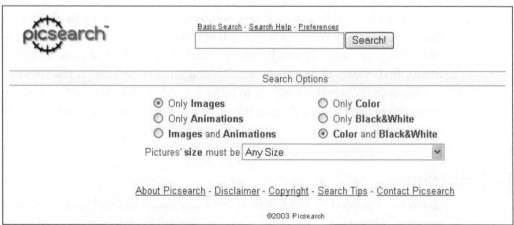

Figure 8.4   The *Picsearch* advanced search interface
© 2003 Picsearch

Search results are displayed in groups of 16, and provide searchers with the option of going directly to the URL that displays the image, or to an intermediate page that gives the user information about the image, such as file size, file type and so on.

Ditto.com

Ditto.com, found at **www.ditto.com/**, is an American company that styles its search engine as 'the world's leading visual search engine'. The search engine provides nine images at a time, with details on the file size, and a direct link to the source website. It also provides a useful list of related searches: my search for *civil war* offered options such as 'The Civil War', 'American Civil War' and 'Abraham Lincoln'. Disappointingly, there was no link to the English Civil War, however, and the first image from that particular conflict wasn't found until I'd scrolled through seven pages of results. I also found a heavy emphasis on the purchase of products related to the search term, which was a little off-putting.

Image collections

Image collections differ from the resources that we have discussed until now because they are exactly that – a collection of images, very often for a specific-subject area, and the details on the images are held in a particular database. As a result it is not possible for the other search engines to visit and index them. While they may in some circumstances be able to provide a link to the search engine itself, they can't index the data. A second major difference is that in many cases human beings will have indexed the images using meta data, so that the pictures that are retrieved will in most instances be much more relevant than the rather hit-and-miss approach adopted by the search engines mentioned above. As a result, a third and final difference is that pornographic material is highly unlikely to be found, although it is possible that some erotica may do, but I shall leave the reader to decide exactly where the difference lies.

The *Corbis* collection

Corbis was founded by Bill Gates in 1989 and has an unrivalled collection of over two million images that are used commercially in advertising, books, television, newspapers, magazines and other media. However, it is not just a commercial service, since it offers images at reasonable prices to individuals. The search function is very impressive – after running a search with some simple keywords the searcher is shown a series of thumbnail images, and the search can be further focused according to various different parameters as given by *Corbis* (such as Historical, Celebrity, Colour and so on). If the searcher clicks onto a thumbnail it is shown in a larger size (with a watermark) with various size options for downloading. Searchers can also rerun searches based on a large selection of suggested keywords. If it is necessary to obtain images to use in a professional environment it would certainly be worth exploring the collection in some detail; it is located at **www.corbis.com/**.

Getty Images

Unlike the *Corbis* collection, *Getty Images* at **http://creative.gettyimages. com/** is clearly aimed at the professional market (images from the collection can often be found on book covers for example). It has created a large database of images due to several partnership deals with organizations such as the Timelife collection, Hulton Archive and National Geographic. The collection offers access to its data via three main databases: Creative, News and Sport, and Film. As with the *Corbis* collection, it has similar advantages and disadvantages.

Free Images

The *Free Images* collection at **www.freeimages.co.uk/** is quite a small collection, having just over 2500 images in 58 galleries. However, the images are all original and of good quality. They are also free to use (although a link back to the site is required), and it's a simple and easy site to search – either by keyword or by category.

The Digital Librarian: images

While this site at **www.digital-librarian.com/images.html** is not a collection of images in its own right it does provide users with a great many links to image collections covering many different subject areas and geographical regions.

Image newsgroups

If you're unfamiliar with the concept of newsgroups this small section will not make a great deal of sense to you until you've read Chapter 13, so it might make sense to read that chapter first, then return here!

A great many newsgroups are dedicated to images. However, whatever the nature of the newsgroup the concept is exactly the same, in that people post photographs and images of different types and formats. These can be downloaded and saved using your newsreading software and used for whatever purpose is required. Be warned though, since a great many illegally copied images turn up in newsgroups, so you need to be extra careful before using them. The main hierarchy is to be found at alt.binaries.pictures.something-else. Your newsreader can be used to track down the particular group that you're interested in, though be aware that you might be disturbed by some of the images newsgroups that you'll scroll past.

Finding sound files

Unlike images, a great many different types of sound files are available and supported on the internet. In order to play a sound file it is necessary to have a utility that can do this (although if you have a recent version of the Windows operating system you'll already have utilities that will play sound files for you without the necessity for you to do anything else), and we'll talk more about such utilities in Chapter 16. However, for the moment, we can limit the discussion by saying that if you don't have such a utility available on your machine your browser should prompt you to download an appropriate one, or you'll get advice from a website that has sound files available to download.

There are a great many resources in which to find and download sound files, but many of these are from movie/television clips, or from popular music. I suspect that the vast majority of them are in breach of copyright, however. Consequently, the warning that I gave at the beginning of the chapter applies especially to sound files. Before you make any use of them please do check to make sure you're allowed to use them by the appropriate organization or copyright holder. Some sites are explicit about what you can or cannot do with sound files, particularly those of film studios and record labels, so there really should not be too much confusion about the legality (or otherwise) of a sound file. But, if in doubt – check first!

Search engines

An increasing number of search engines provide searchers with the opportunity of searching for sounds or web pages that contain them. *AltaVista* provides a search tab called MP3/Audio and searchers simply need to click on this, and then type in keywords as appropriate. In my experience, however, it is not as easy to locate appropriate sound files as it is web pages; better results are achieved with fewer, rather than more keywords, or by searching for a phrase, such as *'whooping cough'*. (Of course, while that's my experience I'm more than happy to accept that others will have found exactly the opposite!) The results of a search at *AltaVista* provide searchers with the file name, file information and page URL for the file. You can then visit the page and click on the link to play the file, and if you don't have the appropriate utility to play it, your browser will inform you of this. *AlltheWeb* also has exactly the same function, although the displayed results are rather more brusque – simply file name, URL, size of file and date. The *HotBot* advanced search function has an option for searchers to limit results to pages that contain specified media types such as audio, though I have to confess that when I did my whooping cough search *HotBot* did return several pages that did not contain any sound files at all, let alone any on the subject I was interested in.

The *Google Directory* has an option for sound files at **http://directory. google.com/Top/Arts/Music/Sound_Files/** which lists over 2000 entries, though these are links to websites, rather than a way of searching for sound files in their own right. *Yahoo!* has a smaller but similar offering at **http://dir.yahoo.com/Computers_and_Internet/Multimedia/Audio/**. Another useful site, although not a search engine as such, is the *World Wide Web Virtual Library: Audio* at **http://archive.museophile.sbu.ac.uk/audio/** which provides links to a large number of repositories of audio material and is an excellent starting point.

FindSounds

The *FindSounds* search engine at **www.findsounds.com/** runs over one million sound searches for more than 100,000 users every month. The search engine is aptly named, since 'sounds' are what it tends to specialize in, as a selection of sounds from its 'office' category demonstrates: briefcase, cash register, elevator, fax, mouse click, pencil sharpener and typewriter.

General repositories and websites

As just mentioned, a comprehensive listing of these can be obtained from the *WWW Virtual Library: Audio*, so I will limit my comments to a few repositories that I think are particularly useful for the general searcher.

Wav Central at **www.wavcentral.com/** provides access to thousands of clips from television programmes, films, sound effects, and commercials. The search interface is very simple, and it also provides an alphabetical listing of film clips for example. The *EARchive* maintained by Bill Auclair at **www.the-earchives.com/** lists over 3700 sound clips which, like *Wav Central*, tend to focus on television and film clips. My American readers may wish to start their explorations at *Sound America* **www.soundamerica.com/** although there is once again a preponderance of movie- and television-related sounds.

If your interest is in popular music probably the most infamous site to visit is *Napster* at **www.napster.com/** which has in the past been at the centre of many legal disputes because of the way that popular music tracks and albums could be downloaded from the internet using its software. However, *Napster* now proudly proclaims that it is 'back and legal', and music files can now be lawfully downloaded using its software packages.

Various speeches and historical sounds can be obtained via the collections provided by *Webcorp* and at **www.webcorp.com/sounds/** there are links to a great many historical sound files.

The *Internet Archive Live Music Archive* at **www.archive.org/audio/** preserves and archives live music concerts.

The *Online Speech Bank* at **www.americanrhetoric.com/speechbank. htm** is an index to a growing database of 5000-plus full-text, audio and video (streaming) versions of public speeches, sermons, legal proceedings, lectures, debates, interviews, other recorded media events, and a declaration or two. The content is varied, but the emphasis (as might be guessed by the URL) is firmly on the USA.

Newsgroups

There are well over 100 newsgroups to post sound files to, and you can be assured that virtually none of them have copyright clearance! For more information on newsgroups you may wish to skip ahead to Chapter 13.

Playing sound files

It depends entirely on the type of sound file and on having the appropriate plug-in utility available. The majority of files are in a .wav, .mid or .mp3 format. You should simply be able to click on the link and your browser will then open a small window on the page, download the file and play it automatically with the appropriate utility. If a website provides access to a sound file which is in any way unusual or requires the use of unusual software it will usually include a link to a site where you can download the appropriate utility.

Multimedia files

So far we have looked at image and sound files, but of course there are other formats, such as moving images. Indeed, as access to the internet is increasingly via broadband connections, this type of data is becoming more common. Video files are available on the internet in a variety of different formats and, consequently, it is necessary to make sure you have the appropriate software installed on your machine. Since different packages are required for different formats there is little point in installing them until you require them, and when this is necessary your browser will alert you to the fact. However, if you do wish to explore the different packages available a good resource is the *Tucows* site at **www.tucows.com/** where you can simply choose your operating system, find the option for multimedia tools and start browsing!

Be aware that it can take some considerable time to download video files, and even with a fast broadband connection a large file may well take several minutes or even longer. If you are connecting to the internet with a modem this may quite easily extend into several hours, so be prepared to be patient!

Search engines

- *Singingfish* at **www.singingfish.com/** provides access to multimedia files, and in a wide variety of subject areas such as music, sport, news, movies, television, finance and live events.
- *AltaVista* has what it claims to be the 'largest video search on the web' at **www.altavista.com/video/default/** and an example of the interface can be seen in Figure 8.5. The search function allows users to search across a range of file formats, all durations (or, alternatively, less than or more than one minute), from its collections that include the web, news sources and Rollingstone.com, for example.

> **DID YOU KNOW? 〉〉**
> Common video or multimedia file types are .mpeg, .avi, quicktime, Windows media and RealPlayer.

- As you would expect, other search engines have not been slow to follow, and *AlltheWeb* has an offering at **www.alltheweb.com/?avkw=fogg&cat=**

vid&cs=utf-8&q=&_sb_lang=pref. This has very similar options to *AltaVista*, although it does provide a little more information about the video clips available.

- *ez2Find* at **www.ez2www.com/** (or its alternative URL of **www.ez2find. com/**) has an excellent multimedia search engine, and it allows users to search for a variety of different media formats such as midi, mp3, webcams and so on.

- *Mediafind* at **http://search.mp3.de/** is a specialized search engine that just looks for files in a variety of media formats.

- The *Lycos* multimedia search engine at **http://multimedia.lycos.com/** provides access to data from licensed collections, audio, mp3 and, of course, video clips.

Figure 8.5   The *AltaVista* video search interface
© 2004 Overture Services, Inc.

Summary

While there is still of course a preponderance of text on the internet and always will be, data is increasingly being made available in a variety of other formats. It's always worthwhile considering the possibility that the information you require may be available as a sound file, picture or a moving image. It is, however, more difficult to find information in formats other than text simply because it is more difficult to index the information found in a multimedia format. Consequently, perhaps the best way of searching for such data is to first look for a site that may possibly contain sound or image files first, and then search the actual site for the particular information you require.

URLs mentioned in this chapter

http://members.aol.com/donnaskani/filetypes.html
http://images.google.com/
www.altavista.com/image/default/
http://images.search.yahoo.com/
http://search.yahoo.com/news/
www.ez2find.com/
www.ixquick.com/
www.fazzle.com/
www.faganfinder.com/img/
www.1stopstock.com/
www.picsearch.com/
www.ditto.com/
www.corbis.com/
http://creative.gettyimages.com/
www.freeimages.co.uk/
www.digital-librarian.com/images.html
http://directory.google.com/Top/Arts/Music/Sound_Files/
http://dir.yahoo.com/Computers_and_Internet/Multimedia/Audio/
http://archive.museophile.sbu.ac.uk/audio/
www.findsounds.com/
www.wavcentral.com/
www.the-earchives.com/
www.soundamerica.com/
www.napster.com/
www.webcorp.com/sounds/
www.archive.org/audio/
www.americanrhetoric.com/speechbank.htm
www.tucows.com/
www.singingfish.com/
www.altavista.com/video/default/
www.alltheweb.com/?avkw=fogg&cat=vid&cs=utf-8&q=&_sb_lang=pref
http://search.mp3.de/
http://multimedia.lycos.com/

Chapter 9 »
Finding people

Introduction

If you talk to people about the internet, and specifically ask what they think it is, you will get a wide variety of answers: technical support people will tell you all about the computers and protocols used to link everything together; information professionals will wax lyrical about the information that can be found and used; sales people will tell you what a great tool it is for selling products and so on.

However, what many of them will not think of saying is that, when it comes right down to it, the internet is about people. It is people who make the computers, create the protocols, put up the information and, once again, people who will be buying the products. So what the internet is about is people, plain and simple. As such, the internet is also a marvellous way to find out all about them, often in much more detail than you would expect. This chapter deals with some of the ways that you can locate particular people and find out more about them.

There are basically four different ways of looking for people on the internet: you can use the standard search engines to look for references to someone's name and then visit the website(s) that are returned to you; you can use search engines that look for a name and relate that to an e-mail address; you can use a 'people finder' to look for particular individuals; or finally you can use a small number of very specific resources that have started to appear in the last couple of years that allow people to add information about themselves to allow others to find them. In this chapter I'll cover all these methods and try to assess (in a very non-scientific way) how useful each of these proved to be when I attempted to use it.

Standard search engines

The standard search engines that we use are obviously the first place to start, and a search for an individual's name is best run using double quotes to put it into a phrase. *"Phil Bradley"* returns about 5400 references in *Google*, while Phil Bradley without the quotes returns over a quarter of a million. Of course, it is also important to remember that people may not use their full name, so always keep in mind that *"William Smith"* might also be found in a search for *"Bill Smith"*, *"Will Smith"* and so on. As an experiment I used some of the major search engines that I've already referred to and ran a search on my name to see what turned up:

AlltheWeb	16,922
AltaVista	3,495
Google	5,440
HotBot	3,587
Lycos	15,467
MSN	3,342.

HINTS & TIPS >>

While putting a person's name into a phrase will certain focus your search more closely, it will exclude results that use a middle name or initial, for example. "George Bush" will not return results that refer to him as "George W Bush", so be aware of this.

To be honest, I'm not entirely sure what, if anything, this proves. Certainly it clearly indicates that there is a huge discrepancy between the results given by different search engines, and if you've read previous chapters in this book that shouldn't come as any surprise. Quite clearly it's necessary to limit the search by various other terms to reduce the recall and increase the precision. If we assume that the *"Phil Bradley"* that we're looking for is me (rather than the baseball player, American general or gay porn star) it's going to be necessary to limit the search further by adding in other search terms. Since I'm a librarian you could add that into the search which, using *AlltheWeb*, brings us down to 287 results; a more manageable figure and the results start to point towards me in rather more detail. Alternatively, and perhaps more usefully, if we simply add in the phrase "home page" although we get more results (5513) the first result is a link to my website at **www.philb.com/**. In this exact instance you'd have got exactly the same result with the first searches, but that's cheating slightly, since my site is optimized with various search engines to come at the top of the results for that specific phrase search.

Consequently, using a general search engine to find a particular individual does have some merit, providing that you have a fairly clear idea of exactly who you are looking for. However, it would not necessarily provide you with contact details, unless that information was included on a web page, for example. This approach certainly wouldn't work terribly well if the person you are looking for has a common name; there are over 240,000 hits with *AltaVista* for *"John Smith"*, for example. (This has almost doubled in number from the figure included in the second edition of this book!)

E-mail search engines

Some search engines are simply databases of names matched to e-mail addresses. The data are collected from a variety of sources – usenet newsgroup postings, web pages, people who register directly with such search engines and so on.

> **DID YOU KNOW? >>**
> **55**% of computer users send e-mail more often than they make long-distance phone calls (www.perfectisite.com/surprise.html).

Some of these are independent engines, while others are associated with more general search engines. *Yahoo!*, for example, has a people search function at **http://people.yahoo.com/** and this can be seen in Figure 9.1 This is, however, of little value to my British readers (assuming they're looking for individuals who are not American), since the facility searches only for people based in the USA; unfortunately there isn't such an option on the UK version of the site. However, out of interest I ran my search for *"Phil Bradley"* in the White Pages option first of all and came up with 170 matches, with further links to commercial databases that offered to further locate addresses, criminal searches and background checks. Since these all required payment in order to proceed further I left at that point. I did have more luck when I asked the search facility to check for e-mail addresses, and it returned 68 results, including addresses from the UK version of the search engine, and my own address of philb@philb.com.

A second e-mail address search engine, *WhoWhere?!* at **www.whowhere.lycos.com/**, was rather more disappointing, giving me only two e-mail addresses, neither of was were appropriate. I moved on to try *MESA*, the MetaE-mailSearchAgent at **http://rzserv.rrzn.uni-hannover.de/mesa/cgi-bin/e-mail.cgi**, which searches through a variety of different resources, and although it returned only a small number of results in total (26) one of

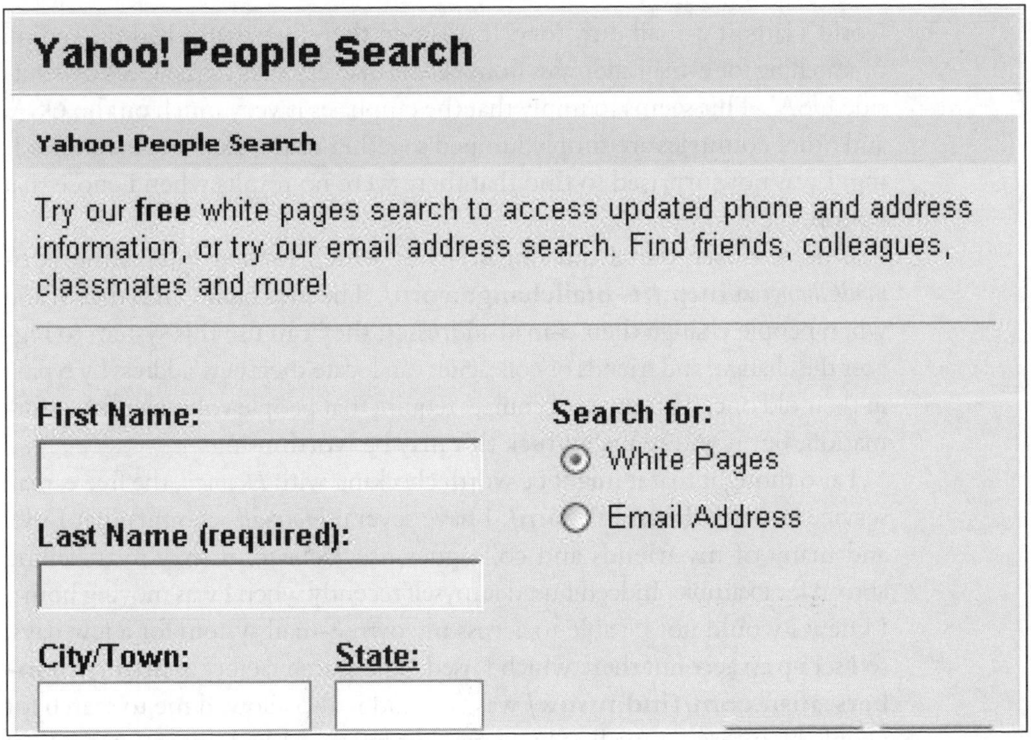

Yahoo! People Search
Yahoo! People Search
Try our **free** white pages search to access updated phone and address information, or try our email address search. Find friends, colleagues, classmates and more!
First Name:
Search for:
White Pages
Email Address
Last Name (required):
City/Town:
State:

Figure 9.1 The *Yahoo!* people search function
© 2004 Yahoo! Inc. All rights reserved

these was an e-mail address that I have used in the past, although of course if you did not know what it was, that would not be of much help.

I next tried a service provided by MIT at **http://usenet-addresses.mit.edu/** which checks the e-mail addresses that people have used when posting to usenet (and for more information on usenet and newsgroups you may wish to jump ahead to Chapter 13), but once again this did not provide anything useful by the way of leads since it was not possible to limit searches Phil AND Bradley; it would look for only Phil OR Bradley, rendering it next to useless, which was a great shame.

My search for my own e-mail address carried on when I visited the *Infospace* e-mail listings at **www.infospace.com/**. I was very impressed with this service; it located a total of 136 Phil Bradleys and both my e-mail addresses were found within the first ten that were returned, although oddly enough my postal address with one was given as being Croydon even though I've never lived there!

Addresses.com at **www.addresses.com/** proudly declares that it is the world's largest e-mail directory. It was odd therefore that it had the option of searching for e-mail addresses from people in every state in the USA or 'Outside USA'. This seems to imply that the emphasis is very much on the USA, and other countries are simply lumped together under that one broad heading. I was not surprised to find that there were no results when I chose that option.

One resource that I did not use, but which looked interesting is *E-mailChange* at **http://e-mailchange.com/**. The idea behind it is that, if and when people change their e-mail addresses, they can use this system to register the change, and friends or colleagues can locate their new address by typing in their old one. This does, of course, require that people volunteer this information, but if you're really stuck this may be worth using.

I also thought that it might be worth checking with *Hotmail*, the free e-mail service at **www.hotmail.com/**. I have several *Hotmail* accounts that I use, and many of my friends and colleagues use *Hotmail*, if they're travelling abroad for example. Indeed I used it myself recently when I was moving home; I knew I would not be able to access my own e-mail system for a few days, so I set up an account there which I used. The search facility at **http://members. msn.com/find.msnw/** was fast, and it also allowed me to search for people by interest as well as by name, but because I had not set up any sort of profile when I set up my account I was unsuccessful in my search. However, if you think it is possible that someone is using a *Hotmail* address, it may be worth trying. But beware that all the usual variants of names have now been taken so names are becoming rather more esoteric and difficult to identify correctly.

Finally I tried the *Internet Address Finder* at **www.iaf.net/frames/ freeresources.htm** but failed to get beyond the opening screen, so I still don't know if it is of any use. However, I have left this resource here, since there may simply have been a glitch in the server, and it may work properly for you if you try it yourself.

Once again, therefore, I had mixed results when using e-mail address finders. Some of them certainly worked very well and returned my e-mail address accurately and quickly. However, I knew the e-mail address that I was looking for – if I hadn't, I suspect that it would have been a rather more touch-and-go operation. I suspect that this problem will continue into the future as more and more people get an increasingly high level of 'spam' e-mail sent to them, and they will use throw away accounts more often.

People finders

These are rather more common than e-mail search engines, and they attempt to provide users with rather more information than just an e-mail address. When possible they also give you a telephone number, street address and, in the case of the USA, even maps of how to get to someone's house. They are often connected to other services, allowing you to send virtual cards, gifts or flowers to the people you find.

Excite has a people finder at **http://directory.superpages.com/people. jsp?SRC=excite** which is US-based and provides information on the individual, their address and telephone number, a map, the option of finding neighbours, and a link to driving instructions on how to get to their home. The UK version at http://people-finder.excite.co.uk/ does not give quite as many options, but it does provide searchers with postal addresses and telephone numbers. It also gives information that it has obtained via the electoral register which includes a map of where the person lives and the option of directions to their home.

DID YOU KNOW? >>
A depressing news item at www. globetechnology.com/servlet/story/ RTGAM.20031219.gtmaps1219/BNStory/ Technology/ goes into some detail about how these services are used to stalk people.

Netscape also has a people finder at **http://wp.netscape.com/netcenter/ whitepages.html** which allows you to search for someone's address or e-mail address. Once again I tried a search for me, and located a total of 77 variations on 'Phil Bradley', but none of them were me. However, the utility was simple and easy to use, and I suspect that, if the individual that you're looking for has a slightly unusual name, it would not be too difficult to track them down.

A British-based resource is *192.com* that can be found at **www.192.com/**. This allows searchers to check a directory enquiries service, the 2002 and 2003 electoral roll, a family search, a relationship tracer and a people tracing service. Many of these options are commercial, however, and it is necessary to register with the site in order to use them.

Given that I'd just tried a directory enquiry service I thought it would be sensible to check with the *British Telecom* site at **www.bt.com/**. This is a very easy service which gives users ten free searches per day. A quick search on my name and initial together with a general location found me immediately. What I found particularly impressive was that the service located me at my new address, which I have been at for about a month. The service is not comprehensive since it does not include ex-directory numbers and of course an increasing number of people do not use the services of British Telecom, but it's a good first step to take in locating someone.

Specific tracking services

A number of these are available if you are trying to trace an old friend or relative, for example.

LookupUK at **www.lookupuk.com/main.html** provides links to UK telephone services, e-mail search services for the UK and Ireland, genealogical services and a message board that allows you to post a message for people that you're looking for – this is also searchable.

In the last few years there has been an explosion of sites that allow you to search for friends from school, based at least in part on the *Friends Re-united* website at **www.friendsreunited.co.uk/**. This site gives people the chance to link themselves to a specific school, college or university, workplace and street. It's very comprehensive, easy to use and well constructed. In fact I've used it myself in the past to locate friends and have been, in turn, found myself. An American equivalent is *Classmates* at **www.classmates.com/**. Other variants of this service that you may wish to explore are:

- *Alumni.Net* at **www.alumni.net/** (a global service)
- *Around People Finder* at **www.around.co.uk/** (a UK service)
- *Forces Reunited* at **www.forcesreunited.org.uk/** (a UK service for members or ex-members of the services)
- *Gradfinder* at **www.reunion.com/** (a US service)
- *Lost school friends* at **www.lostschoolfriends.com/** (a global service)
- *Missing persons worldwide* at **www.missing–persons.info/** (a global service)
- *Netintouch* at **www.netintouch.net/** (a global service)
- *Reunion* at **www.reunion.com/** (a US service)
- *Reunite* at **www.reunite.co.uk/** (a UK service)
- *Roastbeef* at **www.roastbeef.co.uk/** (a UK service)
- *Schoolnews* at **www.schoolnews.com/** (a US and Canadian service).

If you were adopted as a child, or are seeking a child that has been adopted, there are various useful websites, such as the *UK Birth Adoption Register* at **www.ukbirth-adoptionregister.com/** and the *UK Post-adoption Centre* at **www.valleymedia.co.uk/pac/index.htm**. This is obviously an emotive area, and outside the scope of this book, so all I can suggest here is that you should seek advice and assistance before attempting to locate an adopted child or birth parent.

If none of the above services helps find the person that you're looking for, it might be time to start thinking a little more laterally. For example, the

Familysearch database at **www.familysearch.org/** has an excellent selection of genealogical resources online, allowing you to discover a lot of information about relatives, friends and ancestors. Still on the family history angle you may wish to try *GenesConnected* at **www.genesconnected.co.uk/** which is a global resource, although it has a UK emphasis.

Another approach might be to look on an auction site, such as *eBay* at **www.ebay.com/** and search for a particular user, or check through mailing lists and/or newsgroups, which are covered in more detail in Chapter 13.

Summary

As with most internet-related issues, there isn't any one 'best' way of searching for a particular person. Quite clearly, the more you know about a person, the easier they are to track down. However, with a little perseverance and time it may well be possible to locate them.

URLs mentioned in this chapter

http://people.yahoo.com/
www.whowhere.lycos.com/
http://rzserv.rrzn.uni-hannover.de/mesa/cgi-bin/e-mail.cgi
http://usenet-addresses.mit.edu/
www.infospace.com/
www.addresses.com/
http://e-mailchange.com/
www.hotmail.com/
http://members.msn.com/find.msnw/
www.iaf.net/frames/freeresources.htm
http://directory.superpages.com/people.jsp?SRC=excite
http://people-finder.excite.co.uk/
http://wp.netscape.com/netcenter/whitepages.html
www.192.com/
www.bt.com/
www.lookupuk.com/main.html
www.friendsreunited.co.uk/
www.classmates.com/
www.alumni.net/
www.around.co.uk/
www.forcesreunited.org.uk/

www.reunion.com/
www.lostschoolfriends.com/
www.missing-persons.info/
www.netintouch.net/
www.reunion.com/
www.reunite.co.uk/
www.roastbeef.co.uk/
www.schoolnews.com/
www.ukbirth-adoptionregister.com/
www.valleymedia.co.uk/pac/index.htm
www.familysearch.org/
www.genesconnected.co.uk/
www.ebay.com/

Part 2 »

Becoming an expert searcher

Chapter 10 >>
Weblogs

Introduction

When I was writing the second edition of this book in 2001 I was vaguely aware of the existence of what have since become known as 'weblogs' but they didn't seem that important; they didn't even get a mention in the index. Indeed, it was only in that year that a definition for the term became established properly: a BBC news report at **http://news.bbc.co.uk/1/hi/uk/ 1717136.stm** defines weblogs as 'public online journals where cyber diarists let the world in on the latest twists and turns of their love, work and internal lives.' 'The majority . . . are not all that interesting,' says weblog-tracking psychologist John Grohol. A more pertinent, and perhaps more accurate definition, is provided by Peter Scott (a weblog expert at the University of Saskatchewan Library, Canada): 'a web page containing brief, chronologically arranged items of information'. That's about the most general definition that makes any kind of sense, but to try to get a definition that is more specific and is agreed on by the weblog community is doomed to failure.

The term 'weblog' is a generic and all encompassing term for a web page that is produced by an individual (or group of individuals) which is arranged chronologically and generally has entries written around a particular theme. Consequently, some weblogs take the form of person diaries, news services, summaries and links to items of interest, random thoughts and so on. Weblogs generally exhibit some or all of the following characteristics:

- Content changes on a daily (sometimes hourly) basis.
- There is a personal point of view.
- There is an opportunity to contact/collaborate with the author.
- Viewers will find topical material that will (usually) relate to them.
- Issues of the day are generally those that are discussed in detail.
- They respond to rather than create news.
- They are written in a format with the most recent material at the top, while older material is further down the page, or stored in an archive, which is almost like reading backwards through a book.

While I'm sure that personal online diaries can be of great interest, I ignore them in this chapter. I want to focus on weblogs that are, or could be, useful to information professionals in their daily tasks.

Some examples of weblogs

Before we get into the nitty-gritty of weblogs, let's take a look at one or two examples from different ends of the spectrum. One of the most famous weblogs produced by an information professional is Jenny Levine's *ShiftedLibrarian* at **www.theshiftedlibrarian.com/**. Figure 10.1 shows part of the opening page.

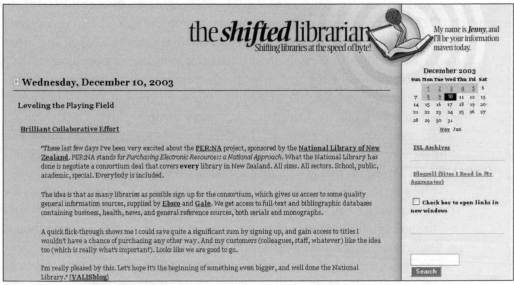

Figure 10.1   *TheShiftedLibrarian* weblog
© 2004 Jenny Levine

Jenny writes about a wide variety of different subjects, although she empha-
sizes weblogs themselves, information technology as used in a library setting
and some other items and observations on things which interest her. Jenny
is without a doubt an expert in her own right, so her comments and observations are of value not only to keep up to date with what is happening in the
library/technology world, but also to gain a feeling for what is an important
development and what is not. Another weblog that exhibits the same general criteria as *TheShiftedLibrarian* is Gary Price's *ResourceShelf* at
www.resourceshelf.com/. You can see a page from Gary's weblog in Figure 10.2. Gary is also well known in the information industry; his weblog
provides brief annotations about various news items relating to search engines
and internet search technologies, with links to the original item or story.

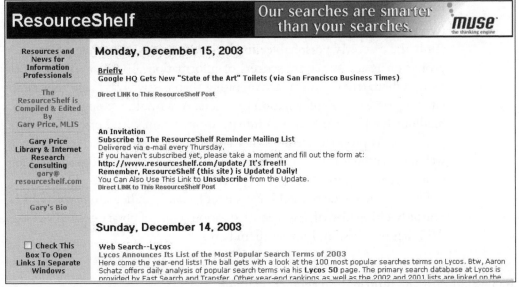

Figure 10.2 Gary Price's *ResourceShelf* weblog
© Gary Price

At the other end of the spectrum is *Slashdot* at **http://slashdot.org/** which
is the work of programmer and graphic artist Rob Malden and some of his
colleagues. *Slashdot* is an extended weblog, in that it carries discussion threads
contributed by various individuals, and on many subject areas, such as games,
hardware, programming and so on.

You may find it useful or interesting to break from reading this book to
take a look at a few other examples of weblogs to get a better feel for them.

Should this be the case, try a few of the following weblogs:

- The *Exploded Library* weblog at **http://explodedlibrary.typepad.com/ salonblog/**
- *Peter Scott's Library Blog* at **http://blog.xrefer.com/**
- The *Stark County Law Library Blawg* at **http://temp.starklawlibrary.org/ blog/**
- *Lady Crumpet's Armoire* at **www.ladycrumpet.com/**
- *Marylaine Block's Neat New Stuff on the Web* at **http://marylaine.com/ neatnew.html**.

Librarians and weblogs

In an article in 2001 Paula J. Hane said that 'blogs are a natural for librarians' (**www.infotoday.com/newslink/newslink0110.htm**) and I think that's certainly the case. My personal feeling is that librarians and other information professionals are by nature seekers of information, observers of the world around them (though in an active, rather than passive way), and they facilitate the provision of information to others. As a result, weblogs are a perfect medium for librarians to disseminate information to others. Information professionals produce weblogs that cover general or specific subject areas, weblogs written for specific user groups, weblogs about weblogs and weblogs produced as a communal effort by various libraries.

Dr L. Anne Clyde of the University of Iceland, on her site at **www.hi.is/ ~anne/weblogs.html**, has identified various types of library-related weblogs. With her permission, I repeat them here.

General library and information science weblogs

We've already seen an example of this type of log: Gary Price's *Resource Shelf*. Weblogs in this category tend to provide information on and brief commentary about news and articles that are of interest to people who work in this particular subject field. They also link back to the original source of the information, although since some stories are carried by various different sources this isn't always possible. Weblogs of this type are useful for information professionals since they allow us to keep up to date with what is happening within the profession, without having to spend a lot of time hunting down news information. Another couple of examples of weblogs in this category are Jessamyn West's library weblog at **www.librarian.net** and *LISNews* at

http://lisnews.com/ which, as the name suggests, keeps people up to date with news and events in the profession.

Weblogs covering specialist topics in library and information science

As well as general weblogs, which are written and designed to cover anything that is of interest in the area of library and information science, an increasing number of weblogs are written by specialists for specialists in various different subject areas:

- The *Handheld Librarian* at **http://handheldlib.blogspot.com/** covers access to the internet using PDAs (personal digital assistants) and how best to be mobile, but still connected to the internet.
- *Sitelines* at **www.workingfaster.com/sitelines/** focuses on better and more effective ways of searching the internet.
- If you're an engineering librarian an absolute must is the *EngLib* blog at **http://englib.info/** which covers information on news, courses, conferences, associations and anything that may appeal to engineering librarians.

Weblogs created by libraries

Interestingly, these are still in the minority; most library and information weblogs are written and produced by individuals, often in their spare time. However, there are a few weblogs produced by various library services, designed primarily for their own users. Consequently, these often have a 'local' feel to them, and may accept submissions from users who can post book reviews, for example. As a result they tend to reflect the interests of their users and cover a wide variety of different subject areas. When I looked, the weblog produced by Gateshead Public Library (which styles itself as 'the first library weblog in the UK') at **www.libraryweblog.com/** covered items on Japanese currency, the history of calendars, home economics and a century of flight!
  Other examples include:

- The Redwood City Public Library weblog at **www.rcpl.info/services/liblog.html**
- *The Leddy Library News* (University of Windsor) at **http://webvoy. uwindsor.ca:8087/mitas/leddyblog/index_html**
- *Chi Lib Rocks!* at **http://radio.weblogs.com/0111803/**. This provides information that is of interest to patrons of the Chicago Library system.

Weblogs created by professional associations and organizations

These have not been as forthcoming or as plentiful as you might expect. Once the value and importance of weblogs becomes clearer I suspect that we shall see an explosion of them. However, some do already exist, and examples of them are:

- The International Association of School Librarianship at **www.iasl–slo. org/happenings.html**
- The Manitoba Library Association, Canada, at **http://mla.blogspot.com/**.

Library and information school weblogs

This type of weblog is often created as part of a project within particular courses by students and so may not always be kept up to date when the originators finish the project. An excellent example of this type of weblog was the *Com-Lib* weblog created in the Library and Information Science Department at the University of Iceland. Although it is no longer maintained it can be seen at **www.iasl-slo.org/comlib.html**.

Weblogs created by librarians

As should already have become clear, librarians like creating and writing blogs. There are as many different types of weblog as there are information professionals who have created them. They are a glorious mix of the silly and sensible, informative and idiotic, and useful and useless! It's worth briefly exploring the following weblogs; some will probably not interest you at all, while others will draw you back time after time. As well as the ones mentioned at the beginning of this chapter, take a look at:

- *Phil Bradley's weblog* at **www.philb.com/blog/blogger.html**
- *Loopy Librarian* at **http://loopylibrarian.blogspot.com/**
- *Electric Ink* at **http://ecphrasis.port5.com/**
- *brary blog* at **www.chickeninthewoods.com/brary/index.php**
- *Open Stacks* at **http://openstacks.lishost.com/os/**
- *Internetsøgning* at **http://erikhoy.blogspot.com/** (please note that this is written in Danish).

Locating weblogs

Anne Clyde's classification scheme is a valuable one. It helps to identify appropriate weblogs, important because the tools available to do this are very limited at the moment. Probably the best way to identify weblogs that will be of interest to you is to locate one weblog that you like (and you should be able to achieve that from those already listed) and follow the links to other weblogs. Almost all weblog authors list weblogs that they in turn read and, if you enjoy reading one individual's weblog, you'll probably also enjoy reading the ones they like. This is, of course, a rather hit-and-miss affair, and it does tend to eat up hours of time, which though pleasantly spent don't exactly help when it comes to doing your job. However, all is not quite lost, since there are a number of other resources that you can use in order to locate weblogs that may be of value to you. In this section I point you towards some resources that you can use in order to find information that's important to you.

Weblog search engines

Possibly the most well known of weblog search engines is *Daypop* at **www.day-pop.com/** which is a current events, news and weblog search engine. *Daypop* searches through almost 60,000 sites for appropriate information for you. The search options are what you would expect, so *+word* will force the engine to include a word, *−word* excludes a word from the search, and *"double quotes"* will search for a phrase. It's also possible to limit the search to news and weblogs, news, weblogs, RSS (Real Simple Syndication; or Rich Site Summary) headlines or RSS weblog posts (referred to a bit later on). *Daypop* has an advanced search function with a date function (particularly important given the timeliness of weblogs and news sources), languages and countries.

The results screen is clear and easy to follow, as can be seen in Figure 10.3 after I had run a search for *xda* (a personal digital assistant).

Daypop does have some particularly interesting features, however. It has a Top 40, which is a list of links that are currently popular with webloggers from around the world. When I wrote this particular section (in the run up to Christmas 2003) a great many links were concerned with the capture of Saddam Hussein. The Top News Stories (based on the number of citations) is self-explanatory, and the Top Posts are those posts that have been cited most often by other weblogs. *Daypop* also highlights what it calls 'word bursts' which relates to the usage of certain words in the past few days; these are good indications of what webloggers are writing about, rather than linking to. The 'news bursts'

Top 40 | Top News | Top Posts | Word Bursts | News Bursts | Top Wishlist | Top Weblogs | Blogstats

DAYPOP xda   Search   News & Weblogs ▾

Searching **All Pages** for **xda**... Found **18** pages matching query. Displaying **1** to **10**.   XML

▨ Superdrewby Gay and Lesbian Online Community - Home Page
... Toys O2 **XDA** The **XDA** is the coolest new mobile phone, PDA, MP3 player
and more on the market today. Available through out the world it is selling ...
www.superdrewby.com - 23K - Cached 12-22 - Citations

▨ tin_the_fatty weblog
... doing a special on the O2 **XDA** II . InfoSync claims a RSP of US $600. 1010
CSL claims a RSP of HK $6,688(!), but with a trade-in price of HK $4,888. I ...
mt.rollingegg.net - 556K - Cached 12-22 - Citations

▨ FOCUS Online | Homepage und News in Kooperation mit MSN
... Gewinnen Sie ein O2 **XDA** II! focus.de/news Saddam schweigt
konsequent Die US-Verhörprofis scheinen sich an dem festgenommenen ...
www.focus.de - 169K - Cached 12-22

▨ The Australian: HANDHELD EDITION
... 540 Series, Qtek and **XDA** Phone Editions (Note: The absence of a
particular device does not mean that it is incompatible with our PDA ...
www.theaustralian.news.com.au/ sectionindex2...- 24K - Cached 12-22

12 results in Headlines
9 results in News
9 results in Weblogs

Sort by: **Relevance** Date
Search: **Full Text** Titles

Narrow by Language

All Languages ▾
More options in
Advanced Search

Daypop Top 40
The Top 40 weblogging links
of the day

Your Site Here

Figure 10.3   The *Daypop* results screen
© Daypop

section of the search engine lists the words that most commonly appear on
the front pages of news sites. Finally, the search engine lists top weblogs, based
on citations, and this can be another useful way of browsing popular weblogs
to get a little more of a feel for them.

This search engine does a significantly different job from those which return
results based on web pages. Some of the most common searches that were run
on *Google* in the few weeks before Christmas 2003 were "*gift guides*" and "*santa
claus*" (though to be fair, the top searched phrase was "*Saddam Hussein*"). However, over at *Daypop*, much more emphasis was placed on the capture of
Hussein, the fact that Libya stated it was giving up weapons of mass destruc-
tion, *Time*'s person of the year, and other end-of-year lists.

Daypop is not, however, the only weblog search tool that is available.
Another one you may like to try is *Feedster* at **www.feedster.com/index.php**.
I have included a screen shot of the home page in Figure 10.4

Feedster is less sophisticated than *Daypop*, in search options and the display
of results, but it does allow users to sort by relevance, date or blogrank. It also
allows searchers to look for images, although this isn't perhaps as useful as it
may sound since most weblogs are text only. Having said all that, it should
also be noted that the results of my test search for *xda* generated 784 results
in comparison to the 16 produced by *Daypop*.

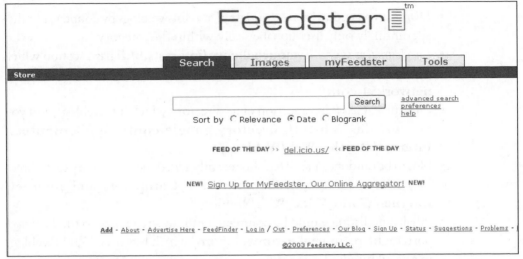

Figure 10.4   The *Feedster* search engine home page
© 2003–4 Feedster, LLC

Other weblog search engines that you may wish to try are:

- *Blogdex* at **http://blogdex.net/search.asp**
- *BlogStreet* at **www.blogstreet.com/**
- *Globe of Blogs* at **www.globeofblogs.com/**
- *Syndic8* at **www.syndic8.com/**
- *Technorati* at **www.technorati.com/**.

Weblog index/directories

If you have read previous chapters of this book you'll already know how I differentiate between search engines and index- or directory-based engines. However, if for some reason you've leapt straight to this chapter, an index or directory is rather more concerned with listing things (websites or weblogs in this case) into various categories. This makes it easier to find weblogs that are of general interest which can then be visited and searched if necessary for specific information. Given that most of us are very new to the whole area of weblogs, this may be a good starting point:

- *Library Weblogs* at **www.libdex.com/weblogs.html** is useful if you have an interest in locating library/information science weblogs according to geographic locations.

- *Diarist* at **www.diarist.net/registry/** also lists weblogs by country, but disappointingly only lists alphabetically within the category.
- *Live Journal* at **www.livejournal.com/interests.bml** has a section which allows users to search for specific interests, as does *Network54* at **www.network54.com/**.
- Of course, *Google* has a section of its directory which lists weblogs, and you can find this at **http://directory.google.com/Top/Computers/Internet/On_the_Web/Weblogs/**.
- Not to be outdone, *Yahoo!* has also recently added such a category to its directory structure at **http://dir.yahoo.com/Computers_and_Internet/Internet/World_Wide_Web/Weblogs/**.
- Finally, no listing would be complete without a reference to the *Eatonweb* portal at **http://portal.eatonweb.com/** which lists over 15,000 weblogs in several hundred categories.

News aggregators

Having read this far, you may think that, although weblogs are of some interest, they really don't deserve all the hype that they've been getting. After all, they are nothing really special – just ordinary web pages that are updated a little more often than most. Well, yes and no. That's certainly one way of looking at weblogs, but it's missing out on an important element that we've not yet covered, and this is RSS. RSS stands for 'Real Simple Syndication' or 'Rich Site Summary', depending on what software the author is using. There are a large number of sites available on the web that allow people to create their own weblogs, and a number of them allow for the creation of an RSS version of the page. An example is the site that I use for my own weblog, called *Blogger*; it can be found at **www.blogger.com/**. When I update my own weblog, two versions are created, an HTML version and an RSS version. If you visit the weblog page you'll see something similar to Figure 10.5.

However, as I've said, another version is also created, and this one looks like Figure 10.6.

I'm sure you'll agree that they don't bear much resemblance to each other! The reason for this is that the RSS version is not meant to be read by the human eye, but by an aggregator. This is a piece of software that is able to look at the RSS version of the page and produce it in another format. At the risk of overexposing this particular weblog, the third version of the page can be seen in Figure 10.7, which has been produced using a news aggregator called *AmphetaDesk*.

Phil Bradley's Blog

about

For librarians and people interested in search engines, searching the net, design issues and general whitterings and rants.

archive

02/01/2003 - 02/28/2003
03/01/2003 - 03/31/2003
04/01/2003 - 04/30/2003
05/01/2003 - 05/31/2003
06/01/2003 - 06/30/2003
07/01/2003 - 07/31/2003
08/01/2003 - 08/31/2003
09/01/2003 - 09/30/2003
10/01/2003 - 10/31/2003
12/01/2003 - 12/31/2003

my links

Useful sites

Tuesday, December 23, 2003

Jakob Nielsen, the web usability guru has highlighted his top ten web design mistakes of 2003. These include an unclear statement of purpose, undated content, bad use of small thumbnails, and pages that link to themselves. Always worth reading.
Phil 10:37 AM

Monday, December 22, 2003

Whichbook is a very nice service indeed. You can choose 4 categories from a total of 12, and decide on how important each one is (so you could go for very sad, disturbing, conventional and short and the system will provide some suggestions for you and, if you're based in the UK, will find a local library that has the title(s) so you can borrow them.
Phil 12:13 PM

TIME magazine has written a very interesting article on Google in which they discuss the possible future of the company and look at the competition. It's not one of the articles knocking Google, but it is saying that they're not the only player. Worth reading.
Phil 10:50 AM

Saturday, December 20, 2003

Figure 10.5 The author's weblog as an HTML-based page
© The author

```xml
<?xml version="1.0" encoding="UTF-8" ?>
- <rdf:RDF xmlns:rdf="http://www.w3.org/1999/02/22-rdf-syntax-ns#" xmlns:dc="http://purl.org/dc/elements/1.1/"
    xmlns="http://purl.org/rss/1.0/" xmlns:admin="http://webns.net/mvcb/" xmlns:l="http://purl.org/rss/1.0/modules/link/"
    xmlns:content="http://purl.org/rss/1.0/modules/content/">
  <!-- Generated by Blogger v5.0 -->
- <channel rdf:about="http://www.philb.com/blog/blogger.html">
    <title>Phil Bradley's Blog</title>
    <link>http://www.philb.com/blog/blogger.html</link>
    <description>For librarians and people interested in search engines, searching the net, design issues and general
      whitterings and rants.</description>
    <dc:date>2003-12-23T10:37:34Z</dc:date>
    <dc:language>en-GB</dc:language>
    <admin:generatorAgent rdf:resource="http://www.blogger.com/" />
    <admin:errorReportsTo rdf:resource="mailto:rss-errors@blogger.com" />
  - <items>
    - <rdf:Seq>
        <rdf:li rdf:resource="http://www.philb.com/blog/2003_12_01_blogarc.htm#107217585430914724" />
        <rdf:li rdf:resource="http://www.philb.com/blog/2003_12_01_blogarc.htm#107209519819626858" />
        <rdf:li rdf:resource="http://www.philb.com/blog/2003_12_01_blogarc.htm#107209025745918428" />
        <rdf:li rdf:resource="http://www.philb.com/blog/2003_12_01_blogarc.htm#107190117913710164" />
        <rdf:li rdf:resource="http://www.philb.com/blog/2003_12_01_blogarc.htm#107174406370403958" />
        <rdf:li rdf:resource="http://www.philb.com/blog/2003_12_01_blogarc.htm#107165985532559419" />
        <rdf:li rdf:resource="http://www.philb.com/blog/2003_12_01_blogarc.htm#107165949515157570" />
        <rdf:li rdf:resource="http://www.philb.com/blog/2003_12_01_blogarc.htm#107165895727618654" />
        <rdf:li rdf:resource="http://www.philb.com/blog/2003_12_01_blogarc.htm#107165776852354724" />
        <rdf:li rdf:resource="http://www.philb.com/blog/2003_12_01_blogarc.htm#107147935015690848" />
        <rdf:li rdf:resource="http://www.philb.com/blog/2003_12_01_blogarc.htm#107147920029459624" />
        <rdf:li rdf:resource="http://www.philb.com/blog/2003_12_01_blogarc.htm#107116672632125558" />
        <rdf:li rdf:resource="http://www.philb.com/blog/2003_12_01_blogarc.htm#107114301131735266" />
```

Figure 10.6 The author's weblog in RSS format
© The author

Phil Bradley's Blog
Last Downloaded: 2003-12-23 12:38:31.   XML ☒

Top Ten Web Design Mistakes of 2003 (Jakob Nielsen's Alertbox) Jakob Nielsen, the web usability guru has highlighted his top ten web design mistakes of 2003. These include an unclear statement of purpose, undated content, bad use of small thumbnails, and pages that link to themselves. Always worth reading.

Whichbook.net Whichbook is a very nice service indeed. You can choose 4 categories from a total of 12, and decide on how important each one is (so you could go for very sad, disturbing, conventional and short and the system will provide some suggestions for you and, if you're based in the UK, will find a local library that has the title(s) so you can borrow them.

Time magazine article on Google TIME magazine has written a very interesting article on Google in which they discuss the possible future of the company and look at the competition. It's not one of the articles knocking Google, but it is saying that they're not the only player. Worth reading.

Globetechnology Online maps direct people to your home shocker! Oh well, duh! Are people really only just now waking up to this? Given that it's very easy to simply type in an individuals name and get details of where they live, their phone number, an arial photograph of their house and so on, it stands to reason that some people will use this in ways that were not intended. Just how obvious is this? It should be - very. I've been talking about it since last century, and we've had at least one high profile murder of a television presenter linked to this sort of service. Jeez.

Google Experiment Provides Internet With Book Excerpts What Amazon can do, so can Google. Apparently there's more information in the world that isn't on the web, which has come as a surprise to Google. They're doing what Amazon has started, which is to allow people to search within books for the information they need. Link goes to New York Times article.

Naked librarians in Calendar surprise! Female librarians in the London Borough of Camden have been taking off their clothes ala the calendar girls movie. Good for them, and lets hope they make lots of money.

Figure 10.7   The author's weblog viewed in a news aggregator
© AmphetaDesk and the author

The advantage of using a news aggregator is that it becomes very much easier for someone to view a large number of weblogs and/or news sites. I currently have over 50 different weblogs and news resources configured in *AmphetaDesk* (which can be downloaded free from **www.disobey.com/amphetadesk/**). It takes about two minutes for the software to visit all 50 sites, pull down the new stories or posted items and display them for me to read. I can then go through them at my leisure, ignoring some and reading others. It is a very fast and effective way to get up to date on all the news that has broken overnight, and it's also very easy for me to keep tabs on what the major players and observers in the information industry are saying about any new developments. It's also useful because it means that I don't have to spend on the internet trying to find news stories for myself. For my sins, I've always enjoyed watching the television series about Buffy the Vampire Slayer and as you can imagine, there are many television and entertainment websites that may, now and then, have articles on the series. I have neither the time nor the inclination to visit all these sites on a daily basis, but one of the weblogs that I take does exactly that. Consequently, although it may at first appear that I've checked 50 weblogs and news resources as I've mentioned, in fact the number is much higher than that, since they in turn have culled data from many other resources.

There are disadvantages with this approach, one being duplication. If there's an important story (such as a new development at *Google*) this will be carried by a lot of the different resources that I take, so I'll see references to the same story over and over again. On the other hand, there's very little chance that I'll miss it. Another disadvantage is that sometimes the software an author uses to turn their weblog into an RSS feed does not work properly, which means in turn that the news aggregator does not collect it. It may be some time before I realize this, since not every log or news resource is updated daily, and consequently I may miss something that is actually quite important. However, if the story is that important, it will be carried by one of the other feeds that I take, so it will not be a disaster.

AmphetaDesk is my preferred news aggregator since it's very easy to install, quick to add new channels and is problem free. Consequently, I've never had need or reason to use another one, but there are many other aggregators that you may wish to try out for yourself. Some of these are as follows:

- *Feedreader* at **www.feedreader.com/**
- *Feedroll* at **www.feedroll.com/rssviewer/**
- *NewsIsFree* at **www.newsisfree.com/**
- *NewsGator* at **www.newsgator.com/**
- *NewsMonster* at **www.newsmonster.org/**
- *RocketNews* at **www.rocketnews.com/search/index.html**
- *Wildgrape NewsDesk* at **www.wildgrape.net/**.

Creating your own weblog

Strictly speaking, given that this volume is about searching the internet, it's not particularly appropriate to have a section on creating your own weblog. However, if you are enthused by reading about weblogs, you will be keen to get more involved. That almost certainly means that you will want to create your own weblog, and it would be churlish to ignore this final, but important element of weblogging.

Before you begin, however, I would strongly suggest that you have a clear idea of what you wish to say in your weblog. Is it to be a very personal one, detailing your inner most thoughts on issues of the day and what you had for breakfast? If so, who will want to read it? Is it to cover a specific subject area? This means that you will need to spend a fair amount of time keeping it up to date, since a weblog with irregular entries or long gaps between entries will not appeal to people. Will you be observing a subject area and pointing people onto other resources? Do you have the time to run a weblog properly? Are you really committed to the idea? The majority of weblogs do not last longer than six months, since for many people they become something of a chore. Once you have a clear idea of what you wish to achieve, you can then progress to the next level, which is to find appropriate software to create your weblog.

At its simplest you could create an HTML page and update it yourself on a regular basis; after all, this is how weblogs started in the first place. However, in order to do this you need to have a reasonable understanding of how to write HTML code in the first instance, and the time available to undertake the task manually. So, while it's possible, it's probably not a sensible use of your time. A much better approach is to make use of one of the software solutions that are readily available. Some of these are commercial products, while others are free. However, what they all do is allow you to create a weblog quickly and easily, and either offer you storage space on their servers, or enable you to publish your log directly onto your own site if you have one. Moreover, many allow you to let others post to the weblog (in case you want to create a community log); some allow your readers to comment on your postings; some let you add photographs; one or two even let you add an 'audio blog' in the form of an aural entry, rather than a written one.

As previously mentioned, I use the software provided by *Blogger.com* located at **www.blogger.com/**. This used to be a commercial product, but was bought by *Google* in 2003 and is now available entirely free of charge. A screenshot of the home page can be seen in Figure 10.8.

Rather than publish my weblog on their servers (which was a possible option) I have configured my system so that all my entries are written directly to the weblog on my own site, both in HTML and RSS format. An advantage that I have found in using this system is that, since it is now owned by *Google*, I have a small icon on my *Google* toolbar that allows me to add a new entry whenever I wish, without having to interrupt what I'm doing; this makes it very easy for me to update my weblog whenever I like, at any point during the day. I should also point out, in the interests of accuracy, that this is the only element of the *Blogger* system that resides on my own computer; the actual software used to create entries is on the *Blogger* site and can be accessed directly by the web browser.

If *Blogger* isn't to your taste, however, there are plenty of other options available to you, and you could do worse than peek at one of the following:

- *b2* at **http://cafelog.com/**
- *Big Blog Tool* at **www.bigblogtool.com/**

Figure 10.8 The *Blogger* home page
© 2000–3 Pyra Labs

- *Geeklog* at **www.geeklog.net/**
- *Movabletype* at **www.movabletype.org/**
- *Radio UserLand* at **http://radio.userland.com/**
- *Xanga* at **www.xanga.com/**.

Alternatively, spend a happy hour or so browsing through the very full listing at *Yahoo!* at **http://dir.yahoo.com/Computers_and_Internet/Internet/World_Wide_Web/Weblogs/Software/**.

Summary

In this chapter we have looked in some detail at the relatively new phenomenon of weblogs; where they come from, what types exist, how you can find them and, to a lesser extent, how you can create your own. I think there is no doubt that 2003 will be the 'Year of the weblog' since that is when they really came of age. I think they are an excellent tool for keeping up to date with both general news and also items of interest to specific user groups and subject areas. They give us quick and easy access to the issues of the day, to the grey ephemera that are so often difficult to track down, the voices, thoughts and opinions of various experts, and they allow searchers to spend more time using information than looking for it. They are, of course, not perfect; opinions are only ever that, however well informed, and while they help us track ephemera they are themselves quite fragile, and many do not survive the initial enthusiasm of their authors. However, enough do exist to do the job they were designed for, and are certainly worth using by anyone – advanced searcher or novice.

URLs mentioned in this chapter

http://news.bbc.co.uk/1/hi/uk/1717136.stm
www.theshiftedlibrarian.com/
www.resourceshelf.com/
http://slashdot.org/
http://explodedlibrary.typepad.com/salonblog/
http://blog.xrefer.com/
http://temp.starklawlibrary.org/blog/
www.ladycrumpet.com/
http://marylaine.com/neatnew.html
www.infotoday.com/newslink/newslink0110.htm
www.hi.is/~anne/weblogs.html
www.librarian.net
http://lisnews.com/
http://handheldlib.blogspot.com/
www.workingfaster.com/sitelines/
http://englib.info/
www.libraryweblog.com/
www.rcpl.info/services/liblog.html
http://webvoy.uwindsor.ca:8087/mitas/leddyblog/index_html
http://radio.weblogs.com/0111803/
www.iasl-slo.org/happenings.html
http://mla.blogspot.com/
www.iasl-slo.org/comlib.html
www.philb.com/blog/blogger.html
http://loopylibrarian.blogspot.com/
http://ecphrasis.port5.com/
www.chickeninthewoods.com/brary/index.php
http://openstacks.lishost.com/os/
http://erikhoy.blogspot.com/
www.daypop.com/
www.feedster.com/index.php

http://blogdex.net/search.asp

www.blogstreet.com/

www.globeofblogs.com/

www.syndic8.com/

www.technorati.com/

www.libdex.com/weblogs.html

www.diarist.net/registry/

www.livejournal.com/interests.bml

www.network54.com/

http://directory.google.com/Top/Computers/Internet/On_the_Web/
Weblogs/

http://dir.yahoo.com/Computers_and_Internet/Internet/World_Wide_
Web/Weblogs/

http://portal.eatonweb.com/

www.blogger.com/

www.disobey.com/amphetadesk/

www.feedreader.com/

www.feedroll.com/rssviewer/

www.newsisfree.com/

www.newsgator.com/

www.newsmonster.org/

www.rocketnews.com/search/index.html

www.wildgrape.net/

http://cafelog.com/

www.bigblogtool.com/

www.geeklog.net/

www.movabletype.org/

http://radio.userland.com/

www.xanga.com/

http://dir.yahoo.com/Computers_and_Internet/Internet/World_Wide_
Web/Weblogs/Software/

Chapter 11 »
Other available database resources

Introduction

Given the size of the internet, and the size of this book, it is not possible to list every information resource that is available to the advanced searcher, or to go into any great detail about what exactly is out there. However, I think that it is important to point you towards as many different ways of obtaining information that I can, so this chapter brings together some of the other ways that you can find out information from internet-database resources.

Some of these are free resources; others you have to subscribe to or pay for on a 'pay as you go' basis. It is important that we cover these, since it is all too easy to limit yourself to material that has been made available for free. While budgetary constraints may make this approach preferable, even a modest expenditure may reap rewards with ease of access to current and reliable information. At the very least, the advanced searcher needs to be aware of a wide variety of resources, and should at least be able to consider the possibility of using commercial as well free resources.

Some of the resources that I look at in this chapter are:

- information provided free of charge by publishers
- online communities
- commercial information
- online journals
- newspapers

- bookshops
- paid services offered by search engines.

Freely available information provided by publishers

It sounds a little bit too good to be true, doesn't it? However, most publishers are indeed offering free material on the internet that you might well expect to pay for. You may rest assured that they have sound financial reasons for providing this information as a 'loss leader' – they hope that you will value the data enough to be prepared to subscribe to the subscription-based service they offer.

I'm aware that at this point I'm racing ahead a little bit, because I've started to talk about 'publishers' without fully explaining what I mean. This is because the term 'publisher' is becoming increasingly difficult to define clearly and neatly. Previously, a publisher was an organization that produced printed books or journals and sold the result to you and me. With the arrival of online services this definition could be expanded to include organizations (sometimes the same ones, more often than not different ones) which published in a digital format, first via large databases stored on mainframe computers, then more recently (in the 1980s and 1990s) onto optical discs such as CD-ROM. The arrival of the internet has made the definition much more difficult, since it could be argued that I 'publish' articles that I write directly onto my website, making me both an author and a publisher. Indeed, anyone who produces a website and makes information available on it can, with justification, be described as a publisher. However, for clarity I am using the term to refer to organizations which have previously made data available either in hard-copy form, via an online database, or in CD-ROM format.

These organizations are very keen to use the internet, since it provides them with another (and these days increasingly their main or only) means of making their data available. Therefore information professionals now have greater flexibility in deciding how to receive their data. I return to this subject in Chapter 14, but all we need to consider at the moment is the fact that one of the ways in which publishers are attracting customers is by offering data for nothing.

Each publisher provides different types of free data:

- My first example is Kluwer Academic Publishers, whose site can be located at **www.wkap.nl/**. You can obtain a full listing of titles, details about each one, sample copies of journals, the tables of contents, a free alerting service and some articles.

- Sweet and Maxwell, a legal publisher, with a website at **www. sweetandmaxwell.co.uk/index.html** offers a whole raft of free information on legal matters, free trials of products and so on directly from the website.
- *Encyclopædia Britannica* at **www.britannica.com/** allows users to browse the 32-volume work (as well as six other resources) to locate articles of interest. An article is provided in brief with the suggestion of subscribing to a full service offered in an advertising-free format.

Online communities

Some companies create an online community based around an area of shared interest. An example of this can be seen at the *BioMedNet* site at **www.bmn.com/.** This is described as 'Elsevier's portal to life sciences'. It currently has over 1.3 million members and, given that there were only 50,000 members when I was writing the first edition of this title, you can see how popular the service is. Membership is free upon registration and this allows access to a library of full-text journals, biological databases, MEDLINE, a job exchange, an alerting service and so on. Members can access much of the content free of charge, but viewing the full text of articles usually requires either a one-off payment or a subscription to the product.

The site is well designed and has the needs and interests of the user at its heart, while being open about the commercial aspects of the site. As a result, users of the system are able to meet online and have discussions; they are informed about new developments in their areas of interest and notified about new publications; they can search existing resources, download articles and generally keep in daily contact with professionals and peers. This has proved to be so popular that other online communities have been established such as *Chemweb* at **www.chemweb.com/**.

Do keep in mind the existence of this material, provided freely by publishers, since it is of high quality, current and with a high level of authority. A slight disadvantage is that you cannot guarantee what information you will find, and it can be a little like going to a car boot or jumble sale. However, if you can identify those publishers who produce material that is relevant to your work, you can obtain some very useful information from them.

Commercial information

Commercial use of the internet could easily take up an entire book in its own right, and I do not intend to go into great detail here. However, it is worth pointing out that publishers are using the internet to increase their revenue, and if you have the budget (which doesn't need to be large) you can make use of these services. I illustrate this by making reference to a small number of companies or organizations that sell products across the internet that are potentially of interest to the advanced searcher.

My first example is the *Oxford Reference Online* collection at **www.oxfordreference.com/**. This is a large and impressive resource that contains more than 120 dictionaries and references titles covering the complete subject spectrum from general reference to science, medicine, the humanities and business. A few examples are the *Oxford Companions* to American Law, American Literature, Military History, Music, British History, Dictionaries of Abbreviations, the Bible, Computing, English Folklore, and so on. The collection is updated three times a year with new material. The cost of the service varies, depending on whether you subscribe as an individual or as an organization, and whether you are an educational establishment. At the time of writing the cost for a prepaid annual subscription for an individual is £95+VAT or US$139 per annum. That's probably less than buying two of the titles, which looks like an interesting proposition to me!

Another example is the collection of resources made available by the *Emerald Group* at **www.emeraldinsight.com/**. The organization says it publishes 'the world's widest range of management and library & information services journals, as well as a strong specialist range of engineering, applied science and technology journals'. Searchers have access to four different databases: *Emerald Full Text*, *Emerald Journals*, *Emerald Abstracts* and *Emerald Management Reviews*. Just to take one example, the *Full Text* database offers 42,000 searchable articles from over 100 different journals. The subjects covered include management, human resources, marketing, librarianship and various aspects of engineering. Full-text articles date back to 1994, and abstracts to 1989. The interface to the database is of a very high quality; field searching is encouraged, with the use of truncation and Boolean operators. Here is a major difference that searchers find when using a commercial product – in almost all instances the interface reflects a complexity that is simply not found with web search engines. The reason for this is clear; it's only serious searchers who purchase a subscription to the particular commercial product and, as such, they are prepared to invest the time needed to learn how to search it most effectively. The databases provided by *Emerald* can be searched free of charge, and basic information on the article can also be displayed on the user's screen. However, in order to view the entire article it is necessary to subscribe to the product. Having said this, *Emerald* is providing a great deal of information entirely free of charge, and it's a very useful resource. *Emerald* also offers a variety of other free resources such as newsletters, updates, free trials, various delivery methods and training guides. Once again, this illustrates the difference between a commercial service and the free search facilities available from search engines such as *Google*. Since *Google* and others make their money from advertisers they tend to focus on their needs, rather than those of the searcher. Because the commercial databases make their money from searchers/subscribers it is in their interests to provide as many resources as possible to make their offerings look more attractive.

My last example in this section is the *LexisNexis* range of products at **www.lexisnexis.com**/. This is a company that I expect most readers are familiar with, even if they've not used the product. The interface allows users to use Boolean to search the full text of 4.1 billion documents in more than 36,000 individual publications or large groups of sources. This by itself is a compelling argument towards use. If you compare this with other news sources that are available from web search engines it's quite clear that the *LexisNexis* product is in an entirely different league. Once you add the quick search function, subject directory, personalized content, archived news, company, public and legal records into the mix it becomes a database that deserves a great deal of consideration. The company has introduced a wide range of pricing structures as well, so it's attractive to companies and individuals, and to those who need access to the data for only a specific period of time.

Online journals

I have already mentioned online journals in connection with databases which can be accessed via the internet, but it is important to make a distinction between these and journals that have their own separate 'life' as electronic journals. There are literally thousands of electronic journals that offer high-quality information totally free of charge. These are often in receipt of funding from one organization or another and exist to promote the free flow of information in their chosen subject area. A good example here is *Ariadne* at **www.ariadne.ac.uk**/ which has as its principle goal 'to report on information service developments and information networking issues worldwide, keeping the busy practitioner abreast of current digital library initiatives'. It is published every quarter; the first issue was in January 1996. The collection can be searched and is therefore a useful and informative repository of information for researchers who have an interest in the subject matter. Another similar journal is the *Internet Resources Newsletter* at **www.hw.ac.uk/ libwww/irn/**. This is published on a monthly basis and at the time of writing issue 112 was published, with issue 1 dated October 1994.

The value of journals of this nature cannot be overestimated. Not only do some of them have very long backruns, as we have seen, but they provide researchers with access to valuable and high-quality data written by acknowledged experts in the field.

Newspapers

Online newspapers are obviously another splendid source of information. I ran a quick search on *Yahoo!* for newspapers and got over 9000 sites (which is almost double the number I found when writing the second edition of this title); I am sure the number will have increased by the time you read this. The range of newspapers is quite phenomenal, from regional or city titles such as the *San Francisco Chronicle* at **www.sfgate.com/** to national newspapers such as the *Electronic Telegraph* at **www.telegraph.co.uk/**. A good resource for locating newspapers is *The Paperboy* at **www.thepaperboy.com/** which lists a large number of newspapers from around the world. As well as listing newspapers, it has a very useful search facility for locating information in headlines.

Each newspaper is obviously unique, and arranges its content as it feels appropriate. Some titles are virtually identical to the printed version; others are entirely electronic; and yet others are a combination of these approaches. Some are updated several times during the day, others daily and yet others once a week. However, they are updated, and whatever the precise content, online newspapers are one of the very best ways to keep up to date with what is happening within a specific region, city or country or throughout the world. A sensible searcher will bookmark at least one or two newspapers to refer to regularly.

There is an increasing possibility that you will have to pay for access to data. This shouldn't really come as anything of a surprise, nor do I think it unreasonable. If companies such as *LexisNexis* are creating revenue out of selling content it seems perfectly sensible that the originators of the data should do so as well. A good example of one newspaper that provides both free content and an enhanced subscription service is the *Financial Times* at **www.ft.com/**. It offers two subscription-based models. These include access to the full online archives, access via a PDA (personal digital assistant), a power search tool, news alerts and so on. The cost for an individual subscription is less than £6 a month at the time of writing, which is a lot less than buying the newspaper. Of course, it's nice to get something for nothing, and the newspaper appreciates this, since it still offers free content, only charging for the extra value added services.

Bookshops

It is an obvious statement, but bookshops are a wonderful source of information. They do have a number of drawbacks, however, chiefly as a result of being a physical entity. You have to go and visit; you need to have a clear idea of what you want (unless you're just browsing); and you need to find the right set of shelves before you can start hunting for an appropriate title. Even when you finally alight on a likely title you may still not be sure if it's exactly what you're after, so it is then necessary to spend time examining the book before purchasing it. All great fun of course, but it does use up a frightening amount of time.

Internet bookshops overcome all these disadvantages and have become very popular. Once again I checked using *Yahoo!* and it currently lists 468 UK or Irish bookstores (up from 151 in the last edition of this title). I'll just explore one or two examples in detail to illustrate their value to the information professional.

Amazon at **www.amazon.com/** or **www.amazon.co.uk/** is one of the largest bookshops (if indeed not the largest) on the internet. *Amazon* has taken an approach similar to that of *BioMedNet*, in that it has tried to create a community feeling to its data. As well as straightforward listings of titles it gives various other useful snippets of information: new and future releases, suggested titles (based on your previous purchases), wish lists and so on. The database can be searched in a number of ways, by keyword, subject, author, ISBN, publisher and date of publication for example. As well as books, *Amazon* has in recent years expanded its offerings to include music, videos, DVDs, electronic goods, kitchen goods and many others. However, since I cannot easily imagine a valid professional reason for running a search for pots and pans, I concentrate on looking at books.

I ran a search for *weblogs* and was presented with a small list of seven titles, sorted in order of bestselling, though I could resort to six other criteria that would be useful if I had a longer list. For each title I was able to read reviews from people who had read it and gain a much greater insight into the book than if I'd been flicking through it in a physical bookshop. I was also able to read through a list of other books about weblogs that an Amazon user had compiled; it gave me some suggestions about books that had sections about weblogs that my own search hadn't picked up.

Needless to say, you can purchase any of the titles that you are interested in, along with a variety of other merchandise. Once you're satisfied with your selection your credit card is debited and the titles are shipped, usually within a couple of days. An internet bookshop offers a useful and easy way to purchase titles or make book selections, partly because of the ease of use of the system, but also because it is possible to see what other readers think about particular products. Moreover, given the discounts that Amazon and other bookshops offer it is almost certainly cheaper to shop there, even once post and packing charges are included. Of course, what you don't have is the immediacy of being able to buy a book, open the cover and start reading. Actually, however, you do, since *Amazon* is offering for sale (and indeed giving away some titles) e-books. These are exactly what you would expect them to be. Once the title has been purchased it can be immediately downloaded and is ready for reading at once. Some titles can also be used on a PDA system, so I can buy my title, download it, transfer it to my handheld device and it's ready for reading.

Other sites offer book-related information that searchers may find useful. An example of this is *Whichbook* at **www.whichbook.net/index.jsp**. This site allows users to choose four criteria from a total of 12, and to indicate along a spectrum how important the criteria are. So, for example, I could choose to see book selections based on my desire to read something very happy, down to earth, very unusual and long. As I'm based in the UK the site also allows me to see if the titles that interest me are available at my local library.

Summary

Effective searchers do not limit themselves to the major search engines or databases, but instead keep a very open mind about using resources across a very wide spectrum. In this chapter we have looked at a variety of these and discussed the ways in which they may be helpful. The best information is not always free and sometimes it is necessary to pay premium prices for premium data, but it is almost always possible to glean some worthwhile information from the free material provided by commercial organizations.

URLs mentioned in this chapter

www.wkap.nl/
www.sweetandmaxwell.co.uk/index.html

www.britannica.com/
www.bmn.com/
www.chemweb.com/
www.oxfordreference.com/
www.emeraldinsight.com/
www.lexisnexis.com/
www.ariadne.ac.uk/
www.hw.ac.uk/libwww/irn/
www.sfgate.com/
www.telegraph.co.uk/
www.thepaperboy.com/
www.ft.com/
www.amazon.com/
www.amazon.co.uk/
www.whichbook.net/index.jsp

Chapter 12 »
Virtual libraries and gateways

Introduction

I have so far concentrated mainly on how to find information on the internet by using a variety of different search engines. This is, of course, a very effective way of obtaining information, but it is not the only way. When you go into a library you do not expect to have to start searching for information immediately; instead you make use of the signposting available, or perhaps a map on the wall to locate the section you are interested in. Moreover, when you get to the shelves you expect that the books and other resources have been selected by the information professionals to cover the subject area and to be trustworthy sources of information.

This does not automatically happen on the internet, since there is no overall 'internet librarian' who can check the authority of the data or provide you with a list of appropriate links. However, there are virtual libraries (also sometimes known as gateways) that can assist in this area. In this chapter I begin by looking at some of the ways in which you can assess and evaluate the resources that you discover, and then I go on to consider the steps that have been taken to provide users with signposts to valuable, authoritative and trustworthy information.

Authority on the internet

You cannot automatically trust the information that you find on the internet. You cannot automatically trust the information that you find on the internet. No, that isn't a typographical error, it's just I felt it was such an important point I decided to repeat it. Since no one is in charge of it, anyone is free to publish almost any type of information or material they wish. I say 'almost' because web authors are constrained by the laws of the land they happen to be in, or which hosts their website(s). In the UK it is not legal for me to libel someone, and making a libellous statement on a website will leave me open to a possible legal action. However, apart from obvious areas such as that, I am free to write and publish anything that I please, and there is no onus on me to ensure that it is factually accurate.

It is necessary therefore to always question the information that you find on the web, and fortunately there are a few helpful ways of being able to do just that.

The domain name

The first thing that I always check when looking at a website is the URL or Uniform Resource Locator, also known as the website address and which generally takes the form **www.somethingorother.com/**. One of the basic ideas behind a URL is to provide an indication about what sort of site a visitor would be likely to find if they visited a particular site or clicked on a link. The following is a list of some of the more common domain name extensions, with a brief explanation about them:

- **.com** The 'dot com' so beloved by the media. This was originally designed to signal that the website was a commercial website from an American organization. However, once people started to realize the importance of domain names it was (and indeed still is) regarded as the 'best' extension to get. Consequently, I registered my own website as philb.com but I neither live in the USA nor host my website there. Almost any and all variations of words in the English language have now been registered as domain names.
- **.co.uk** A 'dot co' website will also be generally regarded as a commercial website, and the two-letter abbreviation after it indicates where it is to be found, or in which country it was registered.
- **.edu** This is the extension most commonly used by American educational establishments.
- **.ac.uk** This is also used by educational establishments, and once again the two letters following the .ac indicate country.

- **.org and .org.uk** This extension is used to denote a charity or non-profit-making organization.
- **.gov or .gov.uk** This indicates the site is a government site, with once again the two letter extension indicating the country in question.
- **.mil** This is used to indicate a site produced by the military.
- **.net** This extension used to be used by companies which had as their main or sole business the internet.
- **.biz** This is a more recent extension and is designed to indicate a business website, used in a similar way to the .com address.
- **.info** This is also a more recent extension, designed to indicate that the site provides information, rather than selling a commercial product.

There are many extensions; others are being added all the time. However, only a small number provide any sort of indication of quality. In order to register either an academic, military or government website it may be necessary to prove to the appropriate registering body that the organization is who it says it is. Consequently, a site that is an .edu site will relate to students, and the information you find on a .mil or .gov website can be trusted – at least to the extent that you might trust anything else a government or military organization says! Other than that, however, there are very few limitations or restrictions on the registration of domain names, since the registration body in each country is primarily interested only in two things – is the money for the registration available, and is the domain name available? As a matter of policy, registration bodies try not to get involved in domain name disputes, particularly since more than one organization may have an equal 'claim' to a particular domain name. For example, the website **www.amex.com/** does not take you to the famous debit card company of that name, but to the American Stock Exchange and **www.aa.com/** takes visitors to the website for American Airlines, and not, as British readers might assume, the Automobile Association, which is instead found at **www.theaa.com/**. I imagine that the US government is (and will forever be) annoyed for not having registered variants of whitehouse.com. (Please be aware that if you visit any of these out of curiosity you may find material that is offensive to you.)

Company logo

The second thing that I check when looking at a website is whether it carries a recognizable company or organization logo. This is not a foolproof method of ensuring the legitimacy of the site, of course, but it does provide further corroborating evidence. Copyright laws exist on the internet in the same way that they do anywhere else, and individuals cannot simply copy any material that they find on websites; if they do, they run the risk of receiving a sharp legal letter telling them to cease and desist. Many companies are very strict on the use that can be made of their logos, sometimes to the extent of refusing to allow them to be used as a graphical link from other sites back to their own.

> **HINTS & TIPS >>**
>
> Since logos are copyright protected, any website using one should obtain permission from the owner to use it.

Contact details

Every site on the web has been created by someone at some time. I am much more likely to treat a site seriously if it provides contact details for the author or person responsible for the site. At least then I know that, if I have problems, either technically or with the information on the site, there is someone that I can contact. If no contact details are given (and this happens surprisingly often) it makes me wonder what is wrong with the site, since no one appears to be prepared to take responsibility for it.

Currency

When I view a website I want to make sure that the data are current. It is usually easy to check in a printed publication, but much harder with a website, unless the author gives details as to when the site or a particular page was last updated. If no date is given I'm much less likely to take the site seriously. A good website is constantly being updated and worked on, and I would expect to find something new, altered or updated at least monthly. Any longer than this can imply that the organization is not taking the site seriously, which casts doubt on the validity of the data. It's also worth being aware of the difference between US and UK date conventions, since 7/6/04 may mean 7 June 2004 or 6 July 2004.

> **HINTS & TIPS >>**
>
> If you want to know when a page was last updated, visit that page and in the address bar type: javascript:alert(document.lastModified) and you'll see a little pop-up box giving you the required information.

Awards

I quite often see sites boasting of the awards they have won, usually accom-

panied by a garish medal of some description. Since there are no official internet bodies, any awards are offered by individuals or companies, and it is
often quite difficult to find out exactly what the criteria are for winning an
award. As a result, I retain a healthy scepticism about them. However, if the
award is a nationally or internationally recognized one, such as the Queen's
Awards for Enterprise (**www.queensawards.org.uk/home1.htm**), and
has been given to the organization concerned, such as a Beacon school
(**www.standards.dfes.gov.uk/beaconschools/**) then this is an entirely
different situation and is well worth mentioning on the site.

Page design

In many cases web page design is entirely down to an individual's personal choice;
simply because the page has a bubblegum pink background does automatically
invalidate the information it contains. However, if an individual or organization cares about their site they should ensure that the pages can be viewed well
using any browser in any screen resolution. Clarity of design and navigation are
important points when it comes to websites and anything less implies that the
authors are not taking their site seriously, are not particularly bothered about
their users and consequently their data may not be accurate or up to date.

Who owns a site?

If I am still in doubt about a site I may check to see who owns it; that is to say,
who it is registered to. Many web-hosting companies provide free utilities for
you to check if a site has already been registered and the one that I generally use
is *Easyspace* at **www.easyspace.com/**. You simply input the name of the site
that you are interested in and, if it has been registered, you can click on an option
for more information. You can then obtain details on who registered the site,
their address, when the site was registered and who the contacts for technical
and administrative details are. If you prefer not to use *Easyspace* a good alternative is the *Check Domain* site at **www.checkdomain.com/**.

Checking links

This is another excellent and quick way of checking the authority of a site. I
think that it is reasonable to assume that most authors link only to sites they
hold in high regard, and that will be useful for their own visitors to go to.
Consequently, one could say that a link to another site is almost a 'vote' for

it. The more votes a site has, the more highly it is regarded and, as we have seen, *Google* in particular does take this into account when returning results. It is very easy to check to see who links to a site and how many links there are by using the syntax link:<address of website>. Consequently, to see who links to my website, you could visit *Google* (or alternatively *AlltheWeb*, which uses the same syntax) and type in link:www.philb.com. This currently gives a figure of 134 sites that link to me, and a quick look through them shows that most of these are either academic sites (that have linked to the articles I've written), or web design companies that link to material on my site. However, it's also worth pointing out that *Google* only lists what it regards as very important sites, and running exactly the same search at *AlltheWeb* gives the rather different figure of 8346 sites in total.

Website history

It may also be possible to see what a website looked like in the past. The *Wayback Machine* at **www.archive.org/** has, since 1996, been visiting and archiving various websites. By visiting the site and keying in the URL that interests you, it is possible to see how the site looked in the past. This may be useful if the domain name has been sold to someone else, or if you just want to see how often the site has been updated. The *Wayback Machine* does not archive all websites, and will remove them at the owner's request, so it's not a foolproof method, but is another option to consider.

Checking against other sources

It almost goes without saying that it is worthwhile checking the information that you retrieve from a web page with a known source of good data. If you have to be certain about the authority of the information you are going to using, simply choose one fact that can be quickly and easily checked against another source. If the results tally, then you can be reasonably reassured that the other data on the site are accurate; if they do not, you may need to do a little more research to be certain that you can reliably use the information.

Recommendations

A final way of being sure that a site is of good quality is to take the word of an expert. If someone who knows what they are talking about tells me that a site is of a high quality with reliable information, I am much more likely to simply accept this as fact, and not look further. Of course, I'm a fairly trusting soul, and you may not be, but nonetheless a recognized authority does impart a certain level of authority by their recommendation. It would be wonderful if we had experts on tap in all subject areas that we could just ask, wouldn't it! Of course we don't, but we do have the next best thing, which is the existence of virtual libraries, and we shall see how they are able to do this job for us.

Virtual libraries

What is a virtual library?

Virtual libraries are called many different things: gateways, digital collections, digital libraries and cyber libraries are just a few of the terms in current use. Whatever they are called, they have certain things in common:

- They are collaborative ventures in which information professionals and other experts in particular areas pool their knowledge and experience to collate information on a specific subject.
- Information is checked for accuracy and authority.
- Their geographical position is not generally important – the focus is on the information they provide, rather than where they are located.
- Data are displayed clearly and concisely, allowing for easy navigation.
- They are kept current.
- Old, out-of-date material is deleted.
- Visitors are kept up to date with news and information as it becomes available.

What does a virtual library contain?

Since all virtual libraries are slightly different it is not possible to give a complete listing of everything that you might find in one – you'll have to discover that for yourself! However, you can generally expect to find a mixture of the following:

- links to other websites and resources
- newsletters, either about the subject area or the virtual library itself
- databases of resources listed at the library and links to databases that cover the particular subject area
- subject guides with more information and background in the various

specialisms covered by the library
- documents, both full text and abstract
- lists of meetings, conferences and exhibitions
- information about mailing lists and newsgroups in the subject areas
- what's new and information announcements
- bibliographies
- books in electronic format
- reports and papers.

When should an information professional use a virtual library?

There are almost as many reasons why you should consider using a virtual library as there are libraries! Some of the major reasons are:

- Virtual libraries provide authoritative, factual information.
- If time is short, they are a useful resource since they contain focused, appropriate information. Search engines, while useful, often return large numbers of hits, even with very precise searches, and many of these may have limited relevance to the subject.
- Virtual libraries generally provide precise, accurate descriptions of information, saving time when trying to decide which resource to look at.
- Virtual libraries are kept current, so there should be few, if any, broken links.
- They collect subject-specific materials in one place.
- They provide an overview of a subject which is useful if you have a limited knowledge or understanding of that subject.
- They are excellent at providing visitors with ready-made lists of 'the best' websites in a subject area.

Virtual libraries currently available

The *WWW Virtual Library* at **www.vlib.org/** is the oldest catalogue of the web. It was begun by Sir Tim Berners-Lee, the 'founding father' of the web, and is in fact a collection of subject-specific libraries. Subject coverage runs from agriculture to west European studies, with gardening, history, sport and many other subjects in between. The libraries associated with it generally display a particular logo which, although it is in the public domain and can be used by anyone, has become associated with them, and this can be seen in Figure 12.1. The home page can be seen in Figure 12.2. There are mirror sites in the UK, Switzerland and Argentina.

Figure 12.1   The *WWW Virtual Library* logo
Courtesy of the WWW Virtual Library

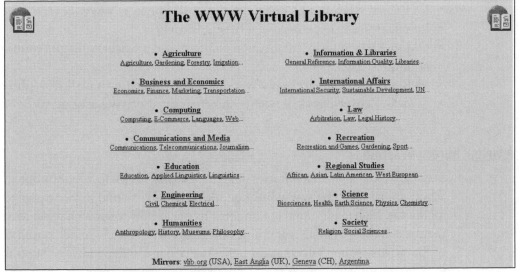

Figure 12.2   The *WWW Virtual Library* home page
Courtesy of the WWW Virtual Library

The *WWW Virtual Library* does not exist in one single place, but is distributed around the world, individual libraries being held and maintained on different servers. The central affairs of the organization are co-ordinated by a council, and major decisions are decided by the membership at large. Consequently, the information you find in each of the component virtual libraries differs in accordance with the subject under consideration.

Of course, given how fluid the internet is, it is simply not possible to list all the virtual libraries available. However, it is not too difficult to discover them for yourself. An obvious approach is to visit your favourite search engine and do a search for "*virtual library*" and then any terms that define what subject area you are interested in. Another good approach is to visit a website called *Pinakes* which can be found at **www.hw.ac.uk/libWWW/irn/ pinakes/pinakes.html** and has a good listing of virtual libraries.

However, if you just want to dip your toe into the water, the following is a short list of some virtual libraries that I've used in the past:

- *ADAM* – art, design, architecture and media information at **www.adam.ac.uk/**
- *ALEX* – a collection of documents in the public domain from UK and US literature at **www.infomotions.com/alex/**
- *Biz/ed* – business and economics at **www.bized.ac.uk/**
- *EEVL* – the Edinburgh engineering virtual library at **www.eevl.ac.uk/**
- *Librarians' Index to the Internet* at **http://lii.org/**
- *OMNI* – a gateway for information on health and medicine at **http://omni. ac.uk/**
- *Philosophy in Cyberspace* at **www–personal.monash.edu.au/~dey/phil/**
- *SOSIG* – covering social science information at **www.sosig.ac.uk/**.

A virtual library in action

Having looked at virtual libraries in general terms, let us now look at one in action. *BUBL*, based at **www.bubl.ac.uk/**, is an information service designed for the UK higher education community. Its use is, however, much wider than that, as it is used by academic communities in the UK and abroad, as well as by librarians, other information professionals and indeed anyone who is looking for information. A major aim of the service is to provide 'clear, fast and reliable access to selected internet resources and services of academic relevance'. A consequence of this is that the data are provided without adverts, animations, very few graphics and with an emphasis on ease of use and speed of loading. The home page can be seen in Figure 12.3.

With *BUBL* it is possible to quickly find a host of information on the UK, such as data on central government, political parties, newspapers, the media, UK web directories, academic information, hospitals, libraries, museums and so on.

DID YOU KNOW? >>

B *UBL* first started in 1990.

BUBL LINK is a database or catalogue of internet resources of academic relevance, with each resource being evaluated, classified and catalogued before being added. However, it also provides access to the data via a *Yahoo!* type approach, as can be seen in Figure 12.4.

BUBL Information Service

LINK / 5:15 | Journals | Search | News | UK | Mail | Archive | Clients | Admin | Feedback

Free User-Friendly Access to Selected Internet Resources Covering all Subject Areas, with a Special Focus on Library and Information Science *

➡ **BUBL LINK / 5:15**
Catalogue of 12,000 selected Internet resources

➡ **BUBL Journals**
Links to current LIS journals/newsletters

➡ **BUBL Search**
Search BUBL or beyond

➡ **BUBL News**
Jobs, events, surveys, offers, updates

➡ **BUBL UK**
Directory of UK organisations and institutions

➡ **BUBL Mail**
Mailing lists and mail archives

➡ **BUBL Archive**
Historical BUBL content

➡ **BUBL Clients**
Pages of organisations hosted by BUBL

BUBL Admin: All about BUBL: contacts, feedback, usage statistics, FAQ, reports

BUBL Information Service, Centre for Digital Library Research, Strathclyde University, 101 St James Road, Glasgow G4 0NS, Scotland
Tel: 0141 548 4752   *Email:* bubl@bubl.ac.uk   *Submit URL:* Suggestions

Figure 12.3   The *BUBL* home page
© BUBL Information Service

BUBL LINK / 5:15

Search | Subject Menus | A-Z | Dewey | Countries | Types | Updates | Random | About | Feedback

Selected Internet resources covering all academic subject areas

Proprietary Rights Notice: Dewey Decimal Classification

A|B|C|D|E|F|G|H|I|J|K|L|M|N|O|P|Q|R|S|T|U|V|W|X|Y|Z

General Reference
books, data, images, journals, maps

Engineering and Technology
aeronautics, electronics, energy, robotics

Creative Arts
art, design, media, music, photography

Health Studies
medicine, nursing, nutrition, pharmacy

Humanities
archaeology, history, philosophy, religion

Life Sciences
agriculture, biology, ecology, genetics, zoology

Language, Literature and Culture
English, ethnography, linguistics, writing

Mathematics and Computing
internet, programming, viruses, statistics

Social Sciences
business, economics, education, law, politics

Physical Sciences
astronomy, chemistry, earth sciences, physics

Featured subjects: Library and Information Science, Archaeology, Music

Figure 12.4   The *BUBL LINK* home page
© BUBL Information Service

The database can be searched in a number of different ways: by using the Dewey Decimal Classification system, by following the links from major headings to subheadings, by country, internet resources or type, or by using the simple or advanced search facility.

Once you have located the subject you are interested in you are presented with a list of (usually) somewhere between five and 15 links (hence the name) to websites that cover your interest in depth. This site listing also includes a short paragraph summarizing the sites, thus enabling you to visit the right site at the first attempt.

I ran a search for "*intelligent agents*" which resulted in seven hits. The same search on *Google* resulted in 1,490,000 matches. This is perhaps not entirely a fair comparison, since I would normally have been much more precise in that search, but even then I would have got far too many hits and would have spent a lot of time visiting sites in order to find exactly what I wanted. Using the *BUBL LINK* service I can rest assured that the sites found are of high quality and will be appropriate to me as an information professional.

Summary

Virtual libraries and gateways are an extremely useful way of ensuring that you limit the results of a search to a manageable number of hits that are current, informative and authoritative. Their strength lies in the fact that the resources made available have been evaluated and selected and, in the case of the summaries particularly, by people who know what they are talking about. Paradoxically, however, this is also their weakness, since this human intervention takes time and a lot of voluntary effort, which may mean that the resources are not always as current as they should be. Nonetheless, a virtual library is always a good way to begin exploring a subject area.

URLs mentioned in this chapter

www.amex.com/
www.aa.com/
www.theaa.com/
www.standards.dfes.gov.uk/beaconschools/
www.queensawards.org.uk/home1.htm
www.easyspace.com/
www.checkdomain.com/
www.archive.org/

www.vlib.org/
www.hw.ac.uk/libWWW/irn/pinakes/pinakes.html
www.adam.ac.uk/
www.infomotions.com/alex/
www.bized.ac.uk/
www.eevl.ac.uk/
http://lii.org/
http://omni.ac.uk/
http://www-personal.monash.edu.au/~dey/phil/
www.sosig.ac.uk/
www.bubl.ac.uk/

Chapter 13 »
Usenet newsgroups and mailing lists

Introduction

The internet is useful for many things, but perhaps it is best used for communication, either between individuals or groups of people. E-mail was the first implementation of this, but it is limited in what it can provide. What is also required is a method of passing information between groups of people, all of whom share the same interests, whether academic or personal. Two methods have been introduced: usenet newsgroups and mailing lists. This chapter discusses the similarities and differences between them, how to make use of them, and the advantages that they can give you as an advanced searcher.

Usenet newsgroups

I expect that you have heard of usenet newsgroups, though you may have heard them described as any of the following: usenet, newsgroups, netnews, discussion groups or just news. For simplicity, I'll refer to them as newsgroups, but it is worth pointing out that, while some of them do carry a lot of news and current events information, that is not their only purpose. Indeed, as other news resources on the internet have developed, this role is becoming less and less important. Newsgroups initially started life as far back as 1980, when two students in North Carolina established a method of transferring up to a dozen messages per day from one machine to another using something called UUCP (UNIX to UNIX Copy). These messages could be read by all the users who logged onto the system and they could respond to the messages by posting their own, which could be copied back to the other machine.

Over the course of time this system has expanded; because the messages dealt with different topics a hierarchy was introduced, allowing people to post to specific newsgroups, to ensure that users did not have to wade through all the messages just to find the two or three which interested them. Newsgroups have become an ever-expanding area of the internet – today there are about 110,000; posts to newsgroups add up to well over six gigabytes per day; over 50 million people participate in them. Please note, however, that no definitive figures are available, though it can be said with certainty that newsgroups are now the largest public information resource in the world, and it is estimated that the data available is up to four times the size of the web.

DID YOU KNOW? >>
1 gigabyte is the equivalent of one thousand 400-page novels.

The method used to send newsgroup messages, commonly referred to as posts or postings, is quite simple. A user posts a message to a particular newsgroup, usually using a piece of software called a 'newsreader' (although it is quite possible to post directly from the web or via the *Microsoft Outlook* program) and this post is sent by the software to the internet service provider's news server. The news server in turn copies the messages it has received to other news servers around the world, thus allowing other users to log onto their providers' news servers, download the post and read it. They can then, if they choose, respond to the posts that interest them and the whole process starts again. This is generally referred to as 'propagation' and, as you can see, it is continual, with people seeing posts, responding to them, having their post copied back around the world and so on. As with most things to do with the internet, it is a 24-hour-a-day, 365-days-a-year activity.

Newsgroups are split into hierarchies, and a newsgroup name is composed of several different elements separated by dots. There is what is known as the 'big seven' hierarchy, and the top level of these seven subject areas is as follows:

- **comp**.   topics related to computing
- **misc**.   miscellaneous topics that don't sit anywhere else in the hierarchy
- **news**.   topics that relate to the internet as a whole
- **rec**.   recreational subjects such as hobbies, sports, the arts and so on
- **sci**.   anything to do with scientific subjects
- **soc**.   social newsgroups, both social interaction and social interests
- **talk**.   generally covers political issues.

Postings to these newsgroups are generally propagated to all news servers around the world, but there are other newsgroups that are only of interest to particular regions or that are regarded as rather more frivolous than the big seven. Examples are:

- **alt**.   alternative, often controversial subjects
- **bionet**.   subjects of interest to biologists
- **uk**.   subjects that may be of interest to people based in, or interested in, the UK.

Later in this chapter I explain how you can get a full list of newsgroups and choose the ones that you find useful. For now, however, let's look a little further into the way that a newsgroup is named, with a few examples:

comp.infosystems.www.authoring.html
misc.education
misc.misc
news.admin.censorship
news.announce.newusers
rec.pets.cats.health+behave
sci.physics.fusion
sci.space.shuttle
soc.history.war.us–civil–war
talk.abortion
uk.local.london
uk.media.tv.misc
alt.books.iain–banks.

You can see from the above examples that there is little by way of a structure to them. They start from the general and move to the specific, but otherwise there is little overall consistency to be found. One of the reasons for this is that there is not a great deal of control over the establishment of newsgroups, although there is a set procedure that must be adhered to in the creation of a newsgroup in the big seven which requires that a proposition be made and voted upon. In general terms, however, it is possible for anyone to set up a newsgroup if enough people think it is a good idea.

Most newsgroups are entirely open, which is to say that anyone can post a message to them. Although these postings are supposed to be 'on topic' to the group in question this does not always happen. Most newsgroups do, however, have a charter which is a statement defining what sort of posts are appropriate to the group. A small number of newsgroups are 'moderated' which means that, before a post can be made available to news servers around the world, someone checks the message for content, validity and so on, and will only clear it for propagation if it satisfies the criteria which have previously been established.

Many newsgroups also have a FAQ, or Frequently Asked Questions list, which lists common questions and answers that people have posted to the newsgroup in the past. They can be a very useful source of information and are usually posted once every two weeks to the group. A good place for a list of them is at **www. faqs.org/faqs/**.

The value of newsgroups to the advanced searcher

The posts that you find on newsgroups are an eclectic mixture of fact, fiction, rumour, advertisements and opinions. Most newsgroups are not moderated, as I've mentioned, so anyone can post anything they wish. In most cases the posts are on topic, however, but sometimes people will 'spam' newsgroups with inappropriate posts. Consequently, it can take some time to sort out the useful information from the nonsense that gets posted. This depends on the number of posts a newsgroup gets every day; some low-volume newsgroups get only two or three posts on an average day, while other newsgroups, especially in the comp. hierarchy, get over 500 per day.

It is worth stressing that a lot of useful information can be gained from different newsgroups – the bug in the original Intel Pentium chip was reported to appropriate newsgroups and the discussions that then took place encouraged Intel to respond to the problem quickly. Many businesses regularly monitor newsgroups and are increasingly using them as a first-line method of communicating with users.

Individuals both pose and answer questions in newsgroups; debates take place; information is shared; new information is made available to each group's user community; and details on new websites, conferences and exhibitions are regularly posted. Consequently, although the information held in newsgroups is often more opinion than fact, it can be a very useful place to begin researching a subject. For example, if I ever get an error message on my computer, I go to the newsgroups to see if anyone else has reported the same error and see a list of possible causes and, more importantly, suggestions on how to fix the problem.

One word of warning here I'm afraid. If you post to newsgroups, within a short space of time you will begin to get unsolicited commercial e-mails (UCE for short) offering anything from the chance to get rich quickly through to cures for baldness or solicitations to visit various dubious websites. This is because unscrupulous companies skim newsgroups for e-mail addresses, which they then sell onto other people who send out UCE. There is very little you can do about this; the best solutions being to post using one of the free e-mail services available, such as *Hotmail*, or to alter your e-mail address to something like philb@removethis. philb.com.

Reading newsgroups

Having whetted your appetite for newsgroups, I shall now explain how you can use them. There are basically two ways of doing this – either using the web to read and post messages or using one of many software packages available for just this purpose.

Web-based utilities

There used to be several websites that you could use to search newsgroups, but these have all either fallen by the wayside or have been subsumed into *Google* at *Google Groups* which can be found at **http://groups.google.com/**. This is a very specialized search engine because all it does is search newsgroups, rather than the web. *Google* has integrated 20 years of archives into the database, with access to over 800 million messages. You can use the system in the same way that you can search its database of web pages, by typing in words or phrases, for example. You can see the opening screen in Figure 13.1.

The results returned give a list of newsgroup postings that contain the searched term(s), together with a list of newsgroups that *Google* feels are particularly appropriate to your search. The details of each post include brief information on the thread, when it was posted, to which group and by which individual. It is also possible to read any responses to the posting.

Google Groups has an advanced function, and you can see the interface screen for this in Figure 13.2. Once you have got used to searching for newsgroup posts the advanced search features make a lot of sense, allowing you to search much more quickly and effectively. As well as searching for messages that

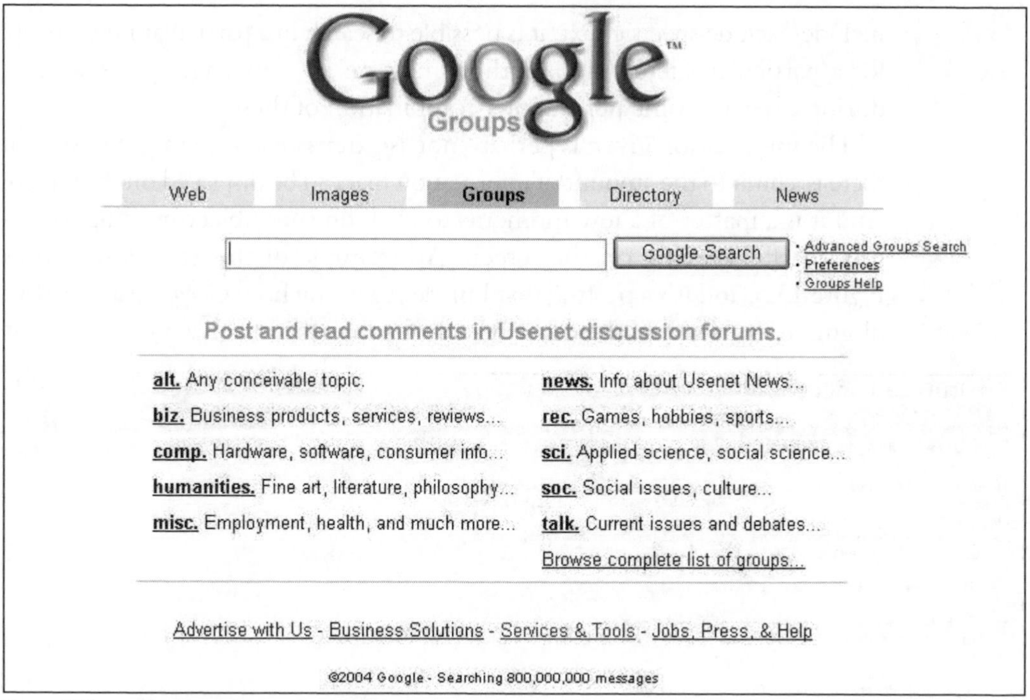

Figure 13.1 The *Google Groups* search interface
© 2004 Google

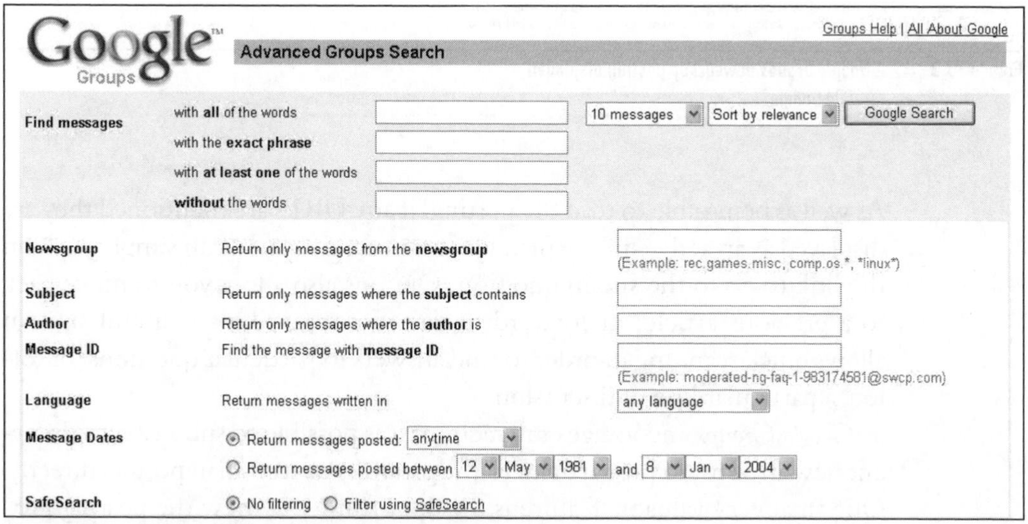

Figure 13.2 The *Google Groups* advanced search interface
© 2004 Google

include/exclude specific text, it is possible to search in a particular newsgroup, for a particular subject line, author, message ID, language, posts written during a specific time period, or a combination of these.

The information given is perhaps not as extensive as one might wish, but there is a limit to the amount of information that can be displayed on the screen. And it is a matter of a few moments to click on the subject heading to display the full posting on the screen. An example of this step is shown in Figure 13.3, and it's a posting that I made regarding how *Google* searches (I've disguised the name of the other posters for the sake of privacy).

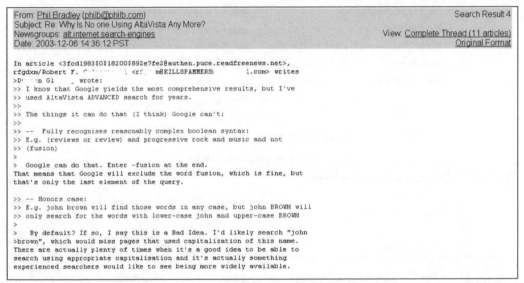

From: Phil Bradley (philb@philb.com)   Search Result 4
Subject: Re: Why Is No one Using AltaVista Any More?
Newsgroups: alt.internet.search-engines   View: Complete Thread (11 articles)
Date: 2003-12-06 14:36:12 PST   Original Format

```
In article <3fcd1983$0$18200$892e7fe2@authen.puce.readfreenews.net>,
rfgdxm/Robert F. C       <rf   m@KILLSPAMMERS    l.com> writes
>D     n Gl    wrote:
>> I know that Google yields the most comprehensive results, but I've
>> used AltaVista ADVANCED search for years.
>>
>> The things it can do that (I think) Google can't:
>>
>> --  Fully recognises reasonably complex boolean syntax:
>> E.g. (reviews or review) and progressive rock and music and not
>> (fusion)
>
>  Google can do that. Enter -fusion at the end.
That means that Google will exclude the word fusion, which is fine, but
that's only the last element of the query.

>> -- Honors case:
>> E.g. john brown will find those words in any case, but john BROWN will
>> only search for the words with lower-case john and upper-case BROWN
>
>  By default? If so, I say this is a Bad Idea. I'd likely search "john
>brown", which would miss pages that used capitalization of this name.
There are actually plenty of times when it's a good idea to be able to
search using appropriate capitalisation and it's actually something
experienced searchers would like to see being more widely available.
```

Figure 13.3   A *Google Groups* newsgroup posting displayed
                  © 2004 Google

As well as being able to read the posting, if any URLs are mentioned they are displayed as an active link, which is very useful since you can simply click on the link to go to the site in question. Options also allow you to move back to a previous article, or forward to any responses. This is useful since it allows quick scanning in order to find answers to particular questions, or follow a particular line of discussion.

Google Groups encourages interaction: it is possible to subscribe to different newsgroups, to post articles to the group(s) or to e-mail posters directly. One final very valuable feature is the opportunity to view the posting profile of the poster whose post you are reading. There are a number of reasons why this is useful: it allows you to identify other posts they have written, and get a feeling for the amount of knowledge they have on a particular subject; and to identify what other groups they post to, on the basis that, if you're interested in what they are writing about, you may be interested in what they are saying to different groups. There is a privacy issue here, but *Google Groups* does have a policy whereby posters can ensure that their postings are not archived.

DID YOU KNOW? >>
A 'thread' is created when someone creates a posting, another person responds to it and so on. The series of messages thus created is generally referred to as a thread and is an easy way to follow a particular discussion.

Reading and posting to newsgroups can take up a frightening amount of time, so if you connect to the internet using a dial-up modem connection this might become an expensive way of reading newsgroups. To give you a quick example, I currently subscribe to about 20 different newsgroups, and it takes me about an hour a day to read and respond to various postings. Even if you connect using broadband you may well find that you need to be very strict with yourself regarding the amount of time that you spend using this particular resource!

Offline newsreaders

A possible solution to both the problems of online costs and the amount of time spent reading newsgroups is to make use of an offline newsreader. The utilities work in a similar fashion to *Google Groups* in that you are able to obtain a list of all of the newsgroups, decide on the ones that interest you and subscribe to them. (Subscribe here is used to mean 'join' rather than 'pay for'.) The major difference is how the information is delivered to you. You connect to the internet normally and start the offline newsreader, which connects to the internet service provider and downloads all the new posts onto your computer's hard disk. Alternatively, the newsreader can be configured to just download the headings of each post (similar to the subject line in an e-mail) to save both space and time.

You are then able to read the postings offline at your leisure and can take as much time as you need to write responses to posts, check any information and so on. Once you are happy with the responses you have written you can log back onto the internet and the offline reader will send the posts back to the news server. If you have simply chosen to download the headings of posts, you can mark those that you think look interesting and the reader will then connect to the news server and download just the content of those posts.

Many different offline newsreaders are available, and a good listing can be obtained from **http://dir.yahoo.com/Computers_and_Internet/ Software/Internet/Usenet/**. They all work in a similar fashion. *Forte Agent* is a commercial product, although there is a free cut-down version available called *Forte Free Agent*. Either product can be downloaded from **www.forteinc.com/main/homepage.php**. The *Forte Agent* main screen can be seen in Figure 13.4. It is quick to configure, in that all you need to do is to provide it with the address of your internet service provider's news server. The program then visits the server and downloads a list of all the newsgroups that the service provider takes. (Not all service providers take all newsgroups – in fact I'd be surprised if any of them did. They are likely to exclude groups that just have a specifically local focus, so my American readers may find it difficult to obtain groups based within the .uk hierarchy, for example, and many providers will also exclude binary or picture groups, since they take up a lot of space.) This list can then be displayed for you to see, and it's an easy job to then subscribe to the groups that interest you. Unsubscribing is just as easy – a simple click on the appropriate icon and the job is done. Reading posts is just a matter of clicking on the heading; replying is just as easy.

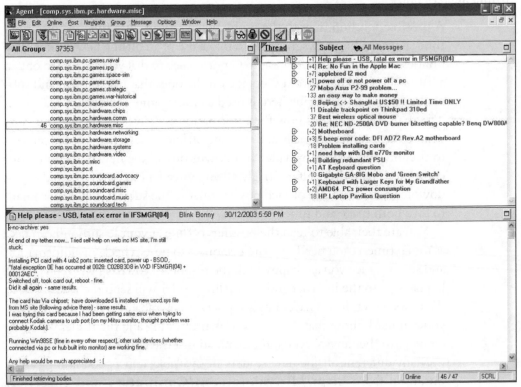

Figure 13.4   The *Forte Agent* main interface screen
© Forte, 1994–2004

Mailing lists

Mailing lists, also called discussion lists or listservs, are very similar to news-groups in concept (allowing one person to contact many, and allowing many to share ideas, thoughts and opinions), but they work quite differently in prac-tical terms, and this leads to an entirely different atmosphere. As we have already seen, newsgroups require newsreading software, or a visit to *Google Groups*. Mailing lists work by using your standard e-mail package; instead of posting via *Google Groups* or *Forte Agent*, you send an e-mail with the text of your mes-sage to a mail server. The mail server is another computer that sits on the internet and is responsible for keeping details about a particular mailing list, including the e-mail addresses of all of the people who have subscribed to that list. The mail server then sends a copy of the e-mail to everyone who is on the list. Your message then arrives in their e-mail accounts for them to read, without you having to know what their e-mail addresses are, or, indeed, have any knowledge of who they are at all. Once your message has been received people can post a response if they wish, either back to you via direct e-mail, back to the mail server which then sends copies of that response to every one on the list (you included), or they can do both.

Characteristics of mailing lists

As you can see from the preceding paragraph, the principle of mailing lists is the same as that of newsgroups – a group of people communicating with each other. However, as the system works using e-mail, there are a number of quite substantial differences in the way in which information profession-als can make use of them, and I'll discuss exactly what they are now.

Joining a mailing list is slightly different to joining a newsgroup. As you now know, you can join a newsgroup by simply selecting it from the list pre-sented by *Forte Agent* or *Google Groups*. Since no one is in charge of a newsgroup (except in the few isolated cases of moderated groups) you can subscribe or unsubscribe as you wish, whenever you wish to. However, to join a mailing list you need to send a message to an appropriate e-mail address requesting to join it. Since each list has an owner, they have to agree to you becoming a member, though in many cases this is automatic. Although this isn't exactly a big hurdle it does require that extra bit of effort, and as a result individuals who simply want to advertise a product or site do not tend to bother. As a result, the traffic is reduced and the posts are more focused than you'll often find with a newsgroup, though this does of course vary with each individ-ual list.

The owner plays an important role in defining the nature and atmosphere of the list by deciding what subjects should be discussed, whether certain types of post (announcements or advertisements, for example) are permitted, and limiting discussion on a topic if it is felt that it has continued for too long. The owner may also decide if the list is moderated or not. A moderated list means that each post has to be checked by the owner, and only if it is approved will it be passed onto all the members to read it. Consequently, moderated lists are generally more on track (the terminology being that the 'signal to noise' ratio is higher), with a smaller number of daily postings. The slight danger of a moderated list is the list owner is all powerful and may delete postings for any number of reasons. This could result in a rather bland series of posts, particularly in mailing lists established by commercial organizations for discussion of their products, since the moderator may decide to delete postings that are critical. However, members of a list in which this occurs generally realize quickly what's happening and unsubscribe. Finally, because moderation is time consuming there may be a delay between a post being sent and its being seen by the list members.

Locating mailing lists

There is no single comprehensive list of mailing lists, so it is necessary to do a little research in order to find ones that may be of interest to you. Disappointingly, many of the resources that I mentioned in the second edition of this book are no longer operating, which makes the challenge even harder. However, there are still some useful places to visit, starting with *Topica* at **www.topica.com/**. *Topica Exchange* lists over 100,000 lists, covering both professional and hobby-related subject areas, and over 12 million people subscribe to them. The directory listing at *Topica* covers subjects such as Computers and the Internet, Government, Humanities, Health, Science and Society. Lists can be located by using the hierarchical approach or the search box. A search for *librarians* resulted in a total of 15 lists, and the details on each cover who the list is aimed at, when it was created, if the archives can be searched, how many subscribers the list has, and how many messages it receives per day. Another resource worth looking at is *Tile.net* at **www.tile.net/**. I found several dozen listed under *librarians*.

HINTS & TIPS >>
Remember that most of the information you retrieve from newsgroups and mailing lists are people's opinions, rather than facts, so be careful not to rely on this information; check other sources as well.

One resource that deserves special mention and that information professionals use a lot is the *National Academic Mailing List Service*, also called *JISCmail*, at **www.jiscmail.ac.uk/**. The focus of the list is centred on the

UK, though not exclusively, and it has thousands of lists, with subscribers representing most, if not all, countries throughout the world. Appropriate lists can be found by searching by name, by using an alphabetical list, by category or by keyword search. A search for *librarians* resulted in 44 matches. Once you have located a list that appeals to you, it's possible to look through the archives and gain a better feeling for the subjects that are covered. Indeed, one does not even need to be a member to search the archives, and these can be a very useful way of finding material that has been published to a particular list.

Joining, leaving and posting to mailing lists

The resources that I've mentioned so far give you precise details on how to join, leave and post to a mailing list, and you should keep that information safe for future reference. However, I also provide as an example one of the lists that I have subscribed to, and found very useful, which is lis–link, described as a 'general Library and Information Science list for news and discussion'. The commands used are specific to this list, but the principle is the same, regardless of the list you join, wherever it might happen to be. To subscribe to the list you simply fill out a form on the web page for the list. I have reproduced part of the form as Figure 13.5. Obviously, you have to provide your name and an e-mail address, and you can choose whether you want to

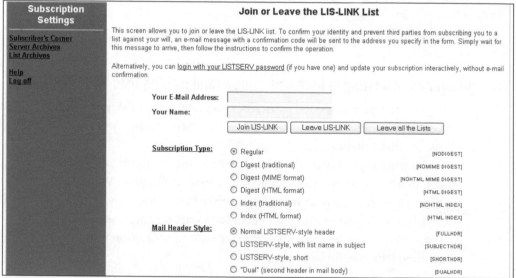

Figure 13.5   The form for joining or leaving *lis-link*
© JISCmail

receive each posting individually or as a 'digest' e-mail once a day, the format in which you wish to receive the postings and various other options. Once you have submitted your application you get an e-mail asking you to confirm the details, after which you are then subscribed. You are given details on how to post to the list (by sending your post to an e-mail address such as lis-link@jiscmail.ac.uk), and another address to send administrative requests to, such as to unsubscribe. It is important that you send requests to the appropriate e-mail address, because if you send a message to leave the list to lis-link@jiscmail.ac.uk it will automatically be distributed to everyone on the list and you will end up looking rather silly!

Why mailing lists are useful for the advanced searcher

Mailing lists are an excellent way of keeping up to date with news and current events in a particular subject area, and I use them to 'check the pulse' of what is happening in the subject fields that interest me. Mailing lists are often the first place that I find out about new courses or conferences, new developments, new websites and current affairs. They are also a superb way to keep in contact with colleagues, and to discuss important issues. A mailing list can also be used to post questions; if I'm completely lost and unable to find information (and this happens to even the best searchers!) I can post my question to a list and usually receive an answer from a helpful person within a few hours. Of course, if I can answer a question posed by another member I always try to return the favour.

> **HINTS & TIPS >>**
> A general rule of thumb is that you receive more serious and accurate information from a mailing list than from a newsgroup.

Some guidelines on posting to both newsgroups and mailing lists

If you are an experienced subscriber you may wish to skip this section since you will already have discovered by observation, trial and error most of the things that I mention.

Newsgroups and mailing lists contain much useful information, and a few moments' research using the archives may well answer your question without you having to post it. On the other hand, you may wish to get more involved than just reading, and decide to start posting yourself. The following are a few pointers that should make your introduction to newsgroups and mailing lists enjoyable and painless:

- Read the newsgroup/mailing list for at least a few days, preferably a few weeks, before you start posting yourself. Each group is its own little community, complete with helpful and knowledgeable people, others who like nothing more than to pick an argument and still others who like to cause problems. Take some time to learn who is who; that way you will quickly see whose posts are worth reading, and whose post you can safely ignore.
- Read the FAQ for the group if it has one. Most publish this once every few weeks or perhaps monthly. The FAQ is a compilation of those questions that are frequently asked and they contain a wealth of information. It is quite possible that your question has already been asked and answered previously and a quick check will confirm this. If you ask a question that's already been answered (and, as is usually the way, often a couple of days before you joined the list) you'll look a little silly, and it won't be a good way of introducing yourself to the group as a whole.
- Do not advertise. Only a very small number of newsgroups and mailing lists allow overt advertisements and they state this when you join. If you post an advertisement to a group or list that does not want them you will find that your mailbox quickly fills up with messages from people telling you (sometimes politely, sometimes not) that advertisements are not welcomed.
- Think about your post before you send it. It is very easy to send a post in the heat of the moment, and if you post when you are angry you will doubtless say things you will later regret. If you are really angry, write the post anyway, but don't send it until the next day when you have calmed down; the chances are that you will decide against sending it, or at the very least will reword it in a rather more tactful manner.
- Don't get involved in a 'flamewar'. This is a situation in which two or more people who hold different views start posting abusive comments to or about each other. Flamewars are unhelpful; they do not add anything constructive to a group. People will quickly regard you as being an offensive or childish poster and will ignore anything that you have to say.
- Ensure that your posts are appropriate for the group or list. There is no point in sending a post about the latest development in search engine optimization to a group that covers the behaviour of cats, for example. If you do so by accident, send another quick posting to apologize for your error and all should be well.
- Resist the urge to 'spam' or cross-post your message. If you post a message to a number of different groups all dealing with the same sort of subject area it's quite likely that the same people will see your posting several times,

and will be less than impressed. If for some reason it is necessary, it's considered polite to apologize for doing so prior to the message body.

- When writing, choose a sensible subject heading that clearly describes the content of your post. Subscribers do not usually read every single post; they scan headings to decide which ones to read. You are more likely to get a good response if your post says something like 'Help needed installing Internet Explorer version 6.1' instead of just 'Help'.

- When replying to another post, don't quote the entire message. Keep your response short and to the point and only quote short sections of the original posting that you are commenting on.

- Don't 'top post'. That is to say, if you are including any of the message that you are responding to in your post, don't write your answer at the very beginning of your post. This is because it will probably not make very much sense to people, and they will then need to read the rest of the post in order to understand what you're talking about.

- Make it clear whether you are speaking for yourself, or on behalf of your organization, particularly if you are posting using a work e-mail account. If in doubt, it's probably best to check with someone in your organization first, or to be explicit and state in your post 'This is my opinion and not necessarily that of my employer'.

- If you ask a question in a newsgroup or mailing list, try to answer two from other people. This isn't a requirement, or even necessarily standard practice, but I think it helps make the newsgroup or mailing list a useful, informative and pleasant place to spend time.

Summary

Newsgroups and mailing lists are a valuable way of keeping up to date with what is happening in a particular subject area. They allow professionals to keep in touch with each other, to share and swap experiences and to ask and answer questions. However, they have the potential to take up considerable amounts of time, and require thought and tact if your experiences there are to be positive ones.

URLs mentioned in this chapter

www.faqs.org/faqs/
http://groups.google.com/
http://dir.yahoo.com/Computers_and_Internet/Software/Internet/Usenet/

www.forteinc.com/main/homepage.php
www.topica.com/
www.tile.net/
http://www.jiscmail.ac.uk/

Part 3 >>
The future

Chapter 14 »

The information mix and into the future

Introduction

I hope that you have found the previous chapters useful and informative, but I am aware that so far I have treated elements such as search engines and intelligent agents (see Chapter 7) largely as discrete elements. Of course, when searching the internet on a daily basis this is an unrealistic way to approach the question 'how do I find the best and most relevant information quickly?', since the best way of obtaining exactly what you need is generally to use a combination of different resources.

In this chapter I attempt to merge all the different elements into a coherent whole, using some real-life examples of internet searching. I also cover a number of other elements related to searching which I have not included so far and, finally, take a quick look into my crystal ball to highlight possible future technologies. The latter is something that I returned to in the second edition, and am going to do again, because I think there's at least as much to be learned from the things that I got wrong as those that I got right!

A quick glance through this chapter, with its many references to information professionals, might lead you to think that unless you have that sort of background it is not relevant to you. This is most certainly not the case, and I'd like to emphasize that anyone may need to find the sort of information that I have referred to in my examples. Furthermore, you may not work in a library or use one each day, but you probably have a collection of books at home, and will find some of my points pertinent to the decisions that you make about what to buy, or how to arrange them.

Where do I go first?

You now have a large array of tools at your disposal which should make the task of searching the internet rather easier. At this point, however, I suspect that you may be a little bewildered, since you have so much choice and so many different starting points! You might well be thinking 'Should I use a search engine and, if so, which one? How about an intelligent agent instead? Or should I ask in a newsgroup, or on a mailing list?'

To begin with, let's go back to basics. If you are finding information for an end–user, the initial approach is no different from any other reference query that you receive, and if you are looking for information for yourself you will have to ask similar questions:

- Has the user clearly identified what information they want?
- Are there any synonyms you should be aware of, particularly when search-ing global resources? The term 'football' means very different things depending on which side of the Atlantic you live.
- Does the user require a very specific piece of information, or an overview of the subject?
- Does the information have to be 'official'? In other words, what level of authority does the user require?
- Does the information have to be current and, if so, current to today, last week or last month?
- What format does the user want? Text, a moving image, a picture, or per-haps a sound file?
- Does the information have to be in a particular language?
- Is the user prepared to pay for the information or does it have to be free?
- Is the information need once only, or is it part of an ongoing project, requir-ing frequent updates?

These are just a few of the questions that you need to be clear on before you can begin your search. I'm sure you ask many of them at the moment, and prob-ably some more besides. However, when using the internet to answer queries you have many more resources available, and it's not difficult to work out from the list above which questions relate specifically to that, rather than to the more traditional searching which you have been doing in the past.

One particular point is 'don't forget other resources!' Quite obviously the emphasis in this book is on the internet, but in most cases you have other resources at your disposal. Just glancing around my own workroom I can see that I have magazines, books, manuals, DVDs, CD-ROMs, a newspaper, a copy of the telephone directory and a Yellow Pages. I expect that I could use the internet to find all of the information contained within all these resources but sometimes it just makes more sense to open the Yellow Pages at the appropriate category, find a telephone number and speak to a real live human being. It's easier, quicker and more effective than locating a Yellow Pages website, running my search, visiting a website, clicking on an e-mail link, writing the e-mail and then hoping I'll get a response in the next couple of days. I'll just say it quietly, because I'll probably never live it down, but the internet is not always the best place to go first. Sometimes it is quicker to say to an enquirer 'The answer you want is in the book with the red cover on the third shelf down over there.' However, for the sake of this chapter, we'll assume that the only resource you have is the computer in front of you.

Some sample searches

Using your initiative

Where can I find information about Christmas traditions?
I need some sample Tarot card spreads.
Where can I book a cheap air ticket?
When did John Lennon die?
Why does my cat eat grass?
Where can I find out more about MI5, Britain's security service?

On the face of it, you would be forgiven for thinking that these are all very different questions without anything to link them together. You would be wrong, since they all have at least one thing in common – it's amazingly easy to find the answers to them. Furthermore, it's not necessary to use a search engine, intelligent agent, virtual library or newsgroup to get the required data; all that you need is to do a little lateral thinking, and try out a few URLs.

Where can I find information about Christmas traditions?

Let's take the Christmas question to begin with. A search at *Google* results in about 666,000 matches for *Christmas traditions*. However, just by typing into the address bar of your browser **www.christmas.com/** you end up at a website that covers, in some detail, information on different traditions, religion and Christmas, and Christmas around the world. It's true to say that there is also a lot of commercial content on which gifts to buy, and where to get them from (which might actually be quite useful if the day is getting closer and the stockings remain unfilled), but it's not difficult to distinguish the commercial data from the information you need.

I need some sample Tarot card spreads.

The tarot card question was a little bit more tricky, since the obvious choice of **www.tarot.com/** is most definitely a commercial site and requires payment for most of its information. Thinking slightly more laterally, going to **www.tarotcards.com/** would appear to be a possibility but, once again, we reach a commercial site, which actually then redirects us to an entirely different site. One final attempt, this time to **www.tarot–cards.com/** doesn't lead to a particularly promising site, since it's only a directory listing, but clicking on a directory called 'tarot' loads a page from the site **www.tarot–cards.com/tarot/** which provides us with some very useful information on several different spreads. Incidentally, three attempts is all that I give myself when using this approach; if I haven't got what I need by then, it's time to be rather more scientific about matters.

Where can I book a cheap air ticket?

The question on cheap air tickets was very simple. Just typing in **www.cheapflights.com/** took me to a very good site, with a wide variety of different flights available, but I noticed within seconds that it was an American site. Not a particular problem this – I simply changed the .com to .co.uk and found a similar site, but with flight information for people from Britain.

When did John Lennon die?

The John Lennon question is an interesting one, since the obvious choice of johnlennon.com did not pull up a web page for me. I was slightly curious about this, since it is such an obvious address and I used the *Easyspace* service to see if it was in fact registered. I quickly discovered that it was, and to Yoko Ono. I assume that she has registered it in her name to ensure that no one else can use it. I tried a variant of the address, and ended up with **www.john-lennon.com/** which gave me the date I was after. This is quite clearly a fan site, rather than an official one, so if I wanted to be absolutely certain the data was correct I would probably have done a proper search, but I'm pretty confident they're right.

Why does my cat eat grass?

I do own a cat, and she does eat grass. My first attempt, at **www.catbehaviour.com/** was no use at all and just led me down a blind alley. I then simply put in an appropriate hyphen, and **www.cat-behaviour.com/** redirected me at once to **www.craftycat.co.uk/**. A brief tour of the site led me to an appropriate section, where my curiosity was satisfied. Although this is obviously a UK-based site, and some of the information such as contact details for cat behaviourists would not be useful for viewers from other countries, I'm confident in assuming that cats in other countries eat grass for the same reasons as British cats, so it's still useful information as far as I'm concerned.

Where can I find out more about MI5, Britain's security service?

How secret is a secret service? Not very would appear to be the answer. Since MI5 is a government department I just went straight to **www.mi5.gov.uk/** and there it was, bold as brass and not a secret agent in site.

I hope that all these illustrations show that you don't have to be a genius to find information on the internet. As long as you are able to think laterally and try one or two possible solutions to your question, just typing in one or two URLs often gets you to a site that will provide your answer. Of course, it's not a foolproof method, and it's easy to end up at fan sites, personal sites or commercial sites that may not take the same rigorous approach as academic and scientific sites, but the approach can often save you a lot of time and energy. As I said, my rule of thumb is that, if I can't find a useful site within three attempts, I try something more scientific. Of course, if you have an enquirer standing right next to you this entire approach may not be appropriate.

Using an index- or directory-based search engine

Which UK newspapers have websites?

This is a very simple and straightforward question; the kind of question that people ask on a daily basis. The answer, however, is not quite so straightforward. A little like a dictionary, in that you have to know how to spell a word in order to find out how to spell it, it's necessary to know which UK newspapers there are in order to see if they have websites. Another particular difficulty with this type of search is deciding exactly what terminology to use. Obvious search terms are of course *UK* and *newspapers*, but this isn't really enough, so it's then necessary to be a little more specific with something like *list* or a phrase *"list of UK newspapers"*. However, for each of these there are equally appropriate synonyms that we could use. I quickly wrote down some terms that I thought I could use:

list	Great Britain
lists	England
listing	Wales
listings	Scotland
listed	Northern Ireland
checklist	Ireland
catalogue	newspaper
category	newspapers
UK	tabloid
United Kingdom	tabloids
GB	press.

That's a total of 22 words, and while some are admittedly not ones that I'd probably choose to search on, or are particularly accurate, I think the point is made. However, I did visit *Google* and ran a search for *uk newspapers list websites*. I felt that this was a reasonably comprehensive search and covered the ground well. There were over 200,000 results and none of the first ten really gave me exactly what I was looking for. I did briefly consider trying different terms but then decided that it was time to turn my attention back to the index/directory-based search engines.

I tried *Yahoo!* first, and with four mouse clicks had a display on my screen, with the option of narrowing the search down further to specific regions. However, I was content with the fact that 36 different titles were immediately available to me. Using the UK and Ireland version of the search engine I was able to get my listing with just two mouse clicks. I next tried the *Google* web directory, and that also took four mouse clicks to obtain a listing, though this was disappointing, being only just over half the number of titles that *Yahoo!* offered me. At this point I could have stopped, since I had my answer. However, as I've pointed out elsewhere in this book, never trust what you find on the internet, and don't expect search engines to be comprehensive. I went back and revisited one of the broader categories at *Yahoo!*, **http://dir.yahoo.com/ News_and_Media/Newspapers/Web_Directories/**, and was offered various options, one of which was a link to *ThePaperboy* at **www.thepaperboy.com.au/welcome.html**. Within a few moments I was able to see a listing of all the UK-based newspapers listed at the site, a total of 357, almost ten times as many as I had been offered by *Yahoo!* I don't think that invalidated the *Yahoo!* search since I did end up finding the information that I wanted from a direct link on its site, and I doubt that I would have seen a listing for *ThePaperboy* in my *Google* search.

Using a free-text search engine

What pantomime holds the record for the most successful run in the USA?

This is another question that looks as though it's very straightforward, but once again we have the problem of terminology and keywords. Thankfully, 'pantomime' is reasonably straightforward since it is just that and not a play, for example. 'USA' could also be found written on pages as 'United States of America' or the shorter though less accurate 'America' or American, so there are four possible terms there. The word 'run' is, contextually, a very accurate term, but when used as a search term it becomes much less precise. Looking at the question being asked we could consider further terms such as 'history', since it's quite possible the most successful run was at some time in the past; 'Broadway' may be another appropriate term to try. One does have to wonder what 'successful' means in this context – longest run, most financially rewarding, seen by the largest number of people could all be used to define 'successful'. However, let's see what we find when using *Google*. *Pantomime* as a single search term isn't very useful since there is at least one piece of software with that name and various other terms, and we have over 225,000 results. *Pantomime USA* reduces that number to 17,000 results, and adding in *run* reduces that still further to 5,400 results. The actual results are interesting, but they still do not provide us with the answer to the query, so it's perhaps a good idea to change the approach, since my 'rule of three' hasn't worked. Given that there are so many results being returned, I thought it might be a good idea to do some phrase searching instead of single word searches and I decided on *"successful pantomime" "American history"* and this resulted in exactly one result: 'Humpty Dumpty', which ran for over 1200 performances in 1868 at the Olympic Theater in New York.

Where can I find information on the different 'weeks' in 2004 promoting various things?

This type of question is very difficult because there's really nothing to get hold of. It doesn't work well with a phrase search, since most of these weeks are phrased as 'national something week' so a search for "*national week*", for example isn't going to work. However, some free-text search engines, such as *AltaVista*, do support the use of the Boolean operator NEAR. I tried a search using its advanced search function for "*National NEAR Week AND NOT 2003*". This provided me with about 132,000 results, listing such events as National Engineers Week, National Youth Week and the interesting National Resurrect Romance Week. None of these would have turned up in the list of results on a search for the phrase "*national week*", so I was satisfied with that element of the search. However, 132,000 results is several orders of magnitude too large to actually look through, so I expanded the search to "*National NEAR Week AND NOT 2003 AND (events OR listing OR lists)*" and this reduced my search to just over 2000 results that did include several sites that provided me with some useful lists of events taking place.

> **HINTS & TIPS >>**
>
> I later discovered a good site that covers the subject of national weeks at www.countmeincalendar.info/countme/ CMIHome.nsf/frmMainHomepage? ReadForm, so if you're actually interested in this sort of information it's a good site to try.

Using specialist search engines

Is the quotation from Casablanca 'Play it again Sam' accurate?

A search for the phrase "*play it again Sam*" at *Google* returns over 30,000 results, and even limiting that to include 'Casablanca' gives over 2000 results. The first of these is from a website subtitled *Play it again, Sam: The Best Quotations from Casablanca*. Of course, the problem here is very clear – if my quotation is inaccurate to begin with, and I'm searching for that, it's highly likely that I'll find websites that contain the same error, thus compounding the problem. As a result, therefore, rather than start by using possibly incorrect data it makes more sense to find a reliable source of information to begin with, and use that to check my query. I happened to know of the existence of the *Internet Movie Database* at **www.imdb.com/** (I could have found it by doing a search for something along the lines of *film quotations database*), which led me directly to the film, to a section on memorable quotes and to the correct quotation.

> **DID YOU KNOW? >>**
>
> The accurate quote is 'Play it Sam', and *Google* found 751 references, but it found over 3000 with the inaccurate quote 'Play it again Sam'. The internet may not lie, but it's not very good at representing the truth!

I then decided that it might be a nice idea to see if I could get a sound file for the actual quote. In order to do this I returned to the general search engine *AlltheWeb* because I knew that it has an option for limiting a search to pages that have audio files (in the advanced search option). It was a matter of a few seconds to identify several websites that had the quote on them in an audio format that I could listen to.

I need addresses of plumbers in Richmond.

The first question that needs to be answered here is of course 'which Richmond?' since there are several of them. Even though I'm based in England, there are at least two different towns with that name, so it's rather important to get that clarified at the outset. A search on *Google* for *plumbers Richmond* doesn't help greatly, since the majority of results on the first couple of pages relate to plumbers in various American towns or cities that have that name. Even including the 'site:.uk' option in the search is not terribly helpful, since the results tend to link to sites that talk about plumbers, but which don't actually give me a list of them. Indeed, there are bound to be plumbers in Richmond that don't have websites, so my search is not going to be particularly comprehensive.

Consequently, it's time once again to stop using a general search engine, and start to use a more specialized one. An obvious choice here is a Yellow Pages site at **www.eyp.co.uk/** that prompts me for the correct Richmond (Yorkshire or Surrey) and then displays matching entries. Once again, the listing may not be comprehensive but, since I'm fairly confident that the Yellow Pages lists the vast majority of businesses (certainly of that type), I'm happy with the results I have obtained.

Using mailing lists

I need someone who is an expert on electronic copyright to speak on a course.

When looking for individuals it's necessary to start with some lateral thinking. We need to find who writes about the whole issue of copyright and more specifically electronic copyright. Good speakers often come from the field of academia, and they're quite likely to post messages on the subject that they're interested in. Therefore, a good starting point is to take a look at a few mailing lists to see who is saying what. *JISCmail* at **www.jiscmail.ac.uk/** provided me with a number of mailing lists where the subject of copyright was being discussed, most particularly a list called, unsurprisingly, 'Copyright'. A quick search through the archives for 'electronic copyright' identified a course that had taken place last year, with a list of speakers and the particular aspects of the subject they had covered. I then ran a quick search on

Amazon to see what they had published in the area and was then able to identify one or two people in particular who were well placed to fulfil the requirements.

Finding factual information using reference books

How many airports are there in the UK?

A friend wanted to know how many airports there are in the UK. I started by using *Google* with the term *airports* and the 'site:.uk' qualifier, but that gave me over half a million results, so I changed the search terms to include the phrase "*number of airports*". That was still too general a term, and the results included pages that, although they had a .uk qualifier in the URL, concerned airports in Russia and Australia. I decided to try the UK government website at **www.ukonline.gov.uk/** and I followed various links that eventually pointed me towards the British Airways Authority website at **www.baa. co.uk/**. This didn't help me since, not only could I not find any statistics quickly, I assumed that they might not cover private airfields (I could be wrong about this of course).

Since this approach clearly wasn't working I decided to try something different. I remembered that the CIA produced a useful world factbook, and it was only a matter of moments to locate it at **www odci.gov/cia/publications/ factbook/**, virtually flip to the section on the UK and scroll down to the section on transportation, to find not only the number of airports (470 in 2002) but also those with paved and unpaved runways.

Incorporating the internet into your overall information strategy

I've previously made the point, and I'm happy to do so again, that the internet isn't the only means of finding out information. I suspect that you have many other resources around you at the moment that you would be loathe to give up, even though there may be similar or even better resources available to you on the internet. In this section I spend some time looking at a selection of these resources to see if any of them are teetering on the edge of the abyss, to be replaced with the monitor screen and log-on page.

Newspapers

All the large daily newspapers are now available on the internet, and most of them do not charge for access, although a move towards this has started. Most newspapers do not, however, put their entire daily content onto their websites, although the *Daily Telegraph* puts up virtually all of each day's paper on the web, with omissions of articles that are not available for copyright reasons. If your information centre requires only current copies of newspapers, it makes a lot of sense to keep them, for a variety of reasons. Users need to come into the library or information centre to read them, which means that you have daily contact with them, and are in a better position to point out new resources to them, for example. However, if you keep back copies of newspapers, it may be worth while considering scrapping these and simply searching the online archives provided by the newspaper sites themselves. Not only will it be much easier, cheaper and simpler to find a particular article, it means that you will be able to save a lot of storage space, since even tabloid newspapers take up a lot of shelf space.

Encyclopaedias

The value of encyclopaedias lies not only in the data, but also in the information held in photographs, charts and other graphical material. There are now several very high-quality encyclopaedias available on the web, such as *Britannica* at **www.britannica.com/** and the sixth edition of the *Columbia Encyclopaedia* at **www.bartleby.com/65/**. They are an effective and fast way of answering reference queries. This, combined with the power to hyperlink to other documents and data in different formats, may tip the balance from a paper-based version to an electronic one.

Commercial databases

Many companies now offer access via the internet rather than by direct dial. Technically there is little difference between these methods of access; both require software, telephone lines and modems. The crucial difference may lie in the different interfaces available, as the web-based version is likely to be easier and more straightforward for the non-professional to use. If you connect to the internet via broadband you'll also find that you are able to retrieve data much more quickly. A small number of databases which are available commercially can also be searched for free via various websites – MEDLINE being a good example. However, although the data are either the same as in the commercial version (or even more current) the web interface may be of inferior quality. CD-ROM versions could still have value, particularly if the software provided allows users to interrogate both locally held and internet resources at the same time – especially useful for combining access to archives and current data. In previous editions of this book I have argued that, if a CD-ROM contains multimedia data it is worth keeping, since it takes much longer to download the same data from the internet, but with the increase of broadband access this is no longer the case. CD-ROM has proved crucial in bringing data to the end-user. I think its role is now moving much more into a mechanism for delivery and perhaps storage, but even this is under threat from DVD technology.

Yellow and White Pages

This is certainly one area in which I would suggest that the paper copy could be disposed of, though more so with the Yellow Pages than the White. Internet Yellow Pages allow for much broader searches, based on company name, location and subject, with links to appropriate websites. The paper-based version is a much inferior product and simply cannot match its electronic cousin for speed and ease of use. White Pages are a little more difficult, at least in the UK, since access to the body of information is carefully restricted. However, it may be worth doing some research to see if the online version provided by, for example, BT at **www.bt.com/directory-enquiries/ dq_home.jsp** is more suitable than a print version. I can certainly vouch for the fact that it's more current. I recently moved and had a new telephone installed; out of interest, I checked four days later and my new number was included in the online directory.

Company annual reports

It is becoming quite common for companies to put their annual reports onto their websites, making them searchable and adding hypertext links. However, it is unlikely that they will do the same with older versions so it may well be necessary to hold onto the archival versions, while managing to do quite well without the current versions.

Dictionaries

Dictionaries can be searched faster and more effectively online than in a paper format and may also suggest appropriate words (in the same way that a word processor's thesaurus might) if you mis-spell the word you are looking for. An online dictionary can overcome the age-old problem of trying to check the spelling of a word when you don't know how to spell it in the first place. Moreover, an increasing number of search engines also have a spell-check function built into them, reducing still further the need to be literate.

Specific reference tools

This of course depends entirely on what the reference tool is, and whether there is an online version of it available, though my default position would be that there probably is. One of the first things that I did when I got access to the internet in my home was throw away all my film- and movie-related reference books, since I knew that I could get a better service from the *Internet Movie Database*. For good measure I also threw away almanacs, a copy of the Bible and so on, simply because I knew that I could find the information that I needed more quickly and easily using the internet. Of course, having a broadband connection helps, since I'm always connected to the internet, so I don't have to waste time logging on to my service provider. If in doubt, it's worth checking such resources as *Refdesk* at **www.refdesk.com/**, the *Virtual Reference Desk* at **www.virtualref.com/** or the *MIT Virtual Reference Collection* at **http://libraries.mit.edu/research/virtualref.html**.

Official papers

Governments are increasingly using the internet to publish information such as papers, discussion documents, legal texts, and press releases. It is certainly worthwhile checking the websites of your own government and ministries in the hope that material you might otherwise have to purchase has been made available for free online.

These are just a few examples to get your mind ticking over to see what else you can perhaps look at very critically with a view to disposing of (or alternatively keeping close to your heart). I'm sure that it's not going to take you much time to draw up your own list, allowing you to save money – or, more likely, redirect it into the purchase of more computers!

Information professionals unite! You have nothing to lose but your books . . .

I am sure that many of you, reading the above points, will be reacting with horror at the idea of throwing away parts of your collections. However, I think this is part of the fundamental change that we are experiencing in the field of information work at the moment. For years we have had to keep collections of books and journals in case they proved useful. As they were produced in paper format, distribution of them was costly and took a long time. Even now, with the fast transport systems we have available, it is expensive to obtain a copy of a city newspaper if that city is 6000 or 12,000 miles away.

It was necessary to have stocks of information simply because it was so difficult to obtain. The internet is quickly changing our perception of knowledge, in terms of its value and its dissemination and storage. As long as I am able to obtain the information that I need within a couple of minutes by using the internet, I have no need to store the same data on a bookshelf. Indeed, in many cases the information that is available electronically is superior to the paper-based version. Not, of course, in terms of the facts themselves; the number of dead in the Civil War does not change however I get the information, but if I obtain those statistics electronically I may be able to import them into a spreadsheet and look at them in any number of different ways. Moreover, electronic contents pages and indexes can be searched more quickly and effectively than their paper counterparts. There will probably always be a need to have some information available in a printed format, and I don't dispute that. However, I firmly believe that we need to move to a situation in which we look at a paper-based product and ask whether we can get rid of it, rather than where to shelve it.

An understandable worry at this point is that if we get rid of all the books and the paper are we not also very successfully doing ourselves out of our jobs? If you have already incorporated electronic access to information in your own service you will understand that this fear is quite unfounded. However, if you are considering embarking on this particular route, I'll go into some detail on how 'less is more' in this instance.

... and an intranet to gain!

Intranets deserve an entire book to themselves, so it not really possible to do them justice here. However, they form an important part of the jigsaw of the emerging information centre, so I'll briefly explain what an intranet is before going on to talk about how it can be used.

An intranet is an organization's internal version of the internet. Information can be stored on a central server, or can be distributed on machines around the organization as required. Information can be made available in HTML format (which is the same format used to create web pages), and links can be made to data contained in other formats, such as word-processed documents, spreadsheets or CD-ROM-based databases. Consequently, the intranet forms an entire knowledge bank for the organization. Information such as telephone lists, draft papers, discussion documents, weblogs and so on can all be published for people to access as and when necessary. If you're frowning at this point and saying 'Yes, but isn't that just a description of the existing network we already have?' I should make the point that existing networks require users to access a wide variety of different tools in order to obtain the information which is required, while an intranet works by providing that access under the umbrella of the web browser.

Furthermore, companies such as *BRS* at **www.opentext.com/brs/** are providing systems to further integrate information into a single cohesive whole. Hypertext links between information increasingly enhance a system in which data can be 'mined', gathered from a variety of different sources and used to create new data sets. Of course, it is also possible to link to sites at other organizations, or to reach out to the rest of the internet (and vice versa) to create an extranet.

The role of the information professional is central to the creation of a successful intranet; after all, we are talking about arranging and creating access to information, albeit in an electronic rather than paper-based system. Who better to take on this role than those who spend their entire time doing just that in more traditional environments? The information professional is perfectly placed to work with technical staff, the marketing department, public relations and so on to structure the information, choose and implement software solutions, train staff and publish information for themselves.

Far from having no work to do, a distributed system such as an intranet means a much more exciting life for the information professional in the future. There are new technical skills to learn, such as HTML authoring, and a requirement to have a better understanding of how all these systems work together. Perhaps more importantly than that, the professional is drawn ever closer into a key position in the organization; a 'just in time' approach means that future information requirements must be anticipated, and resources identified, organized and published on the company intranet. Intelligent agents and news aggregators will be used to a greater extent, because it will be impossible to keep up to date with all the information being published, but someone will need to check the data for accuracy and authority. And the information professional must interrogate the intranet to find out what subjects people are interested in, what topics are of growing importance, and which are of decreasing value to the organization.

> **DID YOU KNOW?** >>
> HTML stands for Hyper Text Markup Language and is the code used to tell a browser how to display the content of a web page on your computer monitor.

Future developments

In 1990, very few people outside academia were aware of the internet; many of us still focused on optical technology as the best or the most innovative way of making information available. Within a decade the internet has taken over as more and more people use it, publish information on it and view it as a first line of publishing and researching. Every day new websites are created, new applications are launched and people discover new uses for it. Consequently, it is a brave person who would attempt to predict what will happen in this fast-changing environment. Perhaps the only certainty is that change will continue at a frightening speed. In the first two editions of this book I looked at some of the advances that I was expecting with the internet, and here I look back at those predictions to see if I was correct, or wildly inaccurate. I also make some new predictions.

The rise of intelligent agents

I have been predicting that these utilities will take off on a grand scale, and that they will become the preferred method of locating information for everything except the 'quick and dirty' search. This has not occurred in the way in which I was expecting, and while there are some good examples of intelligent agents (as discussed in Chapter 7) they have not become as popular as I was expecting. I believe that this is because the vast majority of searchers tend to prefer the 'quick and dirty' approach for one-off searches. Information professionals who need to do more in-depth searching are using intelligent agents, but they are also still making use of commercial databases for much of their ongoing work, obviating the need for an agent. However, news aggregators have recently started to play a much larger role in the automatic gathering of information and they are an excellent way of keeping up to date with what is happening in particular fields of interest. Indeed, Steven M. Cohen in his weblog at **www.librarystuff.net/** says:

> I *never* go to any website on my own anymore (if I'm not doing research, of course). All the information I want to read comes into my aggregator. And, if I happen to miss something, I can probably deal with it. I think that my feeds run the gamut of the type of information I want to read. And if I miss anything in the field of librarianship, someone else is bound to pick it up and post it to their weblog. I'll then read it in my aggregator.

While this is a slightly extreme example, I think it makes the point very well; why bother to do all of the work yourself, if you can get the information that you require to keep up to date from an aggregator? The first thing I do every morning when I start work is fire up *AmphetaDesk* and find out what is happening in the world. While you can argue that an aggregator isn't the same as an intelligent agent, I choose the news feeds that interest me and configure the utility to provide me with exactly the type of information that I want, when I want it.

The role of weblogs

I certainly had not anticipated how important these creations would become in such a short space of time. I have discussed them in Chapter 10. They are so very flexible and informative that I can see them becoming an even more integral part of not only the internet, but in the way in which information professionals share information and keep up to date.

Search engines

In both previous editions of the book, I made the point that search engines are still going to be the single most important way of finding information. At the time I wrote the second edition *Google* was still a relatively minor player in the field and deserved only a small passing mention. Since then of course it has gained its position as the most important search engine of all. While I don't see this changing in the near future *Yahoo!* has been buying competing search engines and will certainly challenge for the number one spot very seriously. Microsoft is also working on its own search engine and by 2006 I believe that we may see another seismic shift in the search engine most people use out of choice. Search engines are becoming more sophisticated as they add in new search features in order to appeal to wider and wider groups of users and this will continue apace.

Broadband technology

Access to the internet is becoming faster as more people are able to connect at speeds ten times faster than by dial-up. The price for this will decrease over time, until it becomes the accepted norm for obtaining access. As a result, the type of data made available will change, as larger files and multimedia formats become more important and readily accessible. This will be supported by ever-

increasing sophistication of computers and the integration of more functionality into the little grey box that sits on the desk. Access to radio stations is
already commonplace and I think it is likely that we'll see the availability of
television channels across the internet.

Mobile computing

My guess is that at the moment, you probably connect to the internet from
your computer at home or at work, and probably both. However, mobile
phones now also have the ability to connect directly into the internet, and the
PDA (Personal Digital Assistant) that I use allows me to connect to the
internet wherever I happen to be – in a café, on a train. Because access is much
slower, we will see a polarization of web-page design to allow access for
both mobile and broadband connectivity. With an increase in Wi-Fi access
(wireless fidelity) a user's physical location will become less and less important. If I'm training a group of people on a sunny day we often joke that it
would be nice to run the course in a local park and, while I don't actually see
this happening, technologically it will not be that difficult. Indeed, with
video conferencing there will be less need for everyone to gather together in
one place, and you will be able to go on a course without leaving your home.

Academic publishing

University presses will need to evolve rapidly as less is published in a paper
format and more electronically. Staff will need to reskill in order to take advantage of more flexible methods of publishing. Printing in traditional formats
fixes an article to its publication date, but in the future I see no reason why
articles should not become almost like discussion documents in their own right.
The peer review process will allow an author to change, alter and add to a document, then electronically republish it. The danger here is that no one will
keep archives of 'work in progress', but it will be necessary to establish systems that store earlier versions of articles in order to keep the historical
perspective. This is an area of flux which I expect to continue for several years
until authors and publishers come to some sort of agreement on the ways in
which the works can be published, amended and archived.

The proliferation of online journals

In both previous editions of this book I said that I expect to see the number of online journals increase, and this is certainly happening. I expect that very specific titles will be created electronically; they will cover very precise subject areas (especially in scientific and medical subject areas) which previously would not have happened because of the unprofitability of a print version.

Summary

In this chapter I've opened up some new avenues for you to explore for yourself. If you have gained anything at all from this chapter I hope that it is an appreciation of the variety of resources and possibilities that the internet provides for the information professional. We will continue to use and hone our skills and, although we may not be using information in a physical format in the future, the role of the information professional still has a long and exciting future.

URLs mentioned in this chapter

www.christmas.com/
www.tarot.com/
www.tarot-cards.com/
www.tarot-cards.com/tarot/
www.cheapflights.com/
www.john-lennon.com/
www.cat-behaviour.com/
www.craftycat.co.uk/
www.mi5.gov.uk/
http://dir.yahoo.com/News_and_Media/Newspapers/Web_Directories/
www.thepaperboy.com.au/welcome.html
www.imdb.com/
www.eyp.co.uk/
www.jiscmail.ac.uk/
www.ukonline.gov.uk/
www.baa.co.uk/
www.odci.gov/cia/publications/factbook/
www.britannica.com/
www.bartleby.com/65/
www.bt.com/directory-enquiries/dq_home.jsp
www.refdesk.com/

www.virtualref.com/
http://libraries.mit.edu/research/virtualref.html
www.opentext.com/brs/
www.librarystuff.net/

Chapter 15

Fifty tips and hints for better and quicker searching

Introduction

Understanding how search engines work, what intelligent agents are and the value of virtual libraries is only one of the skills that a good internet searcher requires. There are a number of other important points to be aware of to ensure that the time you spend on the internet is effective. This chapter is a miscellany of tips and tricks that I've picked up. Some of them may do nothing other than save you a few keystrokes, while others may save you a lot of time. All of them will make your internet life a little easier. Some of these tips are browser specific, and refer to *Microsoft Internet Explorer*; if you don't happen to use that particular browser it's quite likely that the one you do use will allow you to do the same thing, but you may need to hunt around a little bit.

Getting online and moving around the web

1 Get the fastest connection to the internet you can. Of course, in a work environment there may be very little you can do to influence this, but at home there is a lot you can do. If you use a dial-up connection to the internet, make sure that you're using the fastest modem available, and that means a 56K modem. You can find out more about your modem by clicking on Start>Control Panel>Phone and modem. If you have anything less than a 56K modem, consider buying one. They are not expensive and you will recoup the cost in reduced connection

charges. Ideally, move to a broadband or ADSL connection. These are becoming more and more popular; your internet service provider should be able to offer you various packages. In order for it to work properly you will need to have your telephone connection altered and you will need a new modem, which you can either buy yourself or get your service provider to supply for you. A good site to visit for more information is **www.dslforum.org/**; if you're based in the UK, it's worth going to **www.adsl2go.co.uk/** for further advice. While it will cost more than a standard dial-up connection it has the advantage that you can browse the internet more quickly *and* you can use your telephone line for voice calls while you are connected to the internet.

2   Choose when it's best to search. If like me, you spend a lot of time searching American sites you'll find that it is best to search them either in the morning or later in the evening. During the afternoon or early evening you may notice that it takes slightly longer to search, because the Americans are logging on to get their mail and news. Of course, if you're an American user you can safely ignore this advice and instead try using UK sites during your afternoon, since we will all have gone home for the day! You can check to see how busy the internet is by visiting the *Internet Traffic Report* website at **www.internettrafficreport.com/ main.htm**.

3   If you're searching for sites in your own country try to do it at odd hours. If you're awake it's a fair bet that everyone else in your country will be as well, with many of them trying to visit the same sites that you are. The more that you can do first thing in the morning or last thing at night, the quicker your access will be.

Finding web pages

4   The easiest way to find a web page without using a search engine is to guess the URL of the site. It's not infallible, but it's worth a try.

5   Become familiar with the major domain identifiers such as .com, .co.uk, .org and country codes. Organizations will attempt to register memorable combinations of names and identifiers, so if you remembered a website address incorrectly it may be because it is a .org site, rather than a .com site.

6   Shorten the URL. We have all experienced this situation, when we visit a page and we get an error message. This may be because the page address has changed, so simply cut a slice off the end of the address to

the previous forward slash. Eventually you will get to a page that does load, and that may give you some clues as to the location of the page you actually want. Alternatively, just go to the home page and use 'Search this Site' options to find your missing information.

7 If you have problems locating the site, and you are sure that it is on the internet, it may simply be because that site is down for some reason. It's not necessarily because you've typed in the address incorrectly. Try it a second time and, if that still doesn't work, leave it for an hour or so, then try again. If it still fails there may be a serious problem with the site or you might actually have mistyped the URL. Check and try again, or use a site such as *Easyspace* at **www.easyspace.com/** to check that the site still exists.

8 Choose a new home page. When you install a browser it will default to the home page of the company that created it, or perhaps the company that sold you your computer (if you've just bought a new one and the browser comes pre-installed). You'll probably find that this is less than helpful, just irritating. You can change the default start-up (or home) page to one that is more suitable for you – perhaps your favourite search engine. To do this, visit Tools>Internet options>Home Page. Then type in the new home page, or use whatever default page you happen to be on.

9 Write your own home page. If you spend any time at all using the internet, there will be some sites that you return to on a regular basis – they may be search engine sites, personal pages, pages about various hobbies. There is no reason why you shouldn't create your own personal home page; if you've had any experience of using HTML you will be able to create your own page. Once you have done this you can tell your browser to look locally for your created home page using the method described above. It's a quick, simple and easy way of moving yourself around the web with the minimum of effort. If you're not very good at writing HTML, or you don't have the time, I have created a search page on my site which you can download and use yourself – feel free to edit it as appropriate. You can find the source code in Appendix 1, and the version on the web at **www.philb.com/handbookengines.htm**.

10 If you wish to move back several pages, rather than just one, don't waste time clicking on the Back button; simply click and hold the small half diamond to the right of it. That will display your history in the current session and you can jump back to the page you wish to go to.

11   If you've recently visited a web page, and want to return to it, it's always worth trying the History utility in *Internet Explorer*. Clicking on the 'History' icon will allow you to choose a particular day within the last month (depending on how many days' worth of history your browser supports) and the sites that you have visited will be arranged and displayed by day and, within that, alphabetically by site name.

Moving around a web page

12   Once a page has loaded on the screen you may have to spend some time searching through it to find the keyword that you're looking for. If you have installed a search engine toolbar there should be an option allowing you to highlight your search terms on the page. Failing that, use Ctrl + F to bring up a dialogue box to allow you to type in your keyword, and that will then take you to the first and subsequent occurrences of it.

13   Remember to use your 'page up' and 'page down' keys or, if necessary, scroll horizontally across the page. It's possible that the information you are seeking is on the page, but not on the screen in front of you. As well as using these keys you can use the spacebar to move down one screen at a time, or shift and spacebar together to move back up.

14   There may be times when you want to display more of the web page on the screen than you are able to. *Internet Explorer* allows you to display more of the page with the F11 function key; if you use it, the only part of the browser remaining on the screen is a small row of icons – the rest of the screen is used to display the web page.

15   It's not always obvious what is or is not a link. Sometimes links are not underlined, or they may simply be a graphical image that points to another page. In this instance, 'try clicking': anywhere and everywhere to see if you get taken to another page. It's irritating, but sometimes it's the best (or only) approach!

Saving and printing pages

16   Once you have viewed the page on your screen you may wish to save it permanently to disk in order to view again at a later date. The easiest method is to choose 'File' and then 'Save As'. *Internet Explorer* will then prompt you to choose a location, and the default name will be taken from the title element of the page itself, though obviously you can change this if you wish. The page can be saved as a complete page, as

an archive page, a web page (with the HTML intact) or simply as a text file. If for some reason you wish to edit the page, it makes sense to save it as a web page, but if it's long and you're just interested in the text, save as a text file. Please remember that, unless you wrote the page, the copyright belongs to someone else, and you should check with the author before using it.

17 If you wish to save a graphic, position your cursor over the image and right-click. You will then be prompted with a window to print the graphic, save it to disk, make it your Windows background, set it as a desktop item or e-mail it to someone else. Once again, remember copyright!

18 Alternatively you may wish to print the page. It should print out much the same as it appears on the screen, though you may find one or two differences in formatting, particularly if the web page scrolls off the side of the screen. You can check this before printing by choosing File>Print Preview. The main problem will occur if the page does scroll off the right-hand side of the screen. There are two possible solutions to this problem. First, choose to print the page in landscape mode from the 'Page Setup' option. Alternatively, you may find that you can reduce the size of the font by holding down your control key at the same time as you use the mouse wheel – you'll see the font size increase or decrease as you do this. Decrease the font size and check 'Print Preview' again. The page will now fit onto the paper and you can print quite happily.

19 Another way to reduce the size of text (or to increase it) is to go to View>Text Size and choose from smallest to largest.

20 If this still doesn't work, you could simply highlight the text you require, copy and then paste it into a word processor and save it, though you will lose the page formatting this way.

21 Another printing tip. Not every web author types out the URLs hyperlinked on a page and that can be a nuisance when you print the page. When you go to print, click on the 'Options' tab, and choose to also print a table of links, or indeed all the linked pages, though be careful with this last one – you may get through a lot of paper!

22 If you print a lot of pages you may be concerned about the amount of ink that you are using. You can disable the printing of background images by going to Tools>Internet Options>Advanced>Printing and uncheck 'Print background colors and images'.

Faster loading of pages

23   If you find a page is taking a long time to load, it's almost certainly because it is graphic intensive. An easy solution is to turn off the option to automatically load images. Choose Tools>Internet Options>Advanced> Multimedia and uncheck 'Show pictures'. If you do need to see an image, simply reverse the process and reload the page.

24   Understand your browser's cache. When your browser visits a page, it copies the information (both text and graphics) onto a temporary storage area on your own computer. When you view a page that you have recently looked at the browser is intelligent enough to retrieve it from cache, rather than getting the entire thing again from scratch. This is why you generally find that pages you have recently viewed appear on your screen virtually instantaneously. Your browser should provide you with an option of increasing the hard disk space available to temporarily store this data. This can be changed by going to Tools>Internet Options>General>Temporary Internet Files>Settings and moving the bar to the right. Experiment with this until you're happy with the speed of reloading pages, though if you're tight on space on your hard disk, this may not work well; if you have a technical person available, you may wish to seek their advice.

> **DID YOU KNOW?** >>
> The Vatican website is powered by three host computers named after archangels Raphael, Michael and Gabriel, and is run by nuns (www.timesonline.co.uk/article/ 0,,3-538079,00.html).

25   You may wish to view your cache, particularly if you've recently visited a website, but simply cannot remember which one. It's possible to view the cache by following the previous steps and choosing 'view files' but this doesn't provide a very helpful listing. There are various utilities which allow you to view the cache on your machine, such as *Cache View* available from **www. brothersoft.com/Internet_Browsing_Tools_Cache_View_ 16035.html**. This is a commercial product, but you may be able to find free utilities that do the job just as well.

26   If a page is taking a long time to load, click on the 'Stop' and 'Refresh' icons. The chances are that much of the page has already downloaded onto your computer and this will kick the browser back into activity if it has stalled loading the rest of the page.

Using bookmarks

27   I'm sure that you use the 'Favorites' option to bookmark pages that you wish to return to. If you haven't, simply make sure that you are on the page that you wish to keep a note of, and click on the pull-down menu

option 'Favorites'. You can then add the page to the list; just before you do, make sure that the title of the page is something that is meaningful. If the author of the page has done a good job, this should happen, but sometimes a page title may be something such as 'Our home page' or even 'Blank'. Since the Favorites option uses the title element to set the name of the bookmark this is not going to be much help to you a week or so later. If the name isn't meaningful, simply overwrite it with something that is.

28 Give serious thought to how to arrange your bookmarks. You can use the 'Organize Favorites' option to add folders, change the name of folders, or add folders under others. When you save a favorite, make sure that you save it to the correct folder in the first instance, rather than simply appending it to an ever-increasing list.

29 Use a favorites management utility if you find it really is too much of a nuisance to sort your lists into order. There are several utilities that will do this for you, both commercial and free, and a good listing of them can be found in the *Google Directory* at **http://directory.google. com/Top/Computers/Software/Internet/Clients/WWW/ Utilities/Bookmark_Managers/ ?il=1**.

30 Add searches to your list of favorites. If you run various searches on a regular basis, it can be annoying to type them every single time. Once you have run your search once, and you're happy with the syntax and the results that you are getting, add the first page of results to your favorites collection. This will not add that specific page; it will add the search that you ran. When you need to run the search again, simply click on the appropriate favorite, and the search will be rerun for you, with an updated set of results.

31 Instead of adding an often visited page to a list of favorites, you can add it to the link bar instead. This is a bar in *Internet Explorer* where you can store often visited pages. It's slightly quicker to click on a link in this bar than to go up to the 'Favorites' menu and scroll down looking for the page you want. Indeed, there is no reason why you shouldn't actually put a folder into the 'Links' option, so you have slightly quicker access to those pages you visit frequently.

32 If you have problems viewing the text on a page, because the font colour and background colours clash, an easy remedy is to highlight the page by pressing Ctrl+A. This will highlight the entire page, making it much easier to read the text.

33 The previous tip works on a one-off basis, but if you have to do it on a

regular basis, or you need to keep changing the font size, a more permanent measure is to select Tools>Internet Options>General> Accessibility and check 'Ignore font sizes' and/or 'Ignore colors specified on web pages'.

34 Keep up to date with useful sites. I expect that you have some favourite sites that you visit on a regular basis, just to see if anything has been updated since you were there last. It can be a nuisance if you find that the page hasn't changed; you've just wasted a few moments of your valuable time. There are several utilities available that can check web pages for you on a regular basis; they inform you via e-mail once the page changes. At that point you can go back and visit it, and until you get that e-mail you can ignore the page since you know it's not changed. Some of these utilities are free, while others are commercial in nature. Some examples are *WatchThatPage* at **www.watchthatpage. com/**, *Website-Watcher* at **www.aignes.com/** or *InfoMinder* at **www.infominder.com/ webminder/index.jsp**.

Getting the most out of your browser

35 Open two or more copies of the browser. There may be times when you want to have two web pages open at the same time, if you want to check information or compare statistics for example. It can be a nuisance to keep flicking backwards and forwards in your browser, reloading the page each time. Instead of doing that, simply open a second, third or fourth copy of the browser and keep them open at different pages. This can be done very simply by clicking on File>New>Window and going to the page you wish. All copies of the browser will work independently of each other and you can flick backwards and forwards as you need.

36 Use your mouse for quicker access. If you get tired of constantly clicking on back buttons or using pull-down menus, your mouse can automate much of that work. Simply click the right mouse button while you're on a web page and you will have options (as appropriate) to go back or forward a page, create shortcuts or add to Favorites, or view the source code of the page, for example.

37 Alternatively, use keyboard shortcuts, and *Internet Explorer* provides you with a variety of them. Ctrl and enter will add the http:// and .com to a URL in the address bar – put philb into the address bar and then hit both keys – you'll see what I mean:

- Ctrl+N opens a new window
- Ctrl+F performs a find on a page
- Ctrl+P prints
- Ctrl+E searches
- Ctrl+I displays your list of favourites
- Ctrl+H opens the history window
- Ctrl+B opens the Bookmarks or Favorites window
- Alt+D jumps to the address bar.

38 Use the Home key on your keyboard to go directly to the beginning of a page, or End to go to the bottom of it.

39 Use your browser to autocomplete for you. Rather than type the same address in over and over again, or fill in forms with the same information, this process can be automated. Go to Tools>Internet Options> Content>AutoComplete and check 'Web addresses' if you want the browser to complete web addresses, forms, or user names and passwords. Please note that it's probably not a good idea to do the latter on public machines, since that may give someone easy access to your own personal data.

40 If pop-ups are driving you mad you can block them by using the *Google* toolbar or by installing a pop-up killer. There are plenty of these, all doing the same job; the best way of finding them is to do a search for pop-up killer and make your choice from the dozens you'll find.

41 If you are viewing a site that has frames and, for whatever reason, you wish to open up the frame in a new window, simply ensure that your cursor is in the frame you wish to open and right-click with your mouse. You will then be offered the opportunity of opening the frame in a new window.

42 If you are concerned about providing details about yourself, such as an e-mail address, simply create a throwaway account at one of the free e-mail services such as *Hotmail* at **www.hotmail.com/** or *Talk21* at **www.talk21. com/**. Once you're happy with the service provided, or you're sure that the e-mail address isn't going to receive spam you could resubscribe with your 'real' address and close the subscription to the throwaway account.

43 If you have problems remembering lots of different passwords for websites, a useful trick is to use the first letters from a phrase that you'll remember, and then add in a character or two of the site that you're visiting. For example, if your address is 5 High Street, your password could be ila5HS – short for 'I live at 5 High Street'; for a *Hotmail*

account this could be amended to ila5HShm (I live at 5 High Street Hotmail). Since you will be using a combination of letters, numbers and lower and upper case it would be very hard for someone to guess the password you use, but quite easy for you to remember.

44　It can quite often be difficult to remember which websites you've visited and why they're useful. You can, of course, add them to your list of Favorites, and edit the title to add in a little annotation yourself, but this precludes longer notes. A very easy way to keep a note is to create your own weblog using something like *Blogger* at **www.blogger.com/** in conjunction with the *Google* toolbar. This means that when you find a useful page you can simply click on the *Blogger* link and create an entry into your weblog that you can annotate as you desire. While most blogs are designed for others to read you can have a private blog that only you can access, and it's a quick and easy way to keep notes on good sites.

45　If you're really stuck on finding an answer to a query, you might try using the *Google Answers* facility, which allows you to post a query and the amount of money that you're prepared to pay in order to have the question answered, for as little as $2.50. You can explore this facility in depth at **http://answers. google.com/answers/**.

46　If you are out and about and you have a mobile phone or a personal digital assistant you can quickly and easily connect to a version of *Google* designed to be used for this purpose. So, wherever you are, and whatever you're doing, you can get answers to those thorny questions that occur to you. More information on this service is available at **www.google.com/options/wireless.html**.

47　If you find some information in another language that you think might give you the answer to your question, you can always have it translated into a different language using the *AltaVista Babel Fish* utility at **http://world.altavista. com/**. Be aware that the translation is computer generated so will not be perfect. It should, however, be accurate enough to give you the information you need.

48　Don't forget that there are a great many country- or region-specific search engines that search for information in or about one country. In fact there are in excess of 1500 of these; a good listing can be found on my own website at **www.philb.com/countryse.htm**.

49　If you have particular searches that you run on a regular basis at *Google* you might want to try out the *Google Alert* service at **www.googlealert.com/**. This is not provided by the search engine, but by an individual, and it's free, so has to be worth trying.

50   Invest in a stopwatch or alarm clock. It's all too easy to spend way too long searching for the information that you need, particularly if you're the kind of person who gets waylaid by interesting sites that don't actually have anything to do with answering your query! Buy a cheap alarm clock and set it for ten minutes, or perhaps 20 for a really difficult enquiry. Knowing that it is going to go off and frighten anyone close to you may be all that you need to keep you on track.

URLs mentioned in this chapter

www.dslforum.org/

www.adsl2go.co.uk/

www.internettrafficreport.com/main.htm

www.easyspace.com/

www.philb.com/handbookengines.htm

www.brothersoft.com/Internet_Browsing_Tools_Cache_View_16035.
html

http://directory.google.com/Top/Computers/Software/Internet/Clients/
WWW/Utilities/Bookmark_Managers/?il=1

www.watchthatpage.com/

www.aignes.com/

www.infominder.com/webminder/index.jsp

www.hotmail.com/

www.talk21.com/

www.blogger.com/

http://answers.google.com/answers/

www.google.com/options/wireless.html

http://world.altavista.com/

www.philb.com/countryse.htm

www.googlealert.com/

Chapter 16

Utilities to help the advanced searcher

Introduction

While the internet is really all about people talking to other people we must not forget the obvious – we're using computers. There is a tremendous range of utilities and packages to make our lives much easier when it comes to using our computers and, specifically, searching. This chapter covers some of these utilities; what they are, how you can configure them and what you can use them for. It's not a comprehensive listing – that would be impossible – but it will give you some clear ideas on what utilities are available, and where you can get them. Many of these utilities are free of charge or, if they are commercial products, are not terribly expensive, and should be well within the budget of most libraries and individuals. I have not given prices, since these are always subject to change, and pricing structures may differ if you are purchasing on behalf of an organization or buying a copy for your own use – check with the producer of the product for the current price. I refer to the most recent versions of the software, but please remember that such utilities are often updated on a very regular basis, so it's always worth checking to see if there is a more recent version available. Also, as is the way with these things, some of them may no longer be available, or the producer may not support them any more. Finally, if you are in any doubt about using them, or installing them onto your computer, it's always worth seeking the advice of a technical support

> **DID YOU KNOW?** »
> The proposed patron saint of the internet is Isidore of Seville. There's also a prayer you can use prior to using the internet (www.catholic.org/saints/isidore. shtml).

colleague or friend, and remember to back up your system before you install anything, just to be on the safe side.

Browsers

The major browser is of course Microsoft's *Internet Explorer*; the browser finally 'won the war' with *Netscape*. It's almost certain that it's the browser that you use, if not by choice but because it's the one that's been installed on your machine by your technical department, or was preinstalled by the company you purchased your computer from. I've already referred to a lot of the things that you can do with *Internet Explorer* in Chapter 15, so I won't repeat myself here. However, it's always worth remembering that *Internet Explorer* isn't your only option – there are other browsers available to you. In this section I mention some of them for your consideration, although I have to say that I have succumbed to the Microsoft malaise and tend to use *Internet Explorer* virtually all of the time.

DID YOU KNOW? ≫

The very first browser was in actual fact *The Reading Wheel*, by Agostina Ramelli in 1588 (www.qbc.clic.net/Dmephisto/bush/bush.html).

Netscape 7.1

Netscape was the 'browser of choice' for many years, and is still widely available. You can download a copy of the current version at **http://channels. netscape.com/ns/browsers/download.jsp**. It's worth remembering that, even if you tend to use *Internet Explorer*, there is no good technical reason why you shouldn't have this one loaded on your machine as well. In fact, I'd go so far as to say that it is worth having *Netscape* as a backup, since I still sometimes find pages that load better with *Netscape* than with *Internet Explorer*. This is because some authors have coded their pages with HTML (Hyper Text Markup Language) tags that *Netscape* can recognize and understand, but other browsers will not understand or execute correctly.

Most of the facilities you get with *Netscape* are exactly the same as those you'll find with *Explorer*, even down to the wording and keystrokes – only the icons look different. However, a few features are worth mentioning. *Netscape* kills 'pop-up' windows that are the bane of many searchers' lives. Additional controls allow you to accept pop-ups from certain web pages that use the facility to provide you with context-sensitive help. *Netscape* also uses 'tabbed browsing', a feature that allows you to open several web pages at once and flick quickly and easily between them. Of course, it's possible to do this by simply opening another version of the browser, but this is a simple, more elegant method of doing the same thing. *Netscape* also allows you to download several files at the same time, pause and then resume your downloads if you need to use your telephone connection to make a phone call; though, to be fair, if you're using a broadband connection you should be able to do that anyway. There is also a download manager so you can keep an eye on the status of the download, how much of the file has been downloaded and how long it should take to complete. Complete web pages can be downloaded for later viewing without a connection: this can be achieved with one single action, downloading both text and images without separate operations. It is also possible to search from within a web page. You can simply start a new search by selecting the search term with your mouse, right-click and choose the 'Web search' option, thus allowing faster and easier searching. Finally, *Netscape* has an integral e-mail option, with a free account with up to 5MB of space to store your messages. For more details on exactly what you can do with the browser you should visit **http://channels.netscape.com/ns/browsers/browsing.jsp**.

Opera

Opera has been available for almost ten years. You can learn more about *Opera*, or download a copy from the website at **www.opera.com/**. The main selling points with the browser ('selling' being the keyword here, since it is a commercial product) are that it is a smaller program, so is useful if you are short on hard disk space, and it is very fast. *Opera* has all the facilities you would expect a browser to have but also has other features worth mentioning. It provides one-click access to password-protected sites that you have registered with. You can make notes about a particular site using the notes feature to e-mail to a colleague or to simply keep for yourself for later reference. The browser also uses a 'fast forward' approach, by trying to anticipate which page you might be going to visit next, resulting in faster browsing. *Opera* supports the use of keyboard shortcuts, which means that it is easier for people to navigate if they have problems using a mouse. It has a very useful search facility from the address bar and you can also put a link directly into a major search engine without having to actually visit that engine's website. *Opera* can also remember exactly where you were when you were searching – which pages you had open for example – between sessions. This is obviously useful if you have to close the browser down for some reason. The browser also offers functions such as multimedia and plug in support, zoom, toolbars, language customization, a news client and command line options. More details on these and the other features that *Opera* offers can be found at **www.opera.com/features/**.

Firebird 0.7

This is a new browser with a website at **www.mozilla.org/products/ firebird/**. It supports tabbed browsing, pop-up blocking, integrated search, efficient navigation and download support. For more information on all of these aspects of the browser, refer to the very comprehensive Frequently Asked Questions list at **http://texturizer.net/firebird/faq.html**.

More browsers

An excellent site that provides a much more comprehensive listing, with access to other browsers or previous versions is the *Browser News* website at **www. upsdell. com/BrowserNews/**.

Offline browsers

An offline browser allows you to specify a particular site that you want to browse; it goes online and collects the pages for you, downloads them to your hard disk, ensures that all the links work locally, and logs off. You can then view the site offline at your leisure, saving connection charges. Utilities such as these can be very useful if you need to spend a lot of time looking at a large site, want to look at a site while you're on the move (having stored the site onto a laptop), or if you want to run a demonstration without access to a live internet connection.

A good collection of these can be found at *Download.com* at **http:// download.com.com/3150-2377-0.html**. Features that you can expect on any of these utilities include the option of downloading multiple sites at once, support for multimedia formats, flash and java scripting and export to CD. They have the ability to restart a download if you have to close your connection for whatever reason, filter out unnecessary content, or only download pages that have changed since the last time you ran the operation. Most offline browsers are commercial products (though reasonably priced), though they all have an option for trying them out before you buy them, usually limiting you to downloading a small number of pages from a limited number of sites.

Bookmark utilities

As we have already seen, the bookmarks or favorites that can be created with a browser are very useful indeed and, if used correctly, can become your own index to the internet. If you upgrade to a new version of the same browser the installation process is intelligent enough to copy across your existing bookmarks. If you move from one browser to another, whichever browser you move to should also be intelligent enough to provide you with a method of importing your bookmarks from the old browser, though it's always worth checking this in advance. If in any doubt, don't forget that you can run two or more browsers in tandem on the same machine (even to the extent of having both open at the same time looking at the same page) without problems.

If, like me, you're not quite as good at keeping your favorites in order, and you have a huge listing of them in no sensible order, there are utilities that can take care of this process for you. An excellent listing of bookmark managers is at the *E-mail Addresses* website at **www.e-mailaddresses.com/e-mail_bookmarks.htm**; it lists almost 20 different utilities. As you would expect, most of these do exactly the same sort of job. It's possible to easily categorize and manage bookmarks into folders and selectively share them with others using, for example, *Bestlinx* from **www.bestlinx.com/bestlinx20/**. *Bookmax* at **www.bookmax.net/** keeps a list of statistics regarding your bookmarks so you can see which ones you use the most and which ones are actually never used again (which is probably most of them). The *DailyRoutine* utility allows you to set up a small routine of sites that you visit on a daily basis, making it much easier to quickly jump from one site to another; particularly useful if you have certain sites you check on a daily basis for news and current events.

A resource that I use on a regular basis is *Backflip* at **www. backflip. com/login.ihtml**. This allows you to import your bookmarks to your own private web space on its site with the use of a simple icon that you can place into your browser links bar. The value of this is that you have immediate access to all of your bookmarks wherever you are – it's not dependent on you sitting at your own machine. This is particularly useful if you move around a lot and you want to go to a favourite site and cannot remember or find a particular address. Simply visit the *Backflip* site, log in and you have a complete listing of them. It's also possible to share these with friends or colleagues to create a group listing of bookmarks. It's an excellent way of setting up a collection of important websites that you can alert colleagues to, particularly if you want to keep them informed and up to date on new sites. You can see my page in Figure 16.1.

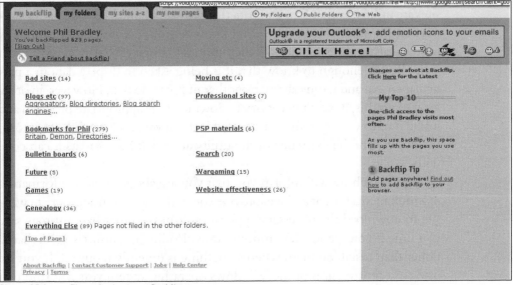

Figure 16.1   The author's page at *Backflip*

Cache viewers

As we have already seen, browsers store recently visited pages in a cache on your local hard drive. They can then be quickly retrieved by the browser and displayed on the screen; the browser does not need to go back to the website to obtain the same data again. The cache is useful because it allows you to view recently visited pages without the necessity of being online, and can also be used to display pages for you when you have forgotten exactly which site you originally retrieved them from. *Internet Explorer* in offline mode will allow you to view pages from the 'History' window, loading them from cache if they are available. A cache viewer is different from an offline browser, since it can only show you pages that you have actually visited, rather than pages you have told it to collect. A listing of various cache viewers can be found at the *Tucows* website at **www.tucows.com/cache95_default.html**. Once again, most of these products are commercial in nature.

Multimedia applications

The web is now a riot of still images, sound files, video and full multimedia. Browsers are able to cope with some of these media without a problem – they can all display images, for example. However, an increasing number of websites are utilizing other forms of data that browsers cannot provide native support for (in other words, they don't know what to do with them), and they need to call on the assistance of other utilities to display the data. The browser is intelligent enough to know that it is being asked to display data in a particular format and it can call upon another utility to do that. However, in order for it to do this, it is first necessary to download the appropriate program and install it onto your system – part of that installation process will be to inform the browser of the existence of the utility and what file formats it can cope with.

A good website will inform you that you are about to view information in a multimedia format and will provide you with a link to an appropriate website to download the necessary application. On the other hand, it may save you time if you spend a few minutes downloading the utilities beforehand, rather than installing them when something is urgently required. If you are using a recent version of the Windows operating system you will find that Windows Media Player is already installed, and this is capable of playing most media formats for you without any work on your part. However, this isn't always the case, so the following is a short listing of some of the most common multimedia applications that you will require in the not too distant future.

RealOne Player

RealOne Player (formerly *RealPlayer*) at **http://uk.real.com/?&src=ZG.uk. idx.rp_ann_loprice.hd.def** is a well known utility that includes an all-purpose media player, allowing users to watch videos and streaming media (media that is transmitted to your computer and played while it is downloading, rather than waiting until the file has downloaded and then played), listen to music or radio stations and so on. *RealOne* supports a wide variety of formats, and can be used to open image files, sound files and video files. The basic player is available free of charge, but users must pay to access advanced features (such as CD burning). The utility is extremely useful due to its flexibility, ease of use and integration into web pages. However, many libraries have not installed it, particularly if they offer public access to machines, because of bandwidth considerations – one user downloading a large file (some multimedia files are extremely large) may slow down overall access to everyone on a network.

QuickTime

This utility is available from **www.apple.com/quicktime/**, and more details on it can be found at **www.apple.com/quicktime/whyqt/**. It is designed to support a wide variety of media files – graphics, sound, video, text and music being a few examples. It was first produced in the early 1990s as a Macintosh program, but is now just as widely used in a Windows-based environment. It is a very popular product and, according to its website, is downloaded 300,000 times a day; a great many websites produce multimedia content in a format designed to be used by *QuickTime*. As you might expect, free and commercial versions are available.

Other multimedia utilities

There are hundreds of different multimedia utilities, and in order to them justice it would require a book twice the size of this one. If you are interested in the subject of multimedia utilities a very good place to start your explorations is the *Tucows* multimedia section at **www.tucows.com/top_section_1570.html.**

Anti-virus protection

Strictly speaking, this has little to do with searching the internet, but it is such an important area for any user that I included a short section here. Sensible users will always be alert to the danger of downloading a file containing a virus, but will not become so completely paranoid that they stop using the internet completely. It is certainly possible to download a virus from a website, usually embedded inside another program, but in my experience it's highly unlikely unless you're downloading cracked, illegal software, in which case you deserve whatever you get! The greatest friend of a virus is anonymity, and many are passed from machine to machine by individuals using floppy disks to transfer files without checking either the files or floppy disk first. This is highly unlikely to happen on the internet, because you are making a specific choice to copy a file and will in all probability remember where you got it from.

DID YOU KNOW? >>
The 'Love Letter' virus cost over US$2 billion in damages worldwide (www.computeruser.com/news/00/05/09/news3.html).

If it later transpires that the file contained a virus it shouldn't be too difficult to track it back to the source. Furthermore, any reputable site regularly checks that the files it makes available do not contain a virus of any sort.

Much more likely is a virus contained as an attachment to an e-mail. For example, a Word document may contain a macro virus designed to harm your system, and many (indeed the majority) of viruses transmit themselves from machine to machine by piggybacking onto an e-mail, or by going through an e-mail address book and sending copies of themselves to all your contacts. If you receive any such attachment from someone you do not know, or indeed that you do, and you're not sure about it, or the attachment has not been referred to in the body of the e-mail, be careful. I suggest that before you open the attachment you write back to the sender and ask who they are, why they've sent you the file and what's in it. Alternatively, just delete it.

It is sensible to back up your hard disk on a regular basis, depending on how valuable your information is. Suggestions range from once a day to once a week, but you should seek the advice of your technical support department. It is also sensible to have effective virus protection software on your machine, since this will catch the majority of viruses that may try to attack your system. However, there are always news stories about the latest virus which spreads 'like wildfire' around the internet. Until a virus checker is aware that something is a virus, and can combat it, the virus can very easily pass into your system. This means that you also need to keep your virus protection software up to date; there's no point in having old or out-of-date software on your system because you really won't be protected. I've given four examples of anti-virus software below, but there are a great many other products. Most of them are commercial products, but they are reasonably priced; and by not buying one you may save money in the short term, but it's going to cost a lot more in terms of your time when (and it will be when, not if) you end up with a ruined machine!

Norton AntiVirus

The *Norton suite* is one of the best known packages, used by over 15 million people worldwide. It can be found at **www.symantec.co.uk/region/uk/product/navbrochure/**. The software provides comprehensive anti-virus support at every possible entry point and subscribers are automatically prompted to update their protection at regular intervals.

Dr Solomon

Dr Solomon provides a wide number of different virus protection packages for work, groupware, servers, home use and so on. Once again, subscribers get updates to their software directly from the internet. More details can be obtained from **www.drsolomon.com/**.

McAfee ViruScan

This is a powerful and well known software package from **www.mcafee. com**/. It includes background and on-demand scanning. As you would expect, updates are available directly from the site.

Housecall

This is a rather different product, since it is a free, web-based utility that checks your machine for viruses while you are online. Although the service is free it may be quite slow, leading to increased telephone charges if you pay for internet access and slow behaviour from your computer while it is doing its job. However, it's an interesting alternative to the other options. You can discover more at **http://housecall.anti-virus.com/**.

Spyware

While not being exactly a virus, this is a particularly nasty form of software that can slow up your system (and as a result your searching) because it spends time and computing power sending details on what you are doing to a third party. It can often be downloaded and installed without your knowledge when you are installing a perfectly legitimate package; information on it will be buried deep in the terms and conditions that you agree to. Consequently, although it's not harming your computer in the same way that a virus does, it's not something you want to have on your system. Luckily there are various software packages that you can use to identify and then delete it from your system.

Ad Aware

Various versions of this software are available, the free version being *Ad Aware Standard*, available from **www.lavasoftusa.com/**. The package is quick to download; it resides on your system, and you can run it whenever you wish to – I usually do so once every month. It checks your computer memory and hard disk and seeks out any spy software and alerts you to it, giving you the option to delete it from your system.

Spybot Search and Destroy

This is a similar package to *Ad Aware* that can be downloaded from

www.safer-networking.org/index.php?page=download. It is free, though you are encouraged to make a donation.

Other spyware utilities

There are almost as many of these utilities as there are spyware packages in the first place. If you don't like either of the two that I have mentioned, you might like to check out a comprehensive listing from *Spychecker* at **www.spy-checker.com/software/antispy.html**, though the majority of products listed are commercial in nature, with free trials.

Firewalls

There is one last internet nasty worth mentioning, and that is a Trojan. As the name suggests, this is a very specific type of virus which, if downloaded, or sent to you in an e-mail, will pass information on your computer back to the person who originated the virus. Your computer then acts as a server, allowing that person access to your computer, to steal passwords, run programs, launch attacks on other machines and worse. A firewall can help prevent this, because it can alert you to any programs trying to access the internet without your knowledge, and can also help block access to your machine from anyone else on the internet. If your computer uses Windows XP it has a built-in firewall that you can activate; if you prefer, you can purchase or use external utilities that do the same job. One of the best known is *ZoneAlarm* which can be obtained from **www.zonelabs.com/store/content/home.jsp**.

Toolbars

I discussed the *Google* toolbar extensively in Chapter 3 but, to save you the time and trouble of rereading that section, a toolbar is a small utility that you can download from a search engine. When you install it, the toolbar will add itself to the browser, so that you can search while you are on any web page, not just on the search page of that particular search engine. It's a fast and easy way to search, and does save some time.

The majority of toolbars work in exactly the same way, and I think there is little point in unnecessarily repeating a list of the functionality. However, there are a few more points that should be made about toolbars generally, since they have advantages and disadvantages. They certainly make life easier for the searcher, since it is no longer necessary to click on a link to get to your favourite search engine and start your search – simply click into the search box towards the top of your browser, type in your keywords and you're away with your search. You'll end up at the search engine website when the list of results are displayed of course, but it does save that little extra time. However, it does mean that searchers don't always get to see the home or opening page of the search engine and, if new features are mentioned there, the danger exists that new and interesting information about the engine may well be missed. Toolbars can also remind searchers of the different functions of the search engine, since it's usually possible to have specific icons included on the bar for advanced searching, searching for news, graphics and so on. Another plus/minus of a toolbar is that it encourages users to use only one search engine. It's the easy option, which of course is one of the reasons why they appeal to both searchers and search engine designers, and it's all too easy to use one as an unthinking default when it comes to searching. However, if you've got this far through the book, you'll be aware of the dangers of just using one search engine rather than several, so as long as you always keep in mind that there are other options available, you shouldn't go too far wrong.

Having said all that, it's time to have a look at a few toolbars, and you'll see below a listing of the search engines and where you can get their toolbars. Try them out until you find one that matches your own requirements, or of course you could just choose the one from your preferred search engine. Please bear in mind that this is an area that most search engines are now exploring, so if your favourite engine isn't listed below it may have developed a toolbar in the intervening period of my writing and your reading; so do check! Below the listing, Table 16.1 gives the options available with the various toolbars, but again remember that they may have changed by the time you read this!

- *AltaVista*   **www.altavista.com/toolbar/default/**
- *Ask Jeeves*   **http://sp.ask.com/docs/toolbar/**
- *Dogpile*   **www.dogpile.com/info.dogpl/tbar/**
- *Google*   **http://toolbar.google.com/**
- *MSN*   **http://toolbar.msn.com/**
- *Teoma*   **http://sp.ask.com/docs/teoma/toolbar/**
- *Vivisimo*   **http://vivisimo.com/toolbar/**
                   toolbar-download.html
- *Webcrawler*   **www.infospace.com/info.wbcrwl/tbar/**
- *Yahoo!*   **http://companion.yahoo.com/**.

Table 16.1 Toolbar options									
Feature	Alta Vista	Ask Jeeves	Dogpile	Google	MSN	Teoma	Vivismo	Webcrawler	Yahoo
Search web	✓	✓	✓	✓	✓	✓	✓		✓
Search news	✓	✓	✓	✓	✓			✓	✓
Search images	✓			✓					✓
Search audio	✓								
Search directory		✓		✓					✓
Advanced search	✓			✓					
Search this site	✓			✓					
Search multiple engines			✓				✓	✓	
Search stocks		✓						✓	
Search weather			✓					✓	
Search products		✓			✓				✓
Clear history		✓	✓	✓	✓	✓	✓		
Translate page	✓								
E-mail page		✓			✓				
Highlight	✓	✓	✓	✓	✓	✓			
Pop-up killer	✓	✓	✓	✓	✓		✓	✓	✓
Configure for print		✓							
Customize	✓	✓	✓	✓	✓		✓	✓	✓

Deskbars

Deskbars are a recent innovation; at the time of writing, only two search engines offer them, *Google* and *HotBot*. A deskbar works independently of the browser; it appears on the Windows taskbar, rather than being embedded in the browser screen. Consequently, you can run a search without having the browser open; the results are displayed in a separate pop-up window. The value of this to the searcher is that it is not necessary to stop what you're doing, or to switch from application to browser and back again; all the commands can be keyboard driven for example. The deskbar extends the use of the toolbar by adding more functionality – it's possible to search for movie reviews using the *Google* offering, or to search for anagrams with the *HotBot* utility. More information on the *Google* deskbar can be found at **http://toolbar.google.com/deskbar/help/index.html**; and information about the *HotBot* version is at **www.hotbot.com/tools/getting-started-with-the-HotBot-Quick-Search-deskbar.html**.

Anonymous browsing

You may be aware that whenever you visit a website your browser provides it with a lot of information about you. This information is stored in a statistics database for later analysis with appropriate software. It's useful information for the site owner to have, since he or she can check to see how often people visit the site, which pages are popular, how long people stay and so on. It's also possible to get a fairly good indication of where a visitor is from. While the statistics would not tell a site owner that Jane Brown paid them a visit, it wouldn't be too hard to work out that someone from West Coast Widgets Incorporated has spent time on the site, and the pages that have been browsed. For most of us, this isn't an issue at all; I really don't care if the owner of a site knows that I've been to visit. However, this can become an issue for people who work in the business field, particularly if the company you work for is considering taking over another one – you may not wish to advertise the fact that you're spending a lot of time exploring its website. It is also not difficult for a site to obtain a copy of any information that you currently have in your Windows clipboard; if you've cut and pasted personal information such as passwords or credit card information here the data can be quickly and easily collected. Consequently it's helpful if you can in some way mask your interest in a site, and this can be achieved using one of the various utilities or websites that specialize in this type of browsing. In this section I point you towards a few sites or utilities that you may wish to explore if you want to browse the net in secret-agent mode.

Anonymizer

The *Anonymizer* website at **www.anonymizer.com/** provides you with a handy utility to check exactly what information you're making freely available (this is in order to encourage you to purchase its software, but it's worth using just to see what information your browser is giving out). *Anonymizer Privacy Manager* can be installed onto your machine to block this leaking of information. It also allows you to browse websites directly from its site with a free 'Private Surfing' option, but this is really just for demonstration purposes, since it will block access to sites at random, and will not allow you to fill in forms online, for example. You will find that it takes considerably longer to download a page using this approach, and it may not load correctly – I tried it out with my own page to find that a lot of data on the page simply were not displayed. However, if you quickly want to check a site without the owner knowing who you are, it's an option you may wish to try. There is a free PrivacyToolbar (yes, another toolbar!) that you can download and use, although once again its use is limited.

Freedom Internet Security & Privacy

This company has a commercial product called *Websecure* with details at **www.freedom.net/products/websecure/index.html**. It protects your identity as you browse websites, blocks malicious scripts and removes annoying advertisements. The service is subscription based.

Idzap

The *Idzap* service at **www.idzap.com/** works by hiding your identity from remote sites. The *Idzap* servers act as proxy between your machine and the remote site. The company sells a commercial product that encrypts all traffic to and from your computer.

Anonbrowse

A page at *Anonbrowse*, located at **http://anonbrowse.cjb.net/**, provides a list of and access to, 11 anonymous browser websites, allowing you to simply input the URL of the site you wish to visit. Once again, however, you may find that the page you're interested in does not load entirely correctly (depending on the scripts, if any, on the page), so be aware that you may be missing useful information.

Other anonymous searching utilities

The *E-mailaddresses* website at **www.e-mailaddresses.com/e-mail_anonymity.htm** provides a valuable listing of various different utilities that you can download and use. The services generally conceal your IP address, disable cookies and JavaScript

Shorter URLs

As you will know by now, the address of my website is **www.philb.com/** and I like to think that it's pretty easy to remember. Even individual pages on my website are not too hard to remember, or to work out what the content is – it doesn't take a genius to guess that **www.philb.com/weblogs.htm**

is a page that discusses weblogs. It's also not going to be that difficult to remember if you decide to send the URL to friends or colleagues. And, if you have a failing memory, you can simply cut and paste it into your e-mail without any difficulties. However, that's not always going to be the case with some URLs which are rather longer. Take, for example, **www.mapquest.com/ maps/map.adp?ovi=1&mqmap.x=300&mqmap.y=75&mapdata= %252bKZmeiIh6N%252bIgpXRP3bylMaN0O4z8OOUkZWYe7NR H6ldDN96YFTIUmSH3Q6OzE5XVqcuc5zb%252fY5wy1MZwTnT 2pu%252bNMjOjsHjvNlygTRMzqazPStrN%252f1YzA0oWEWLw kHdhVHeG9sG6cMrfXNJKHY6fML4o6Nb0SeQm75ET9jAjKelrm qBCNta%252bsKC9n8jslz%252fo188N4g3BvAJYuzx8J8r%252f1fPFW kPYg%252bT9Su5KoQ9YpNSj%252bmo0h0aEK%252bofj3f6vCP** which is a fairly long URL by any method of measurement. Not only will you not remember this, it's very difficult to put into an e-mail, since the word wrapping that takes place may actually stop the URL functioning if your colleague tries to click on the link. There are various utilities that you can use to shorten a URL and make it much more manageable; they ensure that it doesn't 'break' as a result of line wrapping. All of these services are currently free and they are anonymous.

TinyURL

TinyURL at **http://tinyurl.com/** (from which the above long URL example was taken) is a free online utility that you can use to quickly shorten the URL. Simply type (or more probably cut and paste) the long URL into the box and click on 'Make tiny URL'. You will then get a result that looks something **like http://tinyurl.com/6/** which, as you'll agree, is much easier to use. There is also an option on the site whereby you can drag a *TinyURL* favorite into your links bar, and when you reach a page with a long URL you can simply click on that link and create a small URL instantly. In the future, when someone uses the shortened version of the URL that you have provided they will automatically be redirected to the appropriate page. Incidentally, this short URL will never expire. You can see an example of *TinyURL* providing a shorter link to one of my pages in Figure 16.2.

Make a shorter link

This utility is available from **www.makeashorterlink.com/** and works in exactly the same way as *TinyURL*. The major difference between the two util-

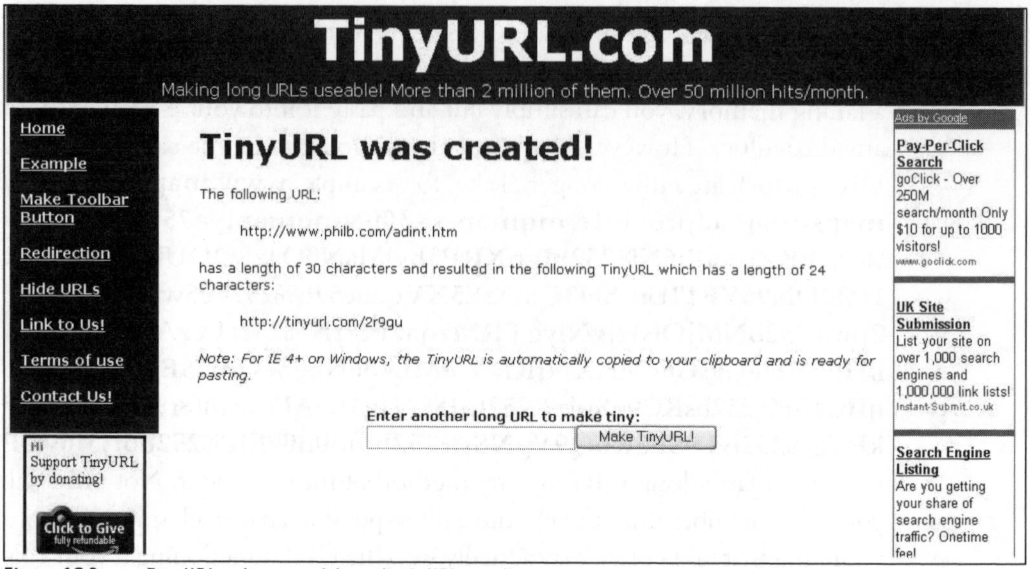

Figure 16.2 *Tiny URL* making one of the author's URLs smaller
© 2002–3 Gilby Productions. All rights reserved. 'Tiny URL' is a trademark of Gilby Productions

ities is that, with the first utility, your browser immediately redirects to the long URL, but with *Make a shorter link* the browser will go to an intermediate 'transition page' that tells the viewer that they will shortly be redirected onwards.

Other shorter URL utilities

For a more comprehensive listing you could visit *Notlong* at **http://notlong.com/links/** which provides links to about 16 utilities in total. One final point to mention with all of these services, while they are free, and the shorter links never expire, this does depend on the people who run the service being able to continue to offer the utility. If they are unable to do this your short links may fail one day; though this is unlikely, it's worthwhile keeping a copy of the full link somewhere on your system.

Web page watchers

I'm sure that there are certain web pages that you visit on a regular basis, just to see if anything has changed. It's an important job, because there are times when you do have to have the most accurate information available at your fingertips. As we've previously seen, search engines are not the best equipped to keep you fully up to date – even the most effective engines do not revisit every web page on a daily basis. Most searchers get into a daily routine of visiting certain sites just to see if anything has changed or been added to a page, and this can be a time-consuming activity. This is where web page watchers come into play. They all work in basically the same way, which is that you register with one, tell it which pages you want to check on a regular basis, and the utility then visits the site on your behalf. If nothing has changed on the page, the utility simply goes back another day. If the page has changed, it sends you an e-mail to alert you. You can then visit the page in question, knowing that something has been altered. Until you get the e-mail from the utility you can ignore the page, safe in the knowledge that it is still exactly the same as the last time you visited. Obviously there is no point in setting up a utility to check something like a news site, such as those of the CNN or the BBC, since they are always changing, but it can be useful with company or personal pages.

TrackEngine

The *TrackEngine* utility at **www.trackengine.com/servlets/com.nexlabs. trackengine.ui.Login/** allows you to quickly add a list of pages you wish to monitor to a list that it keeps on your behalf. It works by adding a link to your browser link bar. When you visit a page that you want to keep track of, you can simply click on this link, which sends a message back to the utility. When it detects new content for you, it sends you an e-mail and you can choose to receive the web page with all the new content highlighted, or a summary report of all the new content on the page. If and when you decide that you no longer need or wish to be notified of changes to a page you can visit the site and amend the list it keeps accordingly.

Morning Paper

This utility is at **www.boutell.com/morning/**. It summarizes the new content on your favourite web pages, and presents it all to you in a single convenient 'newspaper'. It is a utility that you need to download onto your computer and set it to run every time you wish to use it, so it's very similar to the concept used with news aggregators. It is a commercial product, but very reasonably priced.

TracerLock

The *TracerLock* utility at **www.tracerlock.com/** is also a commercial product that works on a subscription basis. It scans thousands of articles published on news sites, online trade journals and e-zines looking for new matches for your information requests. Consequently, it's slightly different to the other utilities mentioned in this section since the emphasis is on keywords you choose to search for, and it does the rest. However, you can also create a list of sites that you want the utility to monitor for changes.

WatchThatPage

This service, from **www.watchthatpage.com/**, allows you to collect new information from your favourite pages. The utility finds pages that have changed, collects the new content for you and presents it to you in an e-mail or a personal web page. You can also specify when the changes should be collected. *WatchThatPage* is a free service.

Miscellaneous utilities

Some utilities do not fall into any of the categories that I've already mentioned. In this section I've added utilities that I either use myself or have looked at and thought they might be a useful addition to the advanced searcher's armoury.

Adobe Reader

This is really one of those resources that you simply cannot do without. I'd be surprised if you don't have it already but, if that's the case, you can download it from **www.adobe.com/products/acrobat/readstep2.html**. It is used to display documents that have been created in the Adobe Portable Document Format (PDF); this is done to keep the original 'look and feel' of the document. It is very often used by government departments for example. Once installed onto your system, your browser recognizes that, if asked to display a .pdf file, it should open and use the *Adobe Reader* to perform this task. The version current to early 2004 is version 6 so, if you have an earlier one, you might want to think about upgrading – it is free to do so.

The Sleuthhound

If, like me, you download articles from the internet to read at a later date, you may find it difficult to remember exactly what you've done with them, and where they are stored. *The Sleuthhound*, available at **http://store3.esellerate. net/store/s.aspx?Cmd=BUY&SKURefNum=SKU3126100860&AffIDC =AFL265521779&coupon=** (or, if you prefer at **http://tinyurl.com/2z99u**), is a document search system for your hard drive. You can create search zones, enter keywords that you remember are contained in the article, and then the utility will display a list of matching documents in your browser window. The utility has a 30-day trial, but is unfortunately a commercial product, although it's very reasonably priced.

AcronymGenie

This utility, which can be downloaded from **www.sofotex.com/ AcronymGenie-download_L14208.html**, is a comprehensive database of acronyms, abbreviations and initialisms drawn from the world of computers, internet, information technology, telecommunications, electronics, embedded systems, biotechnology and so on. You can view and search acronyms with a reverse lookup facility. If you've ever got confused about what an acronym means this is a simple tool to use; it is much quicker and more effective than trying to locate the meaning of an abbreviation using a search engine. It is a free product.

Furl

Furl, which can be found at **www.furl.net/**, was started in the spring of 2003, but has only just become well known. It's a useful utility that allows users to create their own filing cabinet of useful web pages. The idea is very simple – once you find a web page that you feel is useful, and will want to refer to again, you can add it (or *Furl* it) to your own web space provided by *Furl*. You can then refer to the page at any point in the future but, importantly, you can search the pages that you've saved. This can save you a lot of time when hunting down the illusive piece of information that you know you've seen but can't remember where. If you've *Furled* it, simply log onto the site and search through your collection of pages.

Net Snippets

The *Net Snippets* utility, available from **www.netsnippets.com/**, is a powerful utility that allows you to quickly and easily save content from web pages. It is, of course, possible to do this by cutting and pasting into a Word document, but this can be rather slow and laborious. It also requires quite a lot of work to remember to add in details about the site, the URL, authors, date you visited and so on. *Net Snippets* takes care of all of these details for you. When installed on your system it adds another logo to your browser bar; when you wish to capture some useful information you can simply start the utility, cut and paste information as needed, while the utility presents you with factual information about the page you're working on, and this can also be captured. Users can create various folders for different types of information, merge the content into a single file and/or create bibliographies for use in research. It is a commercial product, with different pricing structures depending on individual or site use.

Summary

As you are doubtless aware, this is just a small selection of utilities that the advanced searcher can put to good use. It's not, and cannot be, a complete listing, but it should serve to give you a good idea of the sheer variety of utilities available on the internet. I doubt anyone uses examples of these from all the different categories, but even if you just use one or two of them it will make your use of the internet that much quicker, more effective and, above all, easier.

URLs mentioned in this chapter

http://channels.netscape.com/ns/browsers/download.jsp
http://channels.netscape.com/ns/browsers/browsing.jsp
www.opera.com/
www.opera.com/features/
www.mozilla.org/products/firebird/
http://texturizer.net/firebird/faq.html
www.upsdell.com/BrowserNews/
http://download.com.com/3150-2377-0.html
www.e-mailaddresses.com/e-mail_bookmarks.htm
www.bestlinx.com/bestlinx20/
www.bookmax.net/

www.backflip.com/login.ihtml

www.tucows.com/cache95_default.html

http://uk.real.com/?&src=ZG.uk.idx.rp_ann_loprice.hd.def

www.apple.com/quicktime/

www.apple.com/quicktime/whyqt/

www.tucows.com/top_section_1570.html

www.symantec.co.uk/region/uk/product/navbrochure/

www.drsolomon.com/

www.mcafee.com/

http://housecall.anti-virus.com/

www.lavasoftusa.com/

www.safer-networking.org/index.php?page=download

www.spychecker.com/software/antispy.html

www.zonelabs.com/store/content/home.jsp

www.altavista.com/toolbar/default/

http://sp.ask.com/docs/toolbar/

www.dogpile.com/info.dogpl/tbar/

http://toolbar.google.com/

http://toolbar.msn.com/

http://sp.ask.com/docs/teoma/toolbar/

http://vivisimo.com/toolbar/toolbar-download.html

www.infospace.com/info.wbcrwl/tbar/

http://companion.yahoo.com/

http://toolbar.google.com/deskbar/help/index.html

www.hotbot.com/tools/getting-started-with-the-HotBot-Quick-Search-
    deskbar.html

www.anonymizer.com/

www.freedom.net/products/websecure/index.html

www.idzap.com/

http://anonbrowse.cjb.net/

www.e-mailaddresses.com/e-mail_anonymity.htm

www.philb.com/

www.philb.com/weblogs.htm

http://tinyurl.com/

http://tinyurl.com/6/

www.makeashorterlink.com/

http://notlong.com/links/

www.trackengine.com/servlets/com.nexlabs.trackengine.ui.Login/

www.boutell.com/morning/

www.tracerlock.com/
www.watchthatpage.com/
www.adobe.com/products/acrobat/readstep2.html
http://store3.esellerate.net/store/s.aspx?Cmd=BUY&SKURefNum=SKU3
      126100860&AffIDC=AFL265521779&coupon=
http://tinyurl.com/2z99u/
www.sofotex.com/AcronymGenie-download_L14208.html
www.furl.net/
www.netsnippets.com/

Chapter 17 »
Sources for further help, information and assistance

Introduction

One of the major characteristics of the internet is that it is constantly changing and developing. It is therefore difficult to keep up to date with what is happening with search engine development, the arrival of new ones and the departure of old ones. Once you add in information on new versions of software, new packages, new sites, increased coverage for different subjects, new mailing lists and newsgroups – to mention just a few – the whole process of keeping a grasp on the thing is almost impossible.

In this chapter I bring to your attention a variety of resources that can help you keep on top of what is happening within the world of the internet; if you can spend just half an hour a week checking them, you should stay reasonably informed. Moreover, if you need to obtain a quick overview of a particular subject area, many of the resources that I mention provide useful briefings that cover the major points.

Search engine news and information

Search Engine Watch

This site is run and maintained by Danny Sullivan, who is well known within the industry for providing current and practical information. The site is at **www.searchenginewatch.com/**. Danny keeps very much on top of the industry and his site is always a mine of valuable information, which I check daily by the use of my news aggregator. It is divided into several sections:

- Search engine submission tips. This section is written primarily for web authors and covers information on how to get a better ranking with search engines.
- Web-searching tips. How to do better and more effective searches.
- Search engine listings. Details of all the major search engines, meta/multi-search engines and child-safe services.
- Reviews, ratings and tests. Comparative reviews, most popular search engines, tests and statistics on search engines.
- Search engine resources. A miscellany of useful information.
- Search engine report. A free newsletter that you can subscribe to. If you do not have time to visit the site on a regular basis, this is an excellent backup resource, ensuring that you won't miss the important material – as long as you're able to put aside a few minutes to read it!

Search Engine Showdown

Greg Notess is a writer, speaker and consultant who also happens to be a reference librarian and associate professor at Montana State University. His site at **www.searchengineshowdown.com/** is particularly useful for information professionals. Greg goes into great detail about the major (and some not so major) search engines that you may discover, and he has a very useful news feature. His site is also divided into sections, such as:

- Search engine features. This lists various search engines, what they can do, and how they can do it.
- Analysis. Here you'll find information on how fresh the search engine indexes are, how large they are, and any inconsistencies.
- Reviews. Detailed reviews of the major search engines such as *Google*, *AlltheWeb*, *Gigablast* and *AltaVista*.
- News. This links to various different resources that provide you with useful information.
- Links to other articles. Greg spends much of his time writing articles and he has made some of them available on the web. They are very useful sources of information.

Search Engine Guide

This site at **www.searchengineguide.com/** is targeted rather more at people who market their websites, and need to keep up to date with developments of search engines that will allow them to do this job better. It is also a good source of information for searchers and is well worth visiting.

Search Engine Lowdown

Located at **www.searchenginelowdown.com/** this site tends to focus more on the marketer, but it does contain useful information now and then regarding search engine developments that are of value and interest to the advanced searcher.

Web search tool features

Ian Winship maintains a regularly updated list of features, techniques and syntax used by major search engines. It's short, concise, easy to use and is at **www.unn.ac.uk/central/isd/features.htm**.

The Spider's Apprentice

Subtitled 'A helpful guide to search engines' this site at **www.monash.com/spidap.html** provides users with access to a great many different resources such as:

- a guide to useful search engines
- basic search engine FAQ
- planning a search strategy
- how search engines work
- an in-depth analysis of search engines
- web search wizard.

What's new services

It is difficult to keep up to date with what is happening on the internet generally, as we've already discussed. However, there are plenty of resources that can keep the advanced searcher up to date on new websites, additions to existing ones and so on. Inevitably since these lists are created chronologically they are often almost entirely random collections, and many listings will not be of any interest. However, they are also very quick to browse through and I think it's worth while taking the five or ten minutes a day to find useful nuggets.

FreePint

FreePint at **www.freepint.com/** is a network of 65,828 information researchers globally. It is strong on user interaction and has a useful bulletin board where people can pose and answer queries. This is supplemented with a fortnightly mailing to registered users. An extract from the *FreePint* home page can be seen in Figure 17.1.

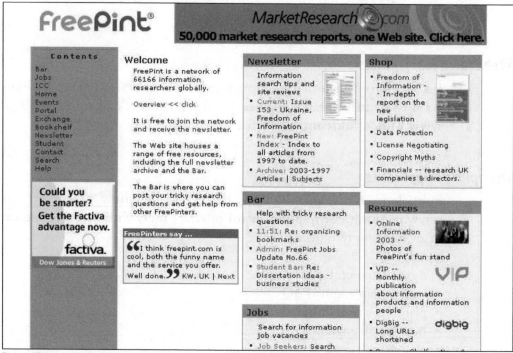

Figure 17.1   The *FreePint* home page
© Free Pint Limited 1997–2004

USA Today Web Guide

This online newspaper at **www.usatoday.com/tech/webguide/front.htm** provides a new list of 'hot sites' on a daily basis. The listing is quite eclectic and designed to appeal to the average person (is there such a creature?), so I think this site would be particularly useful for public librarians who want to bring new and interesting sites to the attention of their users.

Internet Week

This is an electronic newspaper found at **www.internetwk.com/** that provides information on today's news, trends, reviews, resources, awards, an event calendar, articles and highlights. It has a wide coverage and also covers information and news on more general aspects of computing.

The Scout Report

The *Internet Scout Project* at **http://scout.wisc.edu/Reports/ScoutReport/** comes from the Computer Sciences Department of the University of Wisconsin and its weekly publication is of interest to researchers and educators. It provides a fast, convenient way of staying informed about valuable resources on the internet.

Internet News

This particular site, found at **www.internetnews.com/**, is aimed rather more at the IT manager than the information professional or searcher, since the majority of news items discuss software and hardware that most of us have never heard of, nor wish to. However, it does also contain the occasional snippet of information for the searcher.

BUBL updates

A simple alphabetical listing of new sites that *BUBL* has added in the month is at **http://bubl.ac.uk/link/updates/current.html**. Updates for previous months/years can be found at **http://bubl.ac.uk/link/updates/**.

Nethappenings

This is an e-mail list, founded in 1993 by former biology teacher of 20 years, Gleason Sackmann. *Net-happenings* distributes announcements about the latest internet resources, especially education-related, via e-mail. The archives for this list can be found at **www.freelists.org/archives/nethappenings/**

while the sign-up for the list is at **www.edu-cyberpg.com/Community/ NetHappenings.html**.

El Dorado County Library – *What's hot on the internet*

The library provides a large number of links to new or updated sites, arranged alphabetically by site title and it indicates some sites that it thinks are of particular value or interest. This is another site that I think is of particular value to public librarians and you can track it down at **www.eldoradolibrary. org/thisweek.htm**.

Librarians' index to the internet – *New this week*

This eclectic collection of links, covering a wide variety of different subjects, has been chosen by and for librarians and information professionals. Consequently the level of authority on the listed sites is of good quality, and you can try it for yourself by pointing your browser to **http://lii.org/search/ntw**.

Neat New Stuff on the Internet

Marylaine Block is an American librarian who is well known for her articles and training courses. The sites she mentions 'are usually free sites of substantial reference value, authoritative, browsable, searchable, and packed with information, whether educational or aimed at answering everyday questions'. It's located at **http://marylaine.com/neatnew.html**.

ResourceShelf

This is a very well known site, produced and maintained by Gary Price. *Resource Shelf* is updated every day with new listings of valuable information relating to new websites, search engine tips and tricks. The emphasis is on resources and news for information professionals and, as such, this site is one of the most important when it comes to keeping up to date. Visit it at **www. resourceshelf.com/**.

Library Link of the Day

This site at **www.tk421.net/librarylink/** provides readers with a daily link for keeping up to date with the library profession. Sites include the latest library news, good reads on the web, and other valuable resources that a library knowledge worker should know about. The link is presented without commentary.

URLwire announcements of new web launches

This site at **www.urlwire.com/headlines/index.html** is widely used by companies, organizations and individuals who wish to make internet users aware of sites they have newly launched. Sites are listed with a brief annotation.

Sitelines

This site presents a good listing of important trends, new items and search tools, culled from over 50 key alerting services. Visit it at **www.workingfaster. com/sitelines/**.

BBC Technology News

This site is, as you would expect, very regularly updated, and covers news in the area of technology. As a consequence there are lots of articles on aspects of technology that do not relate even indirectly to the internet, but there are at least one or two stories everyday on aspects of the internet. Worth taking a look at, you can find it at **http://news.bbc.co.uk/1/hi/technology/ default.stm**.

ResearchBuzz

This site at **www.researchbuzz.com/about.shtml** attempts to cover the world of internet research and so focuses on search engines, new data-managing software, browser technology, compendiums of information and so on. As is quoted on the site, 'If in doubt, the final question is, "Would a reference librarian find it useful?"' If that's the case, this site is worth a visit.

New York Times Technology

My comments regarding the BBC technology site can be repeated. Both are good sources of data, and I think it simply depends on which site of the Atlantic you live as to which is your first port of call. If you're in the USA, try **www.nytimes.com/pages/technology/index.html** first!

Professional sites

Most if not all library and information science groups are now heavily involved in the internet, by providing publications or training courses, or by funding research. If they're not, I'd have to question their level of professionalism! It's always worth keeping an eye on your preferred professional organization(s) to see what work they are doing in the field. Some national and international organizations' web pages are given below:

- The American Library Association   **www.ala.org/**
- ASLIB   **www.aslib.co.uk/**
- Canadian Library Association   **www.cla.amlibs.ca/**
- CILIP   **www.cilip.org.uk/**
- International Federation of Library   **www.ifla.org/**
  Associations and Institutions
- TFPL   **www.tfpl.com/**
- UKOLUG   **www.ukolug.org.uk/**.

Magazines and journals

Many magazines related to the internet and to the information profession are now published on the internet – either in full or with a table of contents and selected articles. These can prove very useful sources of information; new developments, new sites, 'how to' articles, information on software and so on. *Google* provides a comprehensive list at **http://directory.google.com/Top/ Reference/Journals/**. Another good and broad listing of journals specifically for the information industry can be found at **www.libdex.com/ journals.html** but I have chosen a small sample of the ones that I personally find useful.

ALA *TechSource*

This is produced by the publishing division of the American Library Association and offers the full text of various articles taken from the print version. *TechSource* can be found at **www.techsource.ala.org/**.

Ariadne

Ariadne magazine at **www.ariadne.ac.uk/** is targeted principally at information science professionals in academia, and also to interested lay people both in and beyond the higher education community. Its main geographic focus is the UK, but it is widely read in the USA and worldwide. Archived copies are available right back to the first edition in January 1996. Unlike many magazines this does not have a hard copy version, and the entire journal can be read free of charge at the website.

CILIP Update

This magazine is provided free of charge in hard copy format to members of the organization, and some articles are also made available free of charge to read online, including my own 'Questions and Answers' column. The online version is at **www.cilip.org.uk/update/index.html**.

Information Today

This is a commercial publication, but does provide free access to some leading articles every month directly from the website. You can visit it at **www.infotoday.com/IT/default.shtml**.

Internet Resources Newsletter

This is a free, monthly newsletter at **www.hw.ac.uk/libWWW/irn/irn.html** for academics, students, engineers, scientists and social scientists. It is of global interest and each month highlights new websites, press releases, and book reviews as well as other articles of interest.

Bookshops

I do not include a bibliography or further reading list in this volume. There are several reasons for this: there are already far too many titles available for me to be able to give a comprehensive listing; any bibliography would be out of date before it was printed; it is easier to obtain your own listing using internet bookshops. Internet bookshops exist in large numbers – a quick search on *Google* for *"internet bookshop"* resulted in over 49,000 matches, so I just list the three that I tend to use on a regular basis.

Amazon

Amazon boasts that it has millions of titles available, and it is without a doubt the best known of all the internet bookshops. It provides customer reviews and author interviews and allows you to search by keyword or subject. The information for each title is usually very comprehensive. The global version is at **www.amazon.com/** and the address for the UK site is **www.amazon. co.uk/**.

Blackwell's Online Bookshop

This bookshop has over 2.8 million titles to choose from, with a comprehensive search facility. Its URL is **http://bookshop.blackwell.co.uk/ bobuk/scripts/welcome.jsp**.

The *Internet Bookshop*

This is owned by the W. H. Smith company and provides a similar service to the other two bookshops previously mentioned. Visit it at **www.bookshop. co.uk/**.

Mailing lists

We have previously seen, in Chapter 13, the importance of mailing lists, and I can virtually guarantee that whatever your professional area, there will be several lists that are appropriate for you. You can of course do your own research here, but I've chosen a few lists from the *JISCmail* service at **www.jiscmail.ac.uk/** that you might like to take a look at.

lis-link

This is a general library and information science list for news and discussion. While the emphasis is on UK issues the subject coverage is of interest to information professionals from any country.

lis-pub-libs

This is a forum for the discussion of topics that are of general interest to public librarians in the UK and elsewhere.

lis-ukolug

UKOLUG is a leading UK group for online, CD-ROM and internet searchers. The list contains lots of useful hints, tips and pointers to many resources that are of interest to searchers wherever they are located.

pin

This list, Policing the Net, covers the ethical, moral and political responsibilities of the internet.

Web-research-uk

This mailing list covers UK-specific issues and announcements dealing with internet research.

Spam

I have mentioned 'spam' in passing several times; it is the internet equivalent of junk mail. This is sometimes posted directly to newsgroups and mailing lists, but you will also find it in your e-mail box. If your e-mail address is on a web page, if you post to newsgroups, visit websites or if your e-mail address is to be found in people servers there is a strong possibility that you will end up on various spammers' lists and will be sent unsolicited e-mail. I have discussed this in more detail on my own website, so if you're interested I would suggest you visit **www.philb.com/spamex.htm**. There are a number of websites that provide you with further information, assistance and detailed technical advice on how to combat this particular menace.

DID YOU KNOW? >>

No one can say for certain why the term 'spam' became used for unsolicited e-mails. However, it seems likely that it is related to the Monty Python spam sketch, in which spam is in every item on the menu, and it is impossible to order anything without having at least some of it included in the meal.

Help stop scam spammers

This site at **http://spam.getnetwise.org/** provides a background to spam, lawsuits, legislation, site listings, tips on spotting it and the opportunity to report any that is sent to you.

The Federal Trade Commission

The Federal Trade Commission site at **www.ftc.gov/bcp/conline/edcams/**

spam/index.html is working for consumer protection and provides legal advice and guidance as well as other detailed information on current scams.

SPAM-L FAQ

This document, located at **www.claws-and-paws.com/spam-l/** is the Frequently Asked Questions from the spam mailing list, which is a mailing list for the discussion of the subject, rather than a list used by spammers! As well as being good introductory information, it goes into great detail on how to spot spam, decipher e-mail message headers and report the spam you receive.

> **DID YOU KNOW? >>**
> The top five countries in the world responsible for spam e-mails are the USA, China, South Korea, Brazil and Argentina (www.spamhaus.org/).

Miscellaneous

There are some resources that I really do want to bring to your attention that do not fit into any other category, or which cover so many different categories they are not easy to place. Consequently this is my 'catch all' area for sites that you should visit at least once!

Trade Shows

This is an impressive site listing and detailing major internet related shows, conferences and exhibitions. Find it at **http://events.internet.com/**.

CNET

Styled as 'the source for computers and technology' it covers hardware and software reviews, e-commerce, tech news, web building, latest prices, finance, investment, downloads, help and 'how to' tips. It is at **www.cnet.com/**.

Zdnet

This site at **www.zdnet.com/** provides general information on computers and computing but also has significant amounts of information specifically relating to the internet. It contains new and breaking stories, statistical information and briefings.

The December List

This site is maintained by John December and the URL is **www. december.com/cmc/info/**. It has a wealth of information regarding online communications and the internet. It is a comprehensive collection for both trainers and students, providing access to organizations, forums, articles and bibliographies.

Internet service and access providers

If you ever need to find information on service providers these sites link to over 10,000 of them. Visit them at **http://thelist.internet.com/** and **www.thedirectory.org/**.

Internet hoaxes

Never a week goes by when I am not informed by e-mail of a new virus which is going to destroy my computer. A virus warning should be taken seriously of course, but the first place to check is this site, maintained by the US Department of Energy. The *Computer Incident Advisory Capability (CIAC)* at **http://HoaxBusters.ciac.org/** monitors virus warnings and keeps a list of hoaxes. Please check to see if the virus you have been told about is actually a hoax e-mail (often sent with the best of intentions) before passing it onto colleagues.

Glossary of internet terms

If you've ever wondered what some of those strange little TLAs (three-letter acronyms) mean, this is a good place to start. This site at **www.matisse.net/files/glossary.html** also provides information on four- and five-letter acronyms as well!

Netiquette

As I mentioned in Chapter 13, there are certain things that you should and should not do when posting to newsgroups and mailing lists. This page at **www.fau.edu/netiquette/netiquette.html** tells you everything that you need to know about how to be polite in your dealings with other people on the internet.

Summary

In this chapter I have provide you with some useful links to a number of resources that can assist you in further explorations of the internet. In my opinion all of these sites are worth taking at least a quick look at, since they make the whole process of keeping up to date so much easier. Please remember that it's not a comprehensive listing, and I'm sure that I've not included many other excellent sites, so don't limit yourself to just the sites that I've annotated!

URLs mentioned in this chapter

www.searchenginewatch.com/
www.searchengineshowdown.com/
www.searchengineguide.com/
www.searchenginelowdown.com/
www.unn.ac.uk/central/isd/features.htm
www.monash.com/spidap.html
www.freepint.com/
www.usatoday.com/tech/webguide/front.htm
www.internetwk.com/
http://scout.wisc.edu/Reports/ScoutReport/
www.internetnews.com/
http://bubl.ac.uk/link/updates/current.html
http://bubl.ac.uk/link/updates/
www.edu-cyberpg.com/Community/NetHappenings.html
www.freelists.org/archives/nethappenings/
www.eldoradolibrary.org/thisweek.htm
http://lii.org/search/ntw/
http://marylaine.com/neatnew.html
www.resourceshelf.com/
www.tk421.net/librarylink/
www.urlwire.com/headlines/index.html
www.workingfaster.com/sitelines/
http://news.bbc.co.uk/1/hi/technology/default.stm
www.researchbuzz.com/about.shtml
www.nytimes.com/pages/technology/index.html
www.ala.org/
www.aslib.co.uk/
www.cla.amlibs.ca/
www.cilip.org.uk/

www.ifla.org/
www.tfpl.com/
www.ukolug.org.uk/
http://directory.google.com/Top/Reference/Journals/
www.libdex.com/journals.html
https://www.techsource.ala.org/
www.ariadne.ac.uk/
www.cilip.org.uk/update/index.html
www.infotoday.com/IT/default.shtml
www.hw.ac.uk/libWWW/irn/irn.html
www.amazon.com/
www.amazon.co.uk/
http://bookshop.blackwell.co.uk/bobuk/scripts/welcome.jsp
www.bookshop.co.uk/
www.jiscmail.ac.uk/
www.philb.com/spamex.htm
http://spam.getnetwise.org/
www.ftc.gov/bcp/conline/edcams/spam/index.html
www.claws-and-paws.com/spam-l/
http://events.internet.com/
www.cnet.com/
www.zdnet.com/
www.december.com/cmc/info/
http://thelist.internet.com/
www.thedirectory.org/
http://HoaxBusters.ciac.org/
www.matisse.net/files/glossary.html
www.fau.edu/netiquette/netiquette.html

Appendix 1 »

HTML for a search engine home page

One of the tips mentioned in Chapter 15 is to create a new home page providing links to different search engines. The following HTML code can be used to create such a page. Copy it exactly as it has been given, using a simple text editor or web authoring tool, save it to your local hard disk, giving it a name of your choice, followed by either a .htm or .html extension. Of course, if you wish to choose different search engines, simply replace the URL in the tag <A HREF= "…"> with the new URL and change the link text accordingly. Configure your browser to point to this as your new home page and you're done!

Alternatively, don't type the code out at all. Simply visit **www.philb.com/ handbookengines.htm** and view the source code; the web page version is shown in Appendix Figure 1. Then just cut and paste it and you have a useful home page!

```
<HTML>
<HEAD>
<TITLE>A search engine home page</TITLE>
</HEAD>
<BODY>
<CENTER>
<H1>A search engine home page</H1></CENTER>
<H2>Introduction</H2>
<P>This page provides you with links to some of the main search
engines,divided into the different types of search engine. Feel free to make
use of this page yourself - if you want to copy it and use it as your
own starting page to internet search engines simply download it onto your
```

Free Text Search Engines	Search Engine URL
Google	http://www.google.com
AlltheWeb	http://www.alltheweb.com
AltaVista	http://www.altavista.com
Teoma	http://www.teoma.com
Wisenut	http://www.wisenut.com
Looksmart	http://search.looksmart.com/?tb=web&qt=
AOL Search	http://search.aol.com/aolcom/index.jsp
Euroseek	http://www.euroseek.com/
Gigablast	http://www.gigablast.com
HotBot	http://www.hotbot.com
Lycos	http://www.lycos.com/
MSN	http://search.msn.com/default.aspx
Index/Directory Search Engines	
Yahoo!	http://www.yahoo.com
Yahoo! UK and Ireland	http://uk.yahoo.com/
Google Directory	http://www.google.com/dirhp
Dmoz Open Directory Project	http://dmoz.org/
AltaVista Directory	http://uk.altavista.com/dir/default

Appendix The author's search engine home page
Figure 1   © The author

own computer and use the browser functions to set this as your own home page. Feel free to delete engines or add others to fully customise it to your own requirements. However, if you decide to use it as a publically available page on your own site, please ensure that you add a copyright notice at the bottom: "© Phil Bradley 2004. This page is used with the permission of Phil Bradley and his website can be located at <A HREF="http://www.philb.com">http://www.philb.com</A>" </P>

<H2>Search Engines</H2>

<CENTER>
<TABLE WIDTH="64%" BORDER="1">

<TR> <TD WIDTH="250"><B>Free Text Search Engines</B>
</TD> <TD WIDTH="357"><B>Search Engine URL</B></TD> </TR>

<TR> <TD WIDTH="250">Google</TD> <TD WIDTH="357">
<A HREF="http://www.google.com">http://www.google.com</A> </TD> </TR>

```
<TR> <TD WIDTH="250">AlltheWeb</TD> <TD WIDTH="357">
<A HREF="http://www.alltheweb.com">http://www.alltheweb.com</A></TD> </TR>
<TR> <TD WIDTH="250">AltaVista</TD> <TD WIDTH="357">
<A HREF="http://www.altavista.com">http://www.altavista.com</A> </TD> </TR>

<TR> <TD WIDTH="250">Teoma</TD> <TD WIDTH="357">
<A HREF="http://www.teoma.com">http://www.teoma.com</A></TD> </TR>

<TR> <TD WIDTH="250">Wisenut</TD> <TD WIDTH="357">
<A HREF="http://www.wisenut.com">http://www.wisenut.com</A> </TD> </TR>

<TR> <TD WIDTH="250">Looksmart</TD> <TD WIDTH="357">
<A HREF="http://search.looksmart.com/?tb=web&qt=">http://search.looksmart.
com/?tb=web&amp;qt=</A> </TD> </TR>

<TR> <TD WIDTH="250">AOL Search</TD> <TD WIDTH="357">
<A HREF="http://search.aol.com/aolcom/index.jsp ">http://search.aol.com/
aolcom/index.jsp</A> </TD> </TR>

<TR> <TD WIDTH="250">Euroseek</TD> <TD WIDTH="357">
<A HREF="http://www.euroseek.com/">http://www.euroseek.com/</A> </TD> </TR>

<TR> <TD WIDTH="250">Gigablast</TD> <TD WIDTH="357">
<A HREF="http://www.gigablast.com">http://www.gigablast.com</A> </TD> </TR>

<TR> <TD WIDTH="250">HotBot</TD> <TD WIDTH="357">
<A HREF="http://www.hotbot.com">http://www.hotbot.com</A> </TD> </TR>

<TR> <TD WIDTH="250">Lycos</TD> <TD WIDTH="357">
<A HREF="http://www.lycos.com/">http://www.lycos.com/</A> </TD> </TR>

<TR> <TD WIDTH="250">MSN</TD> <TD WIDTH="357">
<A HREF="http://search.msn.com/default.aspx">http://search.msn.com/default.
aspx
</A></TD> </TR>

<TR> <TD WIDTH="250"> </TD> <TD WIDTH="357"> </TD> </TR>

<TR> <TD WIDTH="250"><B>Index/Directory Search Engines</B> </TD>
<TD WIDTH="357"> </TD> </TR>

<TR> <TD WIDTH="250">Yahoo!</TD> <TD WIDTH="357">
<A HREF="http://www.yahoo.com">http://www.yahoo.com</A> </TD> </TR>

<TR> <TD WIDTH="250">Yahoo! UK and Ireland</TD> <TD WIDTH="357">
<A HREF="http://uk.yahoo.com/">http://uk.yahoo.com/</A>
</TD> </TR>

<TR> <TD WIDTH="250">Google Directory</TD> <TD WIDTH="357">
<A HREF="http://www.google.com/dirhp">http://www.google.com/dirhp</A> </TD>
</TR>

<TR> <TD WIDTH="250">Dmoz Open Directory Project</TD> <TD WIDTH="357">
<A HREF="http://dmoz.org/">http://dmoz.org/</A> </TD> </TR>
```

```
<TR> <TD WIDTH="250">AltaVista Directory</TD> <TD WIDTH="357">
<A HREF="http://uk.altavista.com/dir/default">http://uk.altavista.com/dir/
default</A> </TD> </TR>

<TR> <TD WIDTH="250">AOL Directory</TD> <TD WIDTH="357">
<A HREF="http://search.aol.com/aolcom/browse.jsp">http://search.aol.com/
aolcom/browse.jsp</A> </TD> </TR>

<TR> <TD WIDTH="250"> </TD>  <TD WIDTH="357"> </TD> </TR>
<TR> <TD WIDTH="250"><B>Multi/Meta search engines</B>
</TD> <TD WIDTH="357"> </TD> </TR>

<TR> <TD WIDTH="250">Ixquick</TD>  <TD WIDTH="357">
<A HREF="http://www.ixquick.com">http://www.ixquick.com</A> </TD> </TR>

<TR> <TD WIDTH="250">Search.com</TD>  <TD WIDTH="357">
<A HREF="http://www.search.com">http://www.search.com</A> </TD> </TR>

<TR> <TD WIDTH="250">ez2www</TD> <TD WIDTH="357">
<A HREF="http://www.ez2www.com/">http://www.ez2www.com/</A> </TD> </TR>

<TR> <TD WIDTH="250">Vivisimo</TD>  <TD WIDTH="357">
<A HREF="http://vivisimo.com/">http://vivisimo.com/</A> </TD> </TR>

<TR> <TD WIDTH="250">Dogpile</TD>  <TD WIDTH="357">
<A HREF="http://www.dogpile.com/">http://www.dogpile.com/</A> </TD> </TR>

<TR> <TD WIDTH="250">Zapmeta</TD> <TD WIDTH="357">
<A HREF="http://www.zapmeta.com">http://www.zapmeta.com</A> </TD> </TR>

<TR> <TD WIDTH="250">Fazzle</TD> <TD WIDTH="357">
<A HREF="http://www.fazzle.com">http://www.fazzle.com</A> </TD> </TR>

<TR> <TD WIDTH="250">Kart00</TD> <TD WIDTH="357">
<A HREF="http://www.kartoo.com">http://www.kartoo.com</A> </TD> </TR>

<TR> <TD WIDTH="250"> </TD> <TD WIDTH="357"> </TD> </TR>

<TR> <TD WIDTH="250"><B>Hidden Web search engines</B> </TD> <TD
WIDTH="357">  </TD> </TR>

<TR> <TD WIDTH="250">Infomine</TD> <TD WIDTH="357">
<A HREF="http://infomine.ucr.edu/">http://infomine.ucr.edu/</A> </TD> </TR>

<TR> <TD WIDTH="250">SingingFish</TD> <TD WIDTH="357">
<A HREF="http://www.singingfish.com">http://www.singingfish.com</A> </TD>
</TR>

<TR> <TD WIDTH="250">Scirus</TD> <TD WIDTH="357">
<A HREF="http://www.scirus.com/srsapp/">http://www.scirus.com/srsapp/</A>
</TD> </TR>

<TR> <TD WIDTH="250">Turbo10</TD> <TD WIDTH="357">
<A HREF="http://turbo10.com/">http://turbo10.com/</A> </TD> </TR>
```

```
<TR> <TD WIDTH="250">Complete Planet</TD> <TD WIDTH="357">
<A HREF="http://www.completeplanet.com/">http://www.completeplanet.com/</A>
</TD> </TR>

<TR> <TD WIDTH="250">Invisible Web</TD> <TD WIDTH="357">
<A HREF="http://www.invisible-web.net/">http://www.invisible-web.net/</A>
</TD> </TR>

<TR> <TD WIDTH="250">Direct Search</TD> <TD WIDTH="357">
<A HREF="http://www.freepint.com/gary/direct.htm">http://www.freepint.com/
gary/direct.htm</A> </TD> </TR>

</TABLE>
</CENTER>
</BODY>
</HTML>
```

Appendix 2 >>
Country codes

AD	Andorra	BF	Burkina Faso
AE	United Arab Emirates	BG	Bulgaria
AF	Afghanistan	BH	Bahrain
AG	Antigua and Barbuda	BI	Burundi
AI	Anguilla	BJ	Benin
AL	Albania	BM	Bermuda
AM	Armenia	BN	Brunei Darussalam
AN	Netherlands Antilles	BO	Bolivia
AO	Angola	BR	Brazil
AQ	Antarctica	BS	Bahamas
AR	Argentina	BT	Bhutan
AS	American Samoa	BV	Bouvet Island
AT	Austria	BW	Botswana
AU	Australia	BY	Belarus
AV	Anguila	BZ	Belize
AW	Aruba		
AZ	Azerbaijan	CA	Canada
		CC	Cocos (Keeling) Islands
BA	Bosnia and Herzegovina	CD	Congo, Democratic Republic
BB	Barbados	CF	Central African Republic
BD	Bangladesh	CG	Congo
BE	Belgium	CH	Switzerland

CI	Côte D'Ivoire (Ivory Coast)
CK	Cook Islands
CL	Chile
CM	Cameroon
CN	China
CO	Colombia
CR	Costa Rica
CS	Czechoslovakia (former)
CU	Cuba
CV	Cape Verde
CX	Christmas Island
CY	Cyprus
CZ	Czech Republic
DE	Germany
DJ	Djibouti
DK	Denmark
DM	Dominica
DO	Dominican Republic
DZ	Algeria
EC	Ecuador
EE	Estonia
EG	Egypt
EH	Western Sahara
ER	Eritrea
ES	Spain
ET	Ethiopia
FI	Finland
FJ	Fiji
FK	Falkland Islands
FM	Micronesia
FO	Faroe Islands
FR	France
FX	France, Metropolitan
GA	Gabon
GB	Great Britain (UK)

GD	Grenada
GE	Georgia
GF	French Guiana
GH	Ghana
GI	Gibraltar
GL	Greenland
GM	Gambia
GN	Guinea
GP	Guadeloupe
GQ	Equatorial Guinea
GR	Greece
GS	South Georgia and South Sandwich Islands
GT	Guatemala
GU	Guam
GW	Guinea-Bissau
GY	Guyana
HK	Hong Kong
HM	Heard and McDonald Islands
HN	Honduras
HR	Croatia (Hrvatska)
HT	Haiti
HU	Hungary
ID	Indonesia
IE	Ireland
IL	Israel
IN	India
IO	British Indian Ocean Territory
IQ	Iraq
IR	Iran
IS	Iceland
IT	Italy
JM	Jamaica
JO	Jordan
JP	Japan

KE	Kenya	MU	Mauritius
KG	Kyrgyzstan	MV	Maldives
KH	Cambodia	MW	Malawi
KI	Kiribati	MX	Mexico
KM	Comoros	MY	Malaysia
KN	St Kitts and Nevis	MZ	Mozambique
KP	Korea (North)		
KR	Korea (South)	NA	Namibia
KW	Kuwait	NC	New Caledonia
KY	Cayman Islands	NE	Niger
KZ	Kazakhstan	NF	Norfolk Island
		NG	Nigeria
LA	Laos	NI	Nicaragua
LB	Lebanon	NL	Netherlands
LC	Saint Lucia	NO	Norway
LI	Liechtenstein	NP	Nepal
LK	Sri Lanka	NR	Nauru
LR	Liberia	NT	Neutral Zone
LS	Lesotho	NU	Niue
LT	Lithuania	NZ	New Zealand (Aotearoa)
LU	Luxembourg		
LV	Latvia	OM	Oman
LY	Libya		
		PA	Panama
MA	Morocco	PE	Peru
MC	Monaco	PF	French Polynesia
MD	Moldova	PG	Papua New Guinea
MG	Madagascar	PH	Philippines
MH	Marshall Islands	PK	Pakistan
MK	Macedonia	PL	Poland
ML	Mali	PM	St Pierre and Miquelon
MM	Myanmar	PN	Pitcairn
MN	Mongolia	PR	Puerto Rico
MO	Macau	PT	Portugal
MP	Northern Mariana Islands	PW	Palau
MQ	Martinique	PY	Paraguay
MR	Mauritania		
MS	Montserrat	QA	Qatar
MT	Malta		

RE	Réunion		TO	Tonga
RO	Romania		TP	East Timor
RU	Russian Federation		TR	Turkey
RW	Rwanda		TT	Trinidad and Tobago
			TV	Tuvalu
SA	Saudi Arabia		TW	Taiwan
SB	Solomon Islands		TZ	Tanzania
SC	Seychelles			
SD	Sudan		UA	Ukraine
SE	Sweden		UG	Uganda
SG	Singapore		UK	United Kingdom
SH	St Helena		UM	US Minor Outlying Islands
SI	Slovenia		US	United States
SJ	Svalbard and Jan Mayen Islands		UY	Uruguay
SK	Slovak Republic		UZ	Uzbekistan
SL	Sierra Leone			
SM	San Marino		VA	Vatican City State (Holy See)
SN	Senegal		VC	St Vincent and the Grenadines
SO	Somalia		VE	Venezuela
SR	Suriname		VG	Virgin Islands (British)
ST	São Tomé and Príncipe		VI	Virgin Islands (U.S.)
SU	USSR (former)		VN	Viet Nam
SV	El Salvador		VU	Vanuatu
SY	Syria			
SZ	Swaziland		WF	Wallis and Futuna Islands
			WS	Samoa
TC	Turks and Caicos Islands			
TD	Chad		YE	Yemen
TF	French Southern Territories		YT	Mayotte
TG	Togo		YU	Yugoslavia
TH	Thailand			
TJ	Tajikistan		ZA	South Africa
TK	Tokelau		ZM	Zambia
TM	Turkmenistan		ZR	Zaire
TN	Tunisia		ZW	Zimbabwe

Index

192.com 111
1Blink 76

academic publishing 192
AcronymGenie 225
ADAM 152
AdAware 215
Addresses.com 109
Adobe Reader 224
ALA *TechSource* 236
ALEX 152
AllSearchEngines 76
AlltheWeb 19, 20 182
   advanced search functions
      44–6
   basic search functions 43–4
   image search 96
   link checking 148
   video search 103–4
AltaVista 46–8, 65, 182
   image search 93–4
   sound search 101
   toolbar 217
   video search 103
Alumni.Net 112
Amazon 140–1, 237–8

American Library Association
   236
AmphetaDesk 128
Anonbrowse 220
Anonymizer 219
anti-virus protection 213–16
AOL Search 51, 65
Ariadne 51, 138, 236
Around People Finder 112
Ask Jeeves 29
   toolbar 217
ASLIB 236
Atomz 79

b2 130
Backflip 210
BBC Technology News 235
Beacon schools 147
Beaucoup 76
Bestlinx 210
Big Blog Tool 130
BioMedNet 136
Biz/ed 152
Blackwell's Online Bookshop 238
Blogdex 125
Blogger 40, 126, 130, 204

BlogStreet 125
Bookmax 210
brary blog 122
British Airways Authority 184
British Telecom enquiries 111
broadband technology 191–2
Browser News 209
browsers 207–9
   back button 197
   bookmarks 200–2, 209–10
   cache 200, 211
   functions of 203
   history function 198
   offline browsers 209
   opening copies of 202
browsing anonymously 219–20
BRS 189
BUBL 152–4, 233

Canadian Library Association
   236
Chemweb 136
Chi Lib Rocks! weblog 121
CIA World Factbook 184
CILIP 236
   Update 237

Classmates 112
CNET 240
CNET Search 70, 81
ComLib weblog 122
commercial information 136–8,
    185–6
company annual reports 186
CompletePlanet 87
Copernic 88
Corbis Collection 98–9

Daypop 123–4
December List 241
Deep Query Manager 88
deskbars 218
Diarist 126
dictionaries 186
Digital Librarian 99
Direct Search 85–6
Ditto 98
Dmoz see Open Directory Project
Dogpile 71
    toolbar 217
domain names 144
Download.com 209

Dr Solomon 214

EARchive 102
Easyspace 147, 197
Eatonweb 126
eBay 113
EEVL 152
El Dorado County Library 234
Electric Ink 122
Electronic Telegraph 139
E-mail Addresses 210
E-mailChange 110
Emerald Group 137
Encyclopaedia Britannica 136
encyclopaedias 185
EngLib 121
Eureka! 76
Euroseek 51
Excite 111

Exploded Library 120
ez2Find 71, 96, 104

FaganFinder 96
Familysearch 113
Fazzle 74, 96
Federal Trade Commission 240
Feedreader 129
Feedroll 129
Feedster 124–5
Financial Times 139
FindSounds 101
Firebird 209
firewalls 216
FirstStop WebSearch 89
Forces Reunited 112
Forte Free Agent 164
Free Images 99
free text search engines 19–22,
    46–52
    data collection 20–1
    relevance ranking 22
    searching using 181–2
FreeBMD 80
FreePint 232
Friends Reunited 112
Froogle 37
Furl 225

Geeklog 131
GenesConnected 113
Getty Images 99
Gigablast 51
Globe of Blogs 125
Google 19, 20, 22
    advanced search functions
        35–9
    alerts 204
    answers 204
    basic search functions 32–4
    deskbar 218
    directory 61–3
    history of 32
    image search 92–3
    link checking 148

newsgroups 160–3
shortcuts 38–9
sound files 101
size 32
toolbar *see also* toolbars
    39–42, 217–18
weblog listing 126
Gradfinder 112
Guides to Specialised Search Engines
    89

Handheld Librarian 121
Help stop scam spammers 239
hidden web 83–90
    directories for 87
    intelligent agents for search
        88–9
    introduction to 83–5
    other resources for searching
        89–90
    search engines for 85–7
Highway61 76
home page 197
HotBot 51
    deskbar 218
    sound search function 101
Hotmail 110, 203
Housecall 215

Idzap 220
images *see* multimedia
index/directory search engines
    23–5
    data collection 25
    introduction to 53–4
    searching using 179–81
Infomine 86
Information Today 237
Infospace 109
intelligent agents 88–9, 190–1
International Association of
    School Librarianship
    122
International Federation of
    Library Associations and

Institutions 236
internet
  authority of data 4–5, 143–9
  background 1–13
  commercial databases on 8,
    135–8
  connections to 4, 195
  future of 190–3
  glossary 241
  growth 6–7
  history of 1–3
  hoaxes 241
  mailing lists 9–10
  news aggregators 10, 126–9
  newsgroups 9–10
  online bookshop 140–1
  online journals 138–9
  online newspapers 139–40
  search engines 7–8
  service providers 241
  size 21
  Trade Shows 240
  utilities 206–26
  virtual libraries 8–9
  weblogs 10
Internet Address Finder 110
Internet Archive Live Music Archive
  102
Internet Bookshop 238
Internet Movie Database 182, 187
Internet News 233
Internet Resources Newsletter 139,
  237
Internet Traffic Report 196
Internet Week 233
Internetsøgning 122
intranets 188–9
invisible web *see* hidden web
Invisible-web 87
iTools 76
Ixquick 70, 96

JISCmail 166–7, 183–4, 238

KartOO 75–6

Keyword 76
Kluwer Academic Publishers
  135

Lady Crumpet's Armoire 120
Leddy Library News 121
LexisNexis 138
Librarian.net 120
Librarians' Index to the Internet 89,
  152, 234
Library Link of the Day 234
Library Weblogs 125
LincOn 87
lis-link 238
LISNews 120
lis-pub-libs 238
lis-ukolug 239
LiveJournal 126
LookupUK 112
Loopy Librarian 122
Lost school friends 112
Lycos 51, 65, 104

mailing lists 9–10, 238–9
  characteristics of 165–6
  joining 167
  leaving 167
  locating 166–7
  posting to 168
  searching using 183–4
makeashorterlink 221
MaMMa 76
Manitoba Library Association
  122
Marylaine Block's Neat New Stuff
  120, 234
McAfee ViruScan 215
Mediafind 104
Metacrawler 76
MetaE-mailSearchAgent 108
Missing persons worldwide 112
MIT 109
MIT Virtual Reference Collection
  187
mobile computing 192

MonsterCrawler 76
Morning Paper 223
Movabletype 131
MSN Search 51, 65
  toolbar 217
multimedia
  images; collections 98–9;
    newsgroups 99; search
    engines for 92–9
  introduction 91–2
  sounds; newsgroups 102;
    playing 102–3; repositories
    of 102; search engines for
    101–2
  utilities 212–13
  video; playing 103; search
    engines 103–4
multi/meta-search engines 25–6,
  67–7
  characteristics of 68–71
  data collection 67–8

Napster 102
natural language search engines
  29
Net Snippets 226
Nethappenings 233
Netintouch 112
netiquette 241
Netscape 207–8
Netscape Search 66, 111
New York Times Technology 235
news aggregators 10, 126–9
NewsGator 129
newsgroups 9–10
  examples of 158
  image newsgroups 100
  introduction to 156–9
  offline newsreaders 163–4
  reading 160–5
  sound newsgroups 102
NewsIsFree 129
NewsMonster 129
Norton AntiVirus 214
Notlong 222

official papers 187
OMNI 152
online bookshops 140–1, 237–8
online journals 138–9, 192–3,
    236–7
online newspapers 139–40,
    184–5
Online Speech Bank 102
Open Directory Project 61–4
Open Stacks 122
Opera 208–9
Oxford Reference Online 137

people, finding 106–14
    e-mail addresses 108–11
    introduction 106–7
    people finders 111
    search engines 107–8
    tracking services 112–3
Peter Scott's Library Blog 120
Phil Bradley's weblog 122
Philosophy in Cyberspace 152
Picsearch 96, 97
pin 239
Pinakes 152
pop-up killers 41, 203
publishers 135–8

Queen's Awards for Enterprise
    147
quick reference tools 187
QuickTime 213

Radio UserLand 131
RealOne Player 212
Redwood City Public Library
    weblog 121
Refdesk 187
reference queries 176
ResearchBuzz 235
resource/site-specific search
    engines 26–7, 78–82
ResourceShelf 119, 120, 234
Reunion 112
Reunite 112

Roastbeef 112
RocketNews 129
RSS 126–7

San Francisco Chronicle 139
Schoolnews 112
Scirus 86
Scout Report 233
Search Engine Guide 231
Search Engine Lowdown 231
search engines
    advertising on 28
    cost to use 27–9
    country/regional 29
    free text search engines 19–22,
        46–52; data collection
        20–1; relevance ranking
        22; searching using
        181–2
    future of 191
    growth 18–19
    index/directory search engines
        23–5; data collection 25;
        introduction to 53–4;
        searching using 179–81
    introduction to, 7–8, 17–30
    multi/meta-search engines
        25–6, 67–77; character-
        istics of 68–71; data
        collection 67–8
    natural language 29
    number of 18
    ownership of 27
    relevance ranking 22
    resource/site-specific 26–7,
        78–82
search examples 177–84
Searchengineshowdown 51, 230
Searchenginewatch 51, 229–30
shorter URLs 220–2
Singing Fish 86, 103
Sitelines 121, 235
Slashdot 119
Sleuthhound 225
SOSIG 152

Sound America 102
sounds see multimedia
spam 239–40
SPAM-L FAQ 240
Spider's Apprentice 231
Spybot 215
Spychecker 216
spyware 215–216
Stark County Law Library Blawg
    120
Stopstock 97
Supercrawler 77
Sweet and Maxwell 136
Syndic8 125

Technorati 125
Teoma 48–9
    toolbar 217
TFPL 236
TheBigProject 81
ThePaperboy 139, 180
TheShiftedLibrarian 118
TinyURL 221
toolbars 216–18
    Google 39–42
Topica 166
TracerLock 224
TrackEngine 223
Tucows 211, 213
Turbo10 86

UK Birth Adoption Register 112
UK Government website 184
UK Post-adoption Centre 112
UKOLUG 236
Ungoogle 76
URLwire announcements 235
USA Today Web Guide 232–3
USENET see newsgroups

virtual libraries 8–9, 143–55
    characteristics 149
    contents 149
    examples of 150–4
    use of 150

Vivisimo 71
  toolbar 217

WatchThatPage 224
Wav Central 102
Wayback Machine 148
web page watchers 222–4
web pages
  loading 200
  moving around 198
  printing 198, 199
  text, changing the size of 199
  translating 204
  visiting 198
Web Search Tool Features 231
Webcorp 102
Webcrawler toolbar 217
WebLens Search Portal 90
weblogs 10
  created by information schools
    122
  created by librarians 122
  created by libraries 121

created by professional
    organizations 122
examples of 118–20
future role of 191
general library and information
    science weblogs 120
index/directories of 125–6
introduction to 117–18
news aggregators 126–9
search engines 123–5
specialist topics 121
weblog creation 129–31
WebSearch 77
Websecure 220
what's new services 231–5
Whichbook 141
White Pages 186
WhoWhere?! 108
Wildgrape NewsDesk 129
WiseNut 49–50
*World Wide Web Virtual Library:
  Audio* 101
WWW Virtual Library 150–2

Xanga 131

Yahoo! 23, 180
  arrangement 23–4, 54–5
  e-mail addresses 108
  free text searching 57–9
  functions of 60–1
  image search 94–6
  introduction to 54
  sound search 101
  toolbar 217
  weblog listing 126
Yell 81, 182
Yellow Pages 186

ZapMeta 26, 72–5
  advanced search function 73–4
  basic search function 74
  preferences 72–3
Zdnet 240
ZoneAlarm 216